WOMEN WORLD LEADERS PRESENTS

Unshakable

God Will Sustain You

VISIONARY AUTHORS
Leecy Barnett & Donna Whartenby

Unshakable: God Will Sustain You

Published by World Publishing and Productions
PO Box 8722, Jupiter, FL 33468
Worldpublishingandproductions.com

ISBN: 978-1-957111-34-6
Library of Congress Control Number: 2024917585

Contents

Introduction

Welcome to *Unshakable: God Will Sustain You.* This book will take you through powerful stories written by women whose faith and resilience will amaze you. These authors are not perfect—they have experienced doubts, discouragement, and difficulties. However, their faith is steadfast because it is grounded in God's unwavering love for them. He is the One who sustains them. And they want you to know He will sustain you, too, when you rely on Him. In fact, He will make you *Unshakable.* Bible Scripture teaches: *Cast your cares on the Lord and he will sustain you; he will never let the righteous be shaken* (Psalm 55:22 NIV).

You may have picked up this book because you long to become unshakably rooted in your faith. Martin Luther, instigator of the Protestant Reformation, defined faith this way: "Faith is a living, unshakeable confidence in God's grace; it is so certain, that someone would die a thousand times for it. This kind of trust in and knowledge of God's grace makes a person joyful, confident, and happy with regard to God and all creatures."[1]

This unshakable confidence in God can be yours.

Through the stories within these pages, we invite you to embark on a transformative journey that will inspire change and ignite a fire within you. As you dive into the lives of these unshakable Christ followers, you will encounter the powerful truth found in Psalm 16:8: *I have set the LORD always before me; because he is at my right hand, I shall not be shaken* (ESV).

Between each life story, you will find short take-away teachings designed to help you discover how to become unshakable in different aspects of life, including loneliness, relationships, fear, suffering, and God's forgiveness.

We pray these stories, teachings, and quoted scripture propel you to your own unshakable journey. As you read, we are confident that the Holy Spirit—the Spirit of God Jesus sent to live in believers—will guide and equip you to live a rewarding and fulfilling life built on God Himself, the only unshakable foundation. Hold on tight as God prepares to fuel your inner strength and teach you to proclaim, *He alone is my rock and my salvation, My stronghold; I shall not be greatly shaken* (Psalm 62:2 NASB).

Throughout this Unshakable journey, we will periodically prompt you to take a moment to pray. We invite you to begin this practice now, asking God to speak to your heart.

Dear God, open my eyes and allow me to learn from the journeys, testimonies, and teachings written in this book. Thank You for the opportunity to know You more deeply through these authors' experiences. As I read, teach me to have unshakable faith in You and recognize that no matter what happens in my life, You will sustain me through it all. In Jesus' name, I pray. Amen.

---

[1]Luther, M. (1522). Preface to the Letter of St. Paul to the Romans (Andrew Thornton, Trans.). https://www.ccel.org/l/luther/romans/pref_romans.html

Donna Whartenby

Donna has been a published author with her "Faith and Family" column in *Voice of Truth* magazine since its inception. She loves writing for *Voice of Truth* and is excited about this journey as co-author of *Unshakable: God Will Sustain You.*

Donna grew up in New Jersey, attending church with her family and learning about God's love and Word. She knew she wanted to be a teacher by fifth grade. With her degree in education, she taught in public schools and later became a corporate education facilitator. She developed curricula and taught professional and personal development skills.

Now retired, Donna leads women's ministry church activities and events. She is the co-coordinator of the *Women Encouraging Women* ministry, which encourages women in their walk with Jesus. She loves teaching Bible studies. Donna sings solos, plays the piano, and enjoys singing in choir and praise team.

Donna has been married to her loving and supportive husband, Keith, for over 40 years. They have a son, Bill, who, with his wife, has blessed them with three wonderful grandchildren. Their family vacations often take them where they can discover the beauty of God's creation in nature. Donna and her husband live in South Florida.

Ordinary, Yet Special

By Donna Whartenby

My dear friend and mentor and I meet monthly over coffee. We discussed my new challenge—writing this *Unshakable* chapter. I told her I had no clue what to write. She jokingly asked: "So what makes *you* special?"

As I pondered her question, I realized there had been times in my life when my world was shaken to the core, but I discovered God's unshakable faithfulness in the midst of my struggles; He pulled me out of the mire or walked with me through it.

I realized I needed to explore the question, "*Am I* special to God?"

AN ORDINARY LIFE

I grew up in a middle-class American family with loving parents, a sister, a brother, and a pet. My parents provided for our needs: a dry and warm home, clothes that fit our fast-growing bodies, and delicious meals put on the table as the dollar miraculously stretched. My mother hummed and sang hymns while teaching us cooking and cleaning skills—I developed my love for music because of her joy in music. I took piano lessons and loved to play for myself. As a teen, my dad and I sang in the church choir. We lived what I consider an ordinary life.

My parents followed Proverbs 22:6, *Train up a child in the way he should go* (NKJV), by teaching the importance of loving God and family, being kind and caring for others, and doing your best. We went to church regularly, where I discovered there is One God who loves me, and He is the Creator of the heavens and earth. I heard stories about His Son, Jesus, and what He did for us. I accepted Jesus as my Lord and Savior when I was a teenager, not totally understanding the impact of what that meant.

> *"For I know the plans I have for you," declares the Lord, "plans to prosper you and not to harm you, plans to give you hope and a future"* (Jeremiah 29:11 NIV).

I discovered that my love for teaching was one of my God-given gifts. I worked with children as much as I could—as the kindergarten teacher's assistant in elementary school and, as a teen, working each year at Vacation Bible School and babysitting nearby families. I earned my college degree in education. Teaching was a part of God's plan for me, as evidenced by my burning desire to teach others.

When I was 30 years old, I married the love of my life, Keith, in a steepled church where God, family, and friends witnessed our ceremony. The nine years we dated prior to our marriage must have been part of God's plan to prepare us for what was yet to come. Life was good, and I was loved by God. But was I special?

CHANGED LIVES

Two months before our wedding, my husband's eldest sister was diagnosed with cancer that required surgery. The wedding celebrations went on as planned; the following week, she began chemotherapy and radiation treatments that lasted on and off for almost ten years. One night, while my husband and I were visiting her in the hospital after another surgery, she said she needed to talk to us. She was surviving by the thread of last hopes and maybes but knew she was losing the battle.

We were surprised when she asked us to raise her then nine-year-old son after she was gone.

My sister-in-law knew her husband was not one to raise a child alone. We did not have children yet, and she knew we were financially secure in our employment and took opportunities for family, fun, and travel. She asked us to "raise him up to know God, get his high school diploma, and help him become a man she would be proud of."

Only a few months later, she took her last breath.

The paperwork that made us the child's legal guardians and parents was signed. She handed over her precious gift, her son, for us to raise as our own. Our world was not only shaken by the death of a family member only a few years older than us, but we also became heir to now a ten-year-old boy!

This daunting task was both a blessing and a challenge.

It was a blessing knowing my husband's sister had faith we would love and care for her child as she did. We frequently had to remind ourselves that she had known what she was doing when she gave us her son. I wonder if she knew how many nights we would put our heads on our pillows while strategizing how to stay ahead of this highly intelligent, challenging, and creative boy.

The responsibility of raising a tween boy who was forced to start a new life with us as his parents after the devastating loss of his mother was also an unimaginable challenge. In addition, our son has ADHD (Attention Deficit Hyperactive Disorder), which causes impulsive tendencies, hyperactivity, difficulty focusing, and a short attention span.

Keith and I depended on our God-given strength to show our new son that we loved him and were a family no matter what. Even with the turmoil of our shaken lives and ADHD, we all loved each other and promised to help each other get through this new life God gave us together.

Keith and I relied on our faith in God to help answer the many "why" questions. "Why did mommy have to die?" "Why am I living with you?" "Why did she have to get sick?" And a million other questions we were not prepared to answer. We leaned on God with His unshakable faithfulness to help us deal with the anger, struggles, disobedience, out-of-control behavior, threats of running away, and all the frustrations this teenage boy was dealing with. He nearly flunked out of school multiple times, so we enrolled him in a Christian military school to learn the lessons of respecting himself and others, including *Do what you say you will do. You live the consequences of your choices. Be truthful. Know God loves you.* In our private, weak moments, Keith and I often wished our son would have three children *just like him!*

We tried our best to reflect God's nature with *compassionate hearts, kindness...patience...forgiving each other...and above all these...love, which binds everything together in perfect harmony* (Colossians 3:12-15 ESV) to show our son he was ours no matter what he did or what choices he made. We certainly were not always successful or perfect in our actions. There was not always harmony in our lives. But we taught him about our loving God, who forgives and forgets better than we ever could and loves us unconditionally. Looking back, we realize all the miracles it took to get us through those challenging times. We desperately held onto our unshakable belief that this was part of God's plan. He chose us, and no matter what was thrown at us, it required unshakable faith in our heavenly Father to sustain us.

LIFE'S RELOCATIONS

In addition to dealing with a growing teen wanting to be instantly independent, both my husband and I dealt with job lay-offs and relocations. We moved six times in eight years to various housing, even to a house we built, which we only lived in for a short six months. We had little control over the employment lay-offs and moves. We faithfully prayed to make the best decisions for our family. We did not know or understand why God was taking us through this journey, but we knew He had chosen us and sustained us through these trials. We continued to rely on our faith that God was in control and trust in Him.

When we lived in Tallahassee, Florida, one of our best decisions was to be baptized. My husband became a Christ follower in his late teens but had not been baptized. Our son also decided to commit his life as a Christ follower through baptism, and I re-dedicated my life to Christ; together, we were baptized as a family. That was such a joyous day.

FAITH AND ASSURANCE

> *Now faith is the assurance of things hoped for, the conviction of things not seen* (Hebrews 11:1 ESV).

We were grateful, even when God sent challenges that required our never-ending focus on Him in the path He chose for us. We were determined not to be shaken. God assures us in Isaiah 41:10, *I will strengthen you and help you; I will uphold you with my righteous right hand* (NIV). Psalm 145:13 teaches that God always keeps His promises, as He did for us. Psalm 16:8 tells us to keep our eyes on Him, and we will not be shaken. Although we experienced challenging and shaky times with these relocations, our unshakable God never deserted us. As Philippians 4:19 tells us, He supplies all our needs. Our God provided employment, financial and housing resources, food for our table, gas for our vehicles, new helpful, loving friends, and so much more. We are grateful for God displaying His love by providing abundantly as He promises in John 10:10.

When I was shockingly laid off from the company where I had worked for almost 30 years, I did not know what to do. I wanted and needed to work. I had viable skills. I applied for over 200 jobs but could not find an employer who risked hiring me as I neared retirement age. I was confused that my corporate skills were not valued. I became frustrated because I believed my 50+ years age was too young to retire. Then, I developed shingles, a blistery, extremely painful viral nerve infection that had me walking the floors night and day. It brought me to my knees in prayer. God was determined to get my attention.

While convalescing, I spent hours praying and reading His Word. I knew the Holy Spirit would lead me down the right path because God always has a purpose and plan. This new season became a time of healing and transformation. Soon, the blisters and pain from the shingles diminished and then disappeared.

One day, while finishing my devotion and spending time in prayer, I heard God's voice in my head say, "Stop looking for a job. You are Mine now." God pressed on my heart to teach a women's Bible study.

Who, me? Teach a Bible study? He knew I was not a Bible scholar. *How could I teach a women's study? What made me so special that He chose me?*

As I dug deeper into my study of His Word, Romans 12:11-12 reminded me, *Never be lacking in zeal, but keep your spiritual fervor, serving the Lord. Be joyful in hope, patient in affliction, faithful in prayer* (NIV). God was transforming my heart and mind to teach His Word. And so, I did as I was instructed. I have now taught dozens of studies. His grace allowed me to prepare for some 40 years before He called me to teach for His kingdom's purposes.

What gratefulness and blessings He has provided me as I've helped others discover their spiritual gifts, open doors to discipleship, and welcome the Holy Spirit into their lives. What joy this path has been! God considered me special enough to teach His Word in ways that honor Him while enlightening the students.

SEASONS OF LIFE

Through the years and seasons of my life, I've learned perseverance in life's struggles. God's sovereign grace is sufficient, and my ordinary life has been used in special ways.

We are each uniquely made by God. 1 Peter 2:9 says we are chosen as special. Genesis 1:27 describes us as created in His image. Each person is designed and chosen to bring God glory for His purpose by using our talents, gifts, knowledge, and understanding. Scripture also tells us we are fearfully and wonderfully made (Psalm 139:14).

God chose me to do things I did not think I could do, but I did them. As He presented me with challenges, I learned to trust Him more and discovered His never-ending grace and love. That trust has made *me* unshakable (Psalm 125:1), even unmovable at times. God has provided, protected, and been ever-faithful in my life. Even in what I think of as an "ordinary life," God has blessed and loved me in ways that helped me recognize I am special to Him because He chose me.

To update you on our son, he is now 40+ years old. He is married to a wonderful, supportive wife. They have three children, though I must say there is *only one most like him.* He is the lead pastor of an incredibly supportive, giving church who genuinely loves him. When we listen to him preach, my husband and I quizzically look at each other and ask, "Who is that spiritually wise man that looks and sounds like our son?" He is a godly man and is now working on his doctorate. I am sure his heavenly mom is proud of the man he has become as she desired. People's lives are significantly changed as he shares the gospel, reaches the lost, teaches and preaches God's Word, celebrates those believers who have passed on to eternity, and stands ready to answer any question about the existence of God. Seeing how God has blessed our son and his family brings us such joy.

In the Bible, Esther was tasked with saving the entire Jewish nation from annihilation. She was steadfast and unshaken as her cousin Mordecai told her she was intentionally placed in her position as queen *for such a time as this* (Esther 4:14 NIV). My husband and I were also placed in our son's life by God's perfect timing and provision. And because of God's wisdom, grace, and love, our once devastated and struggling son is now a man after God's own heart, teaching, preaching, and serving in his ministry position for such a time as this.

AM I SPECIAL TO GOD?

God showed me the answer to my question is clearly yes, *I am* special to God. So, what makes me so special?

I am special because God has gifted me with a love of teaching and music, which I use in obedience to Him to bless others. I am so grateful that God considers me so special that He employed me with these gifts, thus making them blessings to me. It brings me joy to know I am following His will.

My husband and I are special because we were chosen by his sister—but ultimately chosen by God—to receive the gift of raising our precious boy as our own son. We have been blessed to help him become the man God made him to be, serving His kingdom. Many years before, God chose our parents to prepare both of us to raise this child, teach him about God, and encourage his spiritual growth, which has gone far beyond what we could fathom. My mom also left me her legacy to celebrate life as we gather for holidays, birthdays, and special times, just as she did. It gives me such wonderful memories, blessings, and joy as I pass this legacy on to our family and grandchildren.

I am special because God transformed my life to teach His Word. He graciously gave me plenty of time to hone my teaching skills to serve His purpose. In gratitude, it brings me such joy that I am considered special by many in my church family for my love of helping others.

I cannot imagine what my life would be if I had missed God's calling and the many opportunities to serve Him. I joyfully serve the Lord. I know I am accomplishing a part of His eternal plan through my obedience and His strength. I am grateful to have the opportunity to teach about our almighty God and His salvation plan through Christ Jesus, bringing joy to others in worship and song.

An entire Jewish nation was grateful to Esther for obeying her call to God's plan. Lives were saved. Souls were spared. A nation survived that still exists today. I am not a queen, but I can only hope I help illuminate people's lives by showcasing who God is, His plan of salvation, and bringing light to a relationship with our heavenly Father.

You've heard my story, still, you may ask, "Am *I* special to God?" The answer for you, too, is a resounding yes! I know that to be true because scripture tells us that God considers each of His children special:

- You are created by God; He designed you in His image (Psalm 139:14-15, Genesis 1:27).
- You have been chosen by God (Ephesians 1:4-5, Romans 8:28-30).
- You are fearfully and wonderfully made (Psalm 139:14-16).
- You are beautiful (Ecclesiastes 3:11, Song of Solomon 4:1-15).
- Your name is written in the Book of Life (Philippians 4:3, Luke 10:20).
- You are given gifts by God (1 Peter 4:10, James 1:17, Romans 12:6-8).
- You are loved by God (John 3:16, Romans 5:8, Romans 8:38-39).
- You are set apart as holy (Deuteronomy 14:2, Jeremiah 1:5).

So much in God's Word teaches us why we are special to Him. I read and re-read scripture to learn His truth and remember my worth. He chose each of us to work for His purposes. You are special in His eyes—allow that to bolster your unshakable faith in almighty God, our Creator and heavenly Father. Allow Him to bring you joy, fulfillment, gratitude, and love as you grow to trust in Him more and more.

If you do not have a relationship with God, ask Him to come into your life, believe that Christ sacrificed His life, dying in your place and paying for your sins. John 3:16 teaches us, *For God so loved the world that he gave his one and only Son, that whoever believes in him shall not perish but have eternal life* (NIV).

Join me with unshakable faith in Him, believing Christ sacrificed His life for you, and love Him as He loves each of His children. Unshakably, God loves you, and He will sustain you. Pray with me:

Lord,

Turn my heart and mind toward You, who You have chosen me to be, and the unshakable life You want me to live. Guide and sustain me as I place Your will and Your purposes as a priority. I humbly come before You, asking for daily direction and guidance in doing Your will. Give me the strength and courage to be obedient as I live out the unique calling You have chosen for me for such a time as this. Give me unshakable faith in You.

Amen.

Unshakable When God Sustains You

By Donna Whartenby

Before you even opened this book, its title, *Unshakable: God Will Sustain You,* offered you hope. But that hope didn't come from us as authors; it is a promise from God's own Word. *Even to your old age and gray hairs I am he, I am he who will sustain you. I have made you and I will carry you; I will sustain you and I will rescue you* (Isaiah 46:4 NIV). (I personally have those gray hairs, so I can attest that this scripture is true.) Our God was so adamant that we hear this truth that He stated it twice within this single verse—God will sustain you! No matter what age. No matter what season in life you are in, even in the tough times of illness, trials, and challenges, God will sustain you as long as you believe in Him.

What does that mean? The answer is multi-faceted. God is all-knowing and is everywhere; you cannot hide from Him. God is all-powerful; He has authority over the heavens and the earth. God alone can carry your burdens, worries, fears, doubts, afflictions, and needs. Dictionary.com includes a varied list of meanings for sustain, including to support, maintain, carry, supply, and endure. God sustains us by helping, comforting, defending, and holding us; by bearing our burdens and supplying our needs. You can trust that He will sustain you through trials, illness, struggles, fear, loss of loved ones, your need for direction, and when you make mistakes and wrong decisions.

God *will* sustain you.

Cast your cares on the Lord and he will sustain you; he will never let the righteous be shaken (Psalm 55:22 NIV).

In Psalm 3:3-6, King David prayed to God for help when he feared being killed. *But you, Lord, are a shield around me, my glory, the One who lifts my head high. I call out to the Lord, and he answers me from his holy mountain. I lie down and sleep; I wake again because the Lord sustains me. I will not fear though tens of thousands assail me on every side* (NIV). We are not strong enough or capable of carrying our burdens alone. We need God. In times of stress, worries, conflict, and fear, humbly call out to Him, saying, "God help me." Trust He is near and hears you. He is your help and shield and will respond in His Sovereign way. Romans 8:28 (NIV) tells us that *in all things God works for the good of those who love him.*

God is the Alpha and Omega, the beginning and end, and everything in between. He sees all and knows all. Despite our own limited view, God knew us before we were born; He knows the ending of our time on earth, and He will be with us through it all.

In fact, if you have given your life to Christ, God will hold and sustain you for eternity. In Matthew 6:34, Jesus explains that it is impossible for any man to spend eternity in heaven by their own striving, but with God, all things are possible. We do not need to worry about the things we cannot control or fear what will happen because our God is in control, nothing can happen without His blessing, and He loves you more than you can imagine. That does not mean we will never have trials, challenges, illnesses, or hardships. But it does mean that God will be with us every day, every hour, every minute, and He will work things out for the good of those who love and believe in Him.

Great is our Lord, and great in power. His understanding has no end. The Lord lifts up those who are suffering, and He brings the sinful down to the ground (Psalm 147:5-6 NLV).

Life is a journey. In each season, we will have different challenges—maybe facing a new beginning, claiming independence, or overcoming physical or health challenges. But God will see you through every season. God is a loving and relational God who promises He will always sustain you. God's Son, Christ Jesus, died on the cross to save you from our unrighteousness and enable you to spend eternity with your heavenly Father. God is faithful to you as His child. You can trust and depend on Him. Rely on His promises; He will never leave you.

If you do not have a relationship with God, ask Him to come into your life today and cleanse your unrighteousness. Place your trust in the unshakable God who will forgive, comfort, and sustain you for eternity.

Almighty God, I need You. I ask that You strengthen and sustain me as I encounter challenges and trials. I humbly and trustingly cast my cares on You, Lord, knowing You will love, care, teach, and protect me no matter what comes my way. I believe Jesus died on the cross to save me from my unacceptable way of living, and I trust You to rescue me and sustain me by Your side for eternity. As I continue to learn more about You, I claim and embrace the unshakable faith You offer me. In Your holy name, I pray. Amen.

Leecy Barnett

Originally from Milwaukee, Wisconsin, Leecy Barnett has lived in Boynton Beach, Florida, for more than 30 years. Education has always been important to Leecy, who has a BA in history from Duke University, an MA in church history from Trinity Evangelical Divinity School, and an MA in Library Science from the University of South Florida. Although she has never married nor had children, Leecy considers being a part of God's forever family for 50+ years a wonderful adventure.

Leecy's first career was in Christian ministry, focusing on college students from America as well as students and scholars from China. After she moved to Florida, Leecy began a second career as a librarian. Now retired, she never stopped her involvement in ministry, teaching the Bible, and writing for her church.

Leecy writes a column for Women World Leaders' *Voice of Truth* magazine, "Power Points: God at Work through Women Leaders Yesterday and Today." She is also the author of two books: *Everything New* (a Bible study for new believers) and *Ten Life Lessons Worth Learning Over and Over Again.* For fun, Leecy enjoys reading, crafts, games, movies, Korean dramas, British television, and cheering on the Duke basketball team.

Unshakable in the Storms of Life

By Leecy Barnett

When I lived in Southern California, I crossed the San Andres Fault every day on my way to work. Since our headquarters building was just down the road from the fault, we always joked we would be the first to go when the big one hit. Being cavalier about earthquakes seemed to be a typical Californian way to cope with the ever-present threat. After I moved back to the Midwest, I watched a documentary about the San Bernardino Valley, where I had lived in California. Evidently, unknown to me when I lived there, San Bernardino was built over a large underground lake. In a major earthquake, the whole valley will sink into the earth—an unbelievable disaster. I had no idea that I was living on such unstable ground.

While growing up, I thought I was on stable ground. I started going to church as a baby. I learned all the Bible stories: Noah and the flood, David and Goliath, Daniel in the lion's den, and Jesus welcoming the children. I thought I was a Christian because I knew about Jesus; however, my religion made no difference in my life. In His Sermon on the Mount, Jesus concluded with a story about people like me:

"Therefore, everyone who hears these words of mine and puts them into practice is like a wise man who built his house on the rock. The rain came down, the streams rose, and the winds blew and beat against that house; yet it did not fall, because it had its foundation on the rock. But everyone who hears these words of mine and does not put them into practice is like a foolish man who built his house on sand. The rain came down, the streams rose, and the winds blew and beat against that house, and it fell with a great crash" (Matthew 7:24-27 NIV).

I had heard Jesus' words but never put them into practice—I was clueless about the faulty foundation of my life. Then, in my first year of college, as I began to see the fissures in my beliefs, some friends told me that I could have a personal relationship with Jesus; all I had to do was put my trust in Him as my Savior and Lord. So, I began the great adventure of listening to Jesus and trying to put His words into practice. I quickly realized that I could not obey Jesus in my own strength. God sent the Holy Spirit to live in me to guide and direct me, help teach me to understand His will and ways, and enable me to hear His voice. Through the Holy Spirit's power, I have been able to obey God and become a doer of His Word. For the last 50+ years, Jesus has sustained me through His Word and His Spirit in the storms of life. I may have experienced storm damage along the way, but my house is still standing. It is unshakable because of Jesus, my faithful and firm foundation.

UNSHAKABLE WHEN YOU WANT TO QUIT

I was undoubtedly the world's worst maid. One summer, a little over a year after I began following Jesus, I went to Lake Tahoe, on the border of California and Nevada, for a "summer project" with other college students from around the country who wanted to learn more about Jesus and share who He is. To support ourselves, we all got jobs in the popular vacation spot. My job was being a maid at the Holiday Lodge Motel. My boss, Erda, was endlessly energetic; she easily made any motel room spotless in 15 minutes. I was supposed to spend no more than 30 minutes on a room since I was paid by the hour. No matter how hard I tried, I could not meet the time constraints. Erda was always on my back. She thought I was lazy and made my life miserable. I wanted to quit, but I felt God wanted me to stick it out to learn perseverance and endurance.

The one thing that got me through that summer was a scripture I memorized and recited over and over while vacuuming:

> *Therefore, since we have so great a cloud of witnesses surrounding us, let us also lay aside every encumbrance and the sin which so easily entangles us, and let us run with endurance the race that is set before us, fixing our eyes on Jesus, the author and perfecter of faith, who for the joy set before Him endured the cross, despising the shame, and has sat down at the right hand of the throne of God. For consider Him who has endured such hostility by sinners against Himself, so that you will not grow weary and lose heart* (Hebrews 12:1-3 NASB1995).

That storm was just a passing shower, but the lesson of endurance I learned from it would prove invaluable in later gale-force storms and hurricanes.

UNSHAKABLE IN HEARTBREAK

At Lake Tahoe, I started dating one of the guys who was also involved in the "summer project." When we went back to our respective colleges in the fall, we continued our relationship long distance. I went to the post office multiple times a day to see if I got any correspondence from Jon. He came to visit me and meet my family over Christmas. By then, I was in love and thought he was "the one." When he decided to attend graduate school just eight miles down the road from my college, I thought this was confirmation that my deepest hopes and dreams would come true.

But shortly after we started the fall semester, it became clear that we were no longer on the same page. I was still crazy about him, but Jon seemed a bit standoffish. In fact, by mid-October, he said we should cool down our relationship, though we did not break up. Soon after, I went to a campus ministry retreat where I had an opportunity to spend time alone with the Lord in the woods of North Carolina.

God spoke to my aching heart through a seemingly unrelated passage of scripture from Hebrews 11:

> *All these died in faith, without receiving the promises, but having seen them and having welcomed them from a distance, and having confessed that they were strangers and exiles on the earth. For those who say such things make it clear that they are seeking a country of their own. And indeed if they had been thinking of that country from which they went out, they would have had opportunity to return. But as it is, they desire a better country, that is, a heavenly one. Therefore God is not ashamed to be called their God; for He has prepared a city for them* (Hebrews 11:13-16 NASB1995).

God was telling me through this scripture that if I wanted to manipulate my relationship with Jon so that things would work out the way I wanted them to, I could do that, but it would mean returning to my old way of life without Him. If I wanted to keep following God, I needed to trust Him to show me what was best and keep seeking His path for my life.

After returning home from the retreat, I felt like it was time to decide about the future of our relationship, so I broke things off completely with Jon.

The next day was amazing—I had total peace from God and was completely confident I had done the right thing. Unfortunately, that peaceful feeling did not last. I literally cried myself to sleep every night for the next two months. Even though my heart was broken into a million pieces, I knew that I made the right choice to follow God.

My dream was to get married and have a family, but that was the closest I ever got to it. Being single has not been an easy path to walk. But God has sustained me. His unconditional love has always been there, even when I didn't feel it. God continually holds me up and keeps me unshakable as I stand on His promises.

UNSHAKABLE IN CONFUSION

Fast forward nearly twenty years. Ironically, a personal category five hurricane, the strongest category with sustained winds over 150 miles per hour, came when I moved to Florida. It was a "perfect storm" of poor choices, bad circumstances, a tragic event, loss of purpose, and general confusion.

I had been living in Virginia, working with a Christian ministry. I loved my work but felt my usefulness was coming to an end. I wanted to teach in some role, so I began to search for teaching positions. I subscribed to a Christian job-hunting service to see what the possibilities might be. One opportunity stood out to me—an opening in a Christian high school teaching history and the Bible, both my fields of study. The school also happened to be in the town where my parents had their winter home. I was excited about the possibility of being closer to my family as my parents were getting older and my dad was battling cancer. This job seemed like a gift from God.

The school flew me down for the interview. My first poor choice came when the principal told me the position I applied for was filled. He asked if I would consider taking a different job, teaching in the middle school. I was not interested in dealing with the raging hormones of early adolescence. In fact, when I did my student teaching in college, I was originally assigned to a middle school. Appalled, I immediately arranged to swap with a classmate so I could teach juniors and seniors in high school.

Because I still felt like God was leading me to Florida and this school, against my better judgment, I told the interviewing principal "yes" to taking the middle school position.

The bad circumstances started two days before classes began—when I stepped on a fire ant hill. I was unfamiliar with these nasty little creatures and the excruciating pain their bites can cause. I believe it was an omen!

A few weeks into the semester, I came down with bronchitis and laryngitis. Being out of school for a week put me perpetually behind in grading papers.

However, the worst circumstance regarding my new job was dealing with middle school students. As individuals, my students were nice; some were even sweet and sympathetic to me. But when they came together as a class, the mob mentality took over. Because I was short in stature, I was unintimidating to my students. From the beginning, I struggled to maintain classroom discipline. On the other hand, it seemed the main goal of the students was to intimidate me and interrupt the possibility of learning. By the end of each day, I was completely frazzled.

Then, tragically, my father's cancer became more severe; medically, nothing more could be done for him. At the beginning of December, my dad went into hospice care, and I took a leave of absence from teaching to help my mom. My dad died less than two weeks later. The rest of December was taken up with funerals—one in Florida and one in my hometown in Wisconsin, which made for a very sad holiday season.

I dreaded returning to teaching after the Christmas break ended. The night before school started, I was so anxious I couldn't sleep—not one wink. I knew that if I were to keep going in the same manner, I would be headed for a nervous breakdown. I told the principal I would finish the last two weeks of the semester but wouldn't complete my contract for the whole year. I am not one to give up easily, but this was the only decision I could make.

I experienced a complete lack of purpose over the next year and a half as I drifted from one temporary job to the next. Since graduating from college, I had worked in different Christian ministries, but now it seemed God was finished using me in ministry. Even after I landed a permanent job in a local public library, which I enjoyed and was successful at, I still wondered how God was planning to use me.

My life was in a state of confusion. It seemed that God led me to Florida and that my teaching job was a divine opportunity. What happened? Sometime during this confusing and chaotic period, I came across this scripture verse: *To You they cried out and were delivered; In You they trusted and were not disappointed* (Psalm 22:5 NASB1995). My first thought was, *This verse must be wrong.* I had trusted in God, but still, I was very disappointed. Then, the thought came to me that this verse *is* true, but I had not trusted in God as He actually is. I relied on the God I wanted Him to be—one who would make my path smooth and never let me undergo hard times.

After I started working in the library, I read a book that seemed to be written directly to me: *When God Doesn't Make Sense* by James Dobson. In the book, Dr. Dobson says believers often come up against a "betrayal barrier." A barrier develops between us and God when we feel He has let us down or not come through as He had promised. Unless we can get past this barrier, our faith in God will eventually wither and die. Dobson said:

My strongest advice is that each of us acknowledge before the crisis occurs, if possible, that our trust in Him must be independent of our understanding. There's nothing wrong with trying to understand, but we must not lean on our ability to comprehend! Sooner or later our intellect will pose questions we cannot possibly answer. At that point we would be wise to remember His words, "As the heavens are higher than the earth, so my ways higher than your ways and my thoughts are higher than your thoughts" (Isaiah 55:9). *And our reply should be, "Not my will but yours be done"* (Luke 22:42).[1]

Taking Dr. Dobson's advice, I decided to stop trying to figure out why all this craziness happened when I first moved to Florida. Even years later, I still don't understand what God was doing, but I have experienced good from it. I learned you do not have to be in "full-time Christian work" for God to use you. As long as you *Work with enthusiasm, as though you were working for the Lord rather than for people* (Ephesians 6:7 NLT), you will be a light to those you work for and with. I also realized that serving God is not limited to our occupation. We serve God with our whole lives: *God has made us what we are. In Christ Jesus, God made us to do good works, which God planned in advance for us to live our lives doing* (Ephesians 2:10 NCV).

Through this time of confusion, my faith was battered and badly bruised by the storms of life. It took me a while to repair the hurricane damage, but I discovered that God is unshakable and will hold on to me throughout my life.

JESUS IS THE UNSHAKABLE ONE

In the last thirty years, I have gone through many more storms. I lost my nephew, my mom, my sister, and a few very close friends to death. I struggle with personal illness and depression and have stress and conflict at work. I've endured financial difficulties and lost my job during the COVID-19 pandemic. I found what my former pastor, Stan Coleman, said over and over to be very true: "You are either about to enter a storm, in the middle of a storm, or just getting over a storm."

We each have our own storms that threaten to destroy our faith. This is why my first lesson on endurance has proved invaluable. The scripture I memorized tells us to go through life, *fixing our eyes on Jesus, the author and perfecter of faith* (Hebrew 12:2 NASB1995). Jesus is the author, originator, founder, leader, ruler, and perfecter of our faith journey. As our Lord and

Savior, Jesus is the creator of our story. He guides us through the twists and turns of life and brings us to the conclusion He planned for us from the beginning. As our perfecter, Jesus is the One who brings us safely through to the end. He completes our faith: *being confident of this, that he who began a good work in you will carry it on to completion until the day of Christ Jesus* (Philippians 1:6 NIV).

At the beginning of my story, I said that God continually holds me up through life's struggles. He alone keeps me unshakable as I stand on His promises. Upon reflection of my life's path, I see that Jesus is really the unshakable One. I am weak and can never make it through the storms on my own: And finally He said to me, *"My grace is enough to cover and sustain you. My power is made perfect in weakness"* (2 Corinthians 12:9 VOICE).

Shortly after I became a Christ follower, I learned an old hymn, which has become a theme song for my life:

My hope is built on nothing less
than Jesus' blood and righteousness;
I dare not trust the sweetest frame,
but wholly lean on Jesus' name.
When darkness veils his lovely face,
I rest on his unchanging grace;
in every high and stormy gale,
my anchor holds within the veil.
On Christ, the solid Rock, I stand:
all other ground is sinking sand
all other ground is sinking sand;[2]

I encourage you to build your hope on Jesus. He is unshakable. All other ground is indeed sinking sand.

---

[1]Dobson. J. (2013). *When God Doesn't Make Sense.* Tyndale, p. 237.
[2]Mote, E. (1834). *My hope is built on nothing less.*

Unshakable Perseverance

By Leecy Barnett

Being a Christian is not easy; it requires perseverance as we endure hardships and battle temptation. Jesus taught us that anyone who comes to Him would have an abundant life (John 10:10), but He also very clearly taught us, *"In this world you will have trouble"* (John 16:33b NIV). Being a Christian does not exempt us from difficult times, but God does promise He will never leave us—so we can have unshakable perseverance by harnessing His wisdom and power. After all, Jesus finishes the statement above by encouraging us, *"...But take heart! I have overcome the world"* (John 16:33c NIV).

To become unshakable in perseverance as we follow Jesus, it may help to know the *REASON* for perseverance, the *ROOT* of perseverance, the *RESULTS* of perseverance, and the *REWARDS* for perseverance.

The *REASON* we must persevere is so we can become like Christ. We, by nature, are sinners, and the world is filled with temptations. When we give our lives to Christ, He washes us clean and sends His Holy Spirit to lead and guide us, but that doesn't mean our propensity to sin vanishes or temptation suddenly dissipates. So, we must persevere in pursuit of the holy calling God has given us as we grow more in His likeness every day. Jesus Himself understands as He persevered against greater temptations than we will ever encounter. Aren't you glad Jesus did not quit before He went to the cross to pay the penalty for our sins? Instead, He *endured the cross, scorning its shame* (Hebrews 12:2 NIV). We are called to be like Christ; that is our reason to remain steadfast in unshakable perseverance.

The *ROOT* of our Christian perseverance is God's love. In writing to the believers in Thessalonica, the Apostle Paul knew that to persevere in all God calls us to, we would need to rely on His love, which God freely offers us. *But the Lord is faithful, and he will strengthen you and protect you from the evil one. We have confidence in the Lord that you are doing and will continue to do the things we command. May the Lord direct your hearts into God's love and Christ's perseverance* (2 Thessalonians 3:3-5 NIV).

And in Corinthians, we are taught that an attribute of love is perseverance: *[Love] always protects, always trusts, always hopes, always perseveres* (1 Corinthians 13:7 NIV).

We have access to true love because, as Christians, *God's love has been poured out into our hearts through the Holy Spirit, who has been given to us* (Romans 5:5 NIV). Both love and perseverance grow in us as we obey the teachings of God's Word. *For everything that was written in the past was written to teach us, so that through the endurance taught in the Scriptures and the encouragement they provide we might have hope. May the God who gives endurance and encouragement give you the same attitude of mind toward each other that Christ Jesus had* (Romans 15:4-5 NIV).

The *RESULTS* of perseverance in Christ are threefold. First, when we persevere in following Christ despite obstacles and roadblocks, we develop character: *We can rejoice, too, when we run into problems and trials, for we know that they help us develop endurance. And endurance develops strength of character, and character strengthens our confident hope of salvation* (Romans 5:3-4 NLT). In today's crazy world, we desperately need to have godlike character and the hope that it brings.

Secondly, persevering in Christ when times get tough can bring us joy. *Don't run from tests and hardships, brothers and sisters. As difficult as they are, you will ultimately find joy in them; if you embrace them, your faith will blossom under pressure and teach you true patience as you endure. And true patience brought on by endurance will equip you to complete the long journey and cross the finish line—mature, complete, and wanting nothing* (James 1:2-

4 VOICE). If you are like me, you may want to become mature in Christ, but look for a shortcut to get there. Unfortunately, the road to maturity leads through trials and takes perseverance.

Thirdly, if we persevere in our calling, we are promised fruitfulness. In Jesus's story of the four types of soil, the good soil is one that perseveres: *But the seed on good soil stands for those with a noble and good heart, who hear the word, retain it, and by persevering produce a crop* (Luke 8:15 NIV). It is easy to get discouraged when we are trying to serve God. Don't quit. God promises us that our perseverance will be worth it. *Let us not become weary in doing good, for at the proper time we will reap a harvest if we do not give up* (Galatians 6:9 NIV).

Finally, the *REWARDS* of our Christian perseverance make all we will encounter worth the cost. *You need to persevere so that when you have done the will of God, you will receive what he has promised* (Hebrews 10:36 NIV). We are promised that the one who endures to the end will be saved (Matthew 24:13 NLT). But we will not just be saved from the penalty of sin—eternal death; we will be saved into a glorious relationship and partnership with God: If we endure, we will also reign with him (2 Timothy 2:12 NIV).

What a joy this will be! *Blessed is the one who perseveres under trial because, having stood the test, that person will receive the crown of life that the Lord has promised to those who love him* (James 1:12 NIV).

When we see the Lord in all His glory, we will be excited to worship Him by casting our crown at His feet (see Revelation 4:10).

Keeping all this in mind is our why! Understanding the *REASON, ROOT, RESULTS,* and *REWARDS* for our Christian perseverance will help us be unshakable as we walk through hardships and stand against temptations.

Lord Jesus, give me the love and perseverance You had. Help me to see trials as opportunities to develop my character and become mature. I thank you for the joy I will have spending eternity with You that will make persevering worth my effort.

....

Loralea Rose Suever

Loralea Rose Suever was born in Washington, grew up in Minnesota, and then lived in South Florida for 30 years. She met her husband, Jeff, in Bible school and celebrated their twenty-fifth anniversary a week before she passed away in April 2024.

Loralea's life was characterized by two things: her love of her Lord Jesus Christ and her love of reading. The first she expressed in countless hours of study, devotion, mentoring others in one-to-one relationships, and teaching in formal settings. Her faith was demonstrated by the way she lived her life; her "special gifts" were apparent to all. One of Loralea's favorite mottos was, "I'd rather see a sermon than hear one any day." Her last request was to hear the Psalms being read to her.

Loralea's love of reading naturally led to a love of writing; she wrote hundreds of poems and other works, occasionally for special purposes such as Easter Church services, but mostly to express the joy of the Lord in her heart. One of her many dreams was to become a published author. Having her story included in *Unshakable* is the realization of her lifelong dream.

What Cannot Be Shaken Remains

By Loralea Rose Suever

On March 18, 2021, I was diagnosed with an uncommon form of cancer that had begun to metastasize. Shortly after my diagnosis, a cancer care worker mentioned that former patients often remarked, "Cancer is the best thing that ever happened to me!" That sounded like poppycock to me, but the phrase kept replaying in my mind over the next few weeks. I finally decided to ponder the options for my outcome. That kind of thinking can seem fruitless and futile, yet we all do it. We do it because sometimes it's a necessary part of the journey to understanding God's plan in whatever shaking or chastening He is allowing.

Due to the massive amount of information coming at me, I got caught up in "paralysis by analysis." And in many ways, I was certainly shaken—shaken in body as everything came crashing down, from nearly bleeding to death in the Emergency Room that first day to when the effects of treatment were just starting to make themselves known. Shaken in my mind by the myriad of questions—many of which did not need to be asked because they only sent my mind down unfruitful paths. And yes, shaken in spirit. For this was not my first bout with physical infirmity—but it was certainly setting out to be the worst. *Can I get through this? Can I be valuable to our Lord and His children? Can I just walk to the car?*

After prayerful consideration and reading the Holy Bible, I decided that being shaken and sifted until only wheat remained and the tares, or weeds, were blown away was the best possible outcome for me and my husband, Jeff.

So, I prayed the Lord would hear my cry, fight the battle for me, and be Jehovah Rapha, our God who heals. And He has been faithful, so kind, and ever-present.

He started by calling to mind those first moments in the hospital when the gastroenterologist seemed to be talking nonsense I could not understand, and my husband and I were trying to make sense of it. Finally clarifying herself, the gastroenterologist very bluntly said, "Didn't she tell you? She has cancer."

When she left, we just held each other and cried. I made a vow as I prayed aloud, "Lord, we do not know where this road leads or how long you have us on it. But we pray, Lord, as long as I am in this hospital, please let us be a light to the doctors and nurses around us so that through this journey, they will see only You when they look at us."

It should be obvious, yet it alludes so many of us at times, me included:

- You cannot become unshakable without first being shaken (sifted).
- Just as surely as one who is intent on being disciplined by the Lord becomes His disciple, one simply is not a disciple by just saying they are. Talk is cheap. If my words challenge or offend, that is not my intention. His Word alone trains us in righteousness as He sanctifies us through remarkable circumstances.

So, as you go on this journey with me, let us learn from and agree with King Solomon, the wisest man who ever lived, along with our Lord's Spirit, the writer of Proverbs 3:11-12: *My son, do not despise the chastening of the Lord, nor detest His correction; For whom the Lord loves He corrects, just as a father the son in whom he delights* (NKJV).

I've heard these things. I've been shaken before. So much so that what could not be shaken was all that remained. I had done my best to endure before, but I must confess, I was not, as the makeup ads try to portray, an "Easy Breezy Covergirl" during those times. Call them trials, tests, chastening, or siftings—the result is the same: you are left with the positive fruit of the effective work of God.

As many as He loves, He chastens:

> *And the Lord said, "Simon, Simon! Indeed, Satan has asked for you, that he may sift you as wheat. But I have prayed for you, that your faith should not fail; and when you have returned to Me, strengthen your brethren"* (Luke 22:31-32).

The writer of Hebrews both encouraged and admonished when he said:

> *Therefore we also, since we are surrounded by so great a cloud of witnesses, let us lay aside every weight, and the sin which so easily ensnares us, and let us run with endurance the race that is set before us, looking unto Jesus, the author and finisher of our faith, who for the joy that was set before Him endured the cross, despising the shame, and has sat down at the right hand of the throne of God* (Hebrews 12:1-2 NKJV).

And then, telling us why we are to rejoice in disciplining or chastening:

> *If you endure chastening, God deals with you as with sons; for what son is there whom a father does not chasten? But if you are without chastening, of which all have become partakers, then you are illegitimate and not sons. Furthermore, we have had human fathers who corrected us, and we paid them respect. Shall we not much more readily be in subjection to the Father of spirits and live? For they indeed for a few days chastened us as seemed best to them, but He for our profit, that we may be partakers of His holiness. Now no chastening seems to be joyful for the present, but painful; nevertheless, afterward it yields the peaceable fruit of righteousness to those who have been trained by it* (Hebrews 12:7-11 NKJV).

As I look back on my life, I see that there were times I had to change as God did His work to make me more and more like Him. I recall that I was not happy about it at the time. Sometimes, change or growth feels like instability—shifting sands—and it can be quite scary. However, the reality was that my foundation remained on the Rock—the blessed and glorious Rock of my salvation.

But how now, in this most uncertain of times, with so many unknowns, when not only is my present turned upside down, but my future as well, do I hold my emotions in check and rest on Him who promised to never leave nor forsake me?

THE EARTHQUAKE

Our reflexive prayer brought on by the Holy Spirit that horrible first morning when we got the news that everything was changing prompted my heart to remain focused on God. It was much like what Jesus told His disciples, *"For the Holy Spirit will teach you in that very hour what you ought to say"* (Luke12:12 NKJV).

In that fearful and broken moment, God gave me the words I should say and the desire to be a light to others. Who am I that my chief goal would be to show His love to others along the journey? My natural inclination would be to think of myself, my fears, and my illness. But no, He awoke in me, just a little "pinkie toe in the body of Christ," to think outside myself. Little did I know that prayer would be the start of a journey where only that which cannot be shaken would remain.

Be Still and Know (Part I)

There is no cell He cannot see.
Before we cry, He knows our plea.
There is no thought He cannot read.

He provides with boundless energy,
For all the world and humanity.
At times, we may wish for a different reply,
But can we trust Him without asking, "Why?"

(Scriptural application of Romans 8:18, 25-28)

THE JOURNEY BEGINS

Radiation. Every day. For months. Being cooked from the inside out like a hot dog. But hey! I finally got my first tattoos! OK, so they are just two small dots on my hips to align the machines, but they are tattoos nonetheless.

This journey is not easy. It is not easy on me and certainly not on my family, who are trying to do so much for me. But two weeks ago, we learned a valuable lesson about the body of Christ.

You see, my husband comes from stubborn German stock and generally refuses to ask for help. I could see the toll that work, taking me to treatments, and trying to maintain our home was taking on him. Against his wishes, I called our church to ask if someone could bring over dinner for us one evening. Several people had offered, and it was time to accept. The end result was that every other day, between 5 PM and 6 PM, someone from church brought enough food for dinner that night and leftovers for the next. They did this joyously for weeks until we no longer needed it.

> *And let us consider one another in order to stir up love and good works, not forsaking the assembling of ourselves together, as is the manner of some, but exhorting one another, and so much the more as you see the Day approaching* (Hebrews 10:24-25 NKJV).

As I lay here most of the day, each day, too weak to do much of anything, I decide not to ask, "Why?" but rather, "What?"

"What can I do in this weakened state?"

I can pray. I can reach out to others and let them know I am praying for them. And I can certainly spend time reading God's Word—or at least listening to it.

Be Still and Know (Part II)

His thoughts aren't our thoughts,
His ways aren't our ways.
Thankfully, He's different than we,
And He is abundant in Mercy!

(Scriptural application of Isaiah 61:1-3)

ROUND ONE IS DONE!

A clear scan! After an absolutely brutal year which included chemotherapy, radiation, five visits to the ER, a horrible bacterial infection, a gall bladder that had to be removed due to radiation damage, severe COVID, and God only knows what else, we have a clear PET scan! I ask the medical oncologist what that means for the next steps. "What do I do now?"

"You go live."

"That's it?"

"Yep. That's it."

Well, it turns out that is not it. You see, there are many effects of the treatment that have to be dealt with, including chronic, often debilitating pain, fatigue, loss of appetite, and the symptoms go on. These are the results of having a treatment that is more aggressive than my aggressive cancer.

However, I make it to church and fellowship with the body of Christ. I understand that first, humbling day I walk in, leaning heavily on my husband's arm, as the congregation turns and begins to applaud, experiencing what the writer of Hebrews meant when he referenced *so great a cloud of witnesses* (Hebrews 12:1 NKJV). I am surrounded. Physically. Spiritually. Near. Far. I cannot see for the tears in my eyes brought on by unbounded love. Love coming from Christ channeled through His church body—both collectively and individually. In that moment, I know and experience His love. Not only do I know what being loved "feels like" or what "it means to be loved," I know love.

Be Still and Know (Part III)

So let your Joy be renewed today,
Know that our God will find a way,

To turn a wrong into a right,
And help you to sleep tonight.

(Scriptural application of Psalm 90:12)

HERE WE GO AGAIN

A new tumor in a new place.
Do I have the strength to run this race?
My heart and head say, "No,"
But my dear husband just says, "Go!"

This time, it rears its ugly head right between my heart and my spine along with "some undefined readings" down by my tailbone. I must confess, I always admired Jeff's stoic, Germanic constancy. Even when it clashed with my "Scottish side." Did you know we had been married over three years before I found out he had ever been mad at something I did? I asked him one time how he never seemed to be mad, and he said, "Oh, I've been mad."

"Really? When?"

And he proceeded to tell me about a time two years prior of something that upset him. Granted, he had to think long and hard to remember it.

"How was I supposed to know? Why didn't you tell me?" I asked.

"It wasn't that big a deal. I knew I'd get over it and forget in a few minutes, and I didn't want to waste the energy I might need for something important."

Well, twenty years later, he's brought that stoic energy to full bear. While I do not know if I have it in me to go through another round of chemo and radiation, he is talking as if there is no discussion to be had. Like there is no decision even to be made. I will never forget the look—shocked, and maybe a little fearful?—on the doctor's face when my normally soft-spoken, "Midwestern nice" husband levels his gaze at the doctor and says, "I am counting on another 20 – 30 years with her. It's your job to make sure that happens. What are you going to do about this?"

It does not appear there is going to be a discussion.

Be Still and Know (Part IV)

Rest in His Goodness,
Remember His Providence.
Cloak yourself in garments of Praise,
Know that He will be with you always.

(Scriptural application of 2 Corinthians 1:3-5)

ANOTHER WIN

As the doctors promised, "Round Two" is nothing like "Round One." The chemo is just an oral pill, and the radiation is "targeted" rather than "wide field, broad spectrum." There is not as much collateral damage to my body. So, we are off to the races. I even drive myself to treatment a few times.

Driving. What joy and freedom there is in the simple things in life. I still struggle with pain and the effects of "Round One." It is like they never went away. The chronic fatigue. Finding out there are terms I had never heard of, like "cancer pain." That is like regular pain—only worse and deeper. Or "chemo brain"—like when you get woken up from a sound sleep, are all disoriented, and can't quite make sense of things. It's like that—only right in the middle of mundane tasks. How does this toaster work again? *Oh, right. Just push the lever down.* It just hits you out of the blue.

The emotions are much more vibrant than before. *Is that because I feel like I stared death so squarely in the face?* Things that I normally would have just shrugged off, I cannot let go. And I find myself crying more. And just wanting to be alone with God. But that's not what He has called me to be.

So, we're taking a vacation! Jeff's oldest sister is turning seventy-five, and we are going to take a road trip. What a wonderful experience this will be. My chemo and radiation are over. The medical team has a plan to treat things "holistically," to "keep things at bay" with the goal of getting those "20-30 years" Jeff keeps bringing up every time I get weary or discouraged. It will be so good to see his family again. And what a surprise it will be!

Be Still and Know (Part V)

He is a Good God, a Man of His Word.
There is no whisper He has not heard.
When our words fail, He reads our minds;
Praying to the Father. Utterly Divine.

(Scriptural application of Philippians 4:4-7)

WEARY

"The thread between this world and the next got very thin." That is what I tell Jeff after the first round of immunotherapy. I cannot explain it, but it has. Physically, I am quite shaken. Spiritually, though, I have never been more solid. I know in whom I believe. Even saying this seems trite compared to the reality in my heart.

I've not been able to do much as I try to manage the symptoms of pain and the ongoing issues from the radiation treatment. Who knew there was a thing called "Radiation Seepage" that could last for years? I have tried to be an encouragement to my husband and others when I can. He has tried so hard to make our dream of a little "homestead" come true. He has truly morphed into the "Gentleman farmer" during this time.

However, I'm getting quite weary. I don't know if it is the treatment, the cancer has returned again, there is a cumulative effect, or what else it could be. But it's hard to eat much at all. I am so grateful to all the wonderful people God has placed in my life. Those true and faithful friends who truly are the "hands and feet" of Christ in practical ways. I know this is hard for them, too. I know some of them "just want me to be better," and they so want to "get the old Lori back." They are truly dear to me. I certainly don't know what the next day or week or month may bring, but I love that *cloud of witnesses* God has surrounded me with.

Be Still and Know (Part VI)

There is no place where we can flee,
And find ourselves apart from He.
Be still and Know that He IS God.
Let His Spirit refresh you and be awed.
For all creation shall kneel and bow;
To the God of forever, the Lord of our now.

(Scriptural application of Philippians 4:8-9)

THE END OF LORALEA'S STORY
Told by her husband, Jeff

Loralea's chapter on earth closed on April 11, 2024. I will not say she "lost her battle with cancer" because the battle was never hers to fight, and she knew that early on. But rather, against all earthly wisdom and the efforts of man, her heavenly Father called her home where He surely declared, *"Well done, good and faithful servant...Enter into the joy of your Lord"* (Matthew 25:21 NKJV). For the wisdom of man is foolishness to God.

The prayer she was so moved to pray on that first morning was answered throughout her journey, as evidenced by the number of nurses who came to visit her each of the many times she was admitted to the hospital, even though they had since been assigned to other floors. Cards came from health care providers and insurance and financial counselors, remarking what a "light" she was and what a "joy she was to talk to and how it came through in her voice."

That final afternoon, no less than seven hospital staff came up to me to express not only their sorrow but also their recognition that her faith and trust in God was "special." One of the nurses, who had worked in the ICU for over four years, had been in the ER for years before that, and even did a stint as the wound care specialist for the entire hospital, came up to me after it was all over with tears in her eyes. I don't think she even heard Lori speak, but she knew Lori loved others by the way she responded non-verbally those last couple of days.

It wasn't always sad. One day at the oncologist's office during treatment, the "flashlight app" on one of the nurse's phones was on. That was all the prompting Lori needed to have the whole ward—all the nurses and all the patients who were receiving chemotherapy and other treatments—sing, "This little light of mine." It was hysterical. And loud!

Before Solomon took over the nation of Israel from King David, he prayed and asked God for wisdom rather than success or riches. Lori's prayer that morning was for the ability to show the love of God to others through her journey, rather than for herself. And He granted her that prayer and strengthened her faith in Him throughout it all.

Unshakable to Lori meant, as Job said in Job 13:15, *Though He slay me, yet will I trust Him* (NKJV).

In those last days, Lori asked to hear the books of Job, Esther, and the Psalms—because she knew those were books where people had been shaken, but only as much as was necessary to show that God, the Rock of our foundation, remained.

Unshakable in Sickness

By Leecy Barnett

You just received the diagnosis. It knocks the wind completely out of you. As your illness progresses, you plead with God: *Be gracious to me, Lord, for I am weak; heal me, Lord, for my bones are shaking; my whole being is shaken with terror. And you, Lord—how long?* (Psalm 6:2-3 CSB). The idea of being unshakable in this situation can seem unimaginable, like a cruel joke. You may be tempted to ask God, What do you want me to do? *Pretend I am not sick; deny the reality of what I am going through?* But denying reality is not what trusting God is all about. Pastor Rick Warren said in his Daily Hope Podcast, "Faith does not ignore reality. Faith does not pretend you don't have a problem. Faith does not act like there's no difficulty.... Faith is facing the facts in your life without being discouraged by them."

Even when you are going through a devastating illness, you can be unshakable by relying on God's love, understanding, presence, and provision.

First, remember God loves you: *"I have loved you with an everlasting love; Therefore, with lovingkindness I have drawn you and continued My faithfulness to you"* (Jeremiah 31:3 AMP). Everlasting love means that God's love doesn't quit; it lasts forever and always; it is eternal and will never end. Even when you don't feel God's love, you can trust it is there. You may hear a whisper telling you, "If God really loves you, He wouldn't have let this happen to you." Believe me, that is not the voice of your Father. It is the voice of Satan, the deceiver. We live in an imperfect world where bad things happen to all people. Even a debilitating illness cannot and will not block God's love.

> *And I am convinced that nothing can ever separate us from God's love. Neither death nor life, neither angels nor demons, neither our fears for today nor our worries about tomorrow—not even the powers of hell can separate us from God's love* (Romans 8:38 NLT).

The second truth that helps you be unshakable in sickness is remembering that God's Son, Jesus, understands what you are going through. Isaiah prophesied that the Messiah would be *a man of suffering, and familiar with pain* (Isaiah 53:3 NIV). And true to that prophesy, when Jesus was about to face His own death, He was stressed beyond what most of us could even imagine: *And being in agony, He prayed more earnestly. Then His sweat became like great drops of blood falling down to the ground* (Luke 22:44 NKJV). Jesus understands everything you go through.

The third truth is that God is always with you: *Even though I walk through the valley of the shadow of death, I will fear no evil, for you are with me* (Psalm 23:4 ESV). You can embrace your illness knowing God is with you every step of the way, and He will bring healing and restoration in His perfect way and timing. He'll give you the strength to fight, hope to live, and grace in your weakness. Romans 8:28 reminds us that *God causes everything to work together for the good of those who love God and are called according to his purpose for them* (NLT).

Finally, we can be unshakable in our sickness knowing that God's provision is perfect. Even in our most difficult moments, we can look forward to the time when God will wipe away our tears. *He will wipe every tear from their eyes, and there will be no more death or sorrow or crying or pain. All these things are gone forever* (Revelation 21: 4 NLT).

Because of sin, our bodies are defective, and we will all experience sickness. However, as Christians, we will be blessed with an eternity with God in perfect health.

> Therefore we do not lose heart. Though outwardly we are wasting away, yet inwardly we are being renewed day by day. For our light and momentary troubles are achieving for us an eternal glory that far outweighs them all. So, we fix our eyes not on what is seen, but on what is unseen, since what is seen is temporary, but what is unseen is eternal (2 Corinthians 4:16-18 NIV).

Father, I thank You that nothing can separate me from Your love. Even when suffering and sickness are so real, Your love is a greater reality. Jesus, thank You for leaving your eternal home to be born as one of us. I am so grateful that You understand everything I am going through. Thank You for Your constant presence even as You have gone before me to prepare a place for me to live in eternity free from illness. I proclaim myself unshakable in You!

Carol Ann Whipkey

[illegible]

Carol Ann Whipkey

Carol Ann Whipkey is a best-selling published author. She is a Christ follower, and much of her retired time is devoted to serving in the Women World Leaders ministry as a writer and encourager through her uplifting, joyful spirit, guidance, and love for writing.

Carol enjoyed her career as a beauty consultant and worked in an accounting position at UPS until retirement.

She is an artist trained by the world-renowned wood carver Joe Leanord, whose work is in the New York Museum of Art and Disney in Paris and the USA. As a hobby, Carol spends much of her time carving horses, birds, and other commissioned work that comes her way.

Carol lives in her own park-like setting on 52 acres in Thompson, Ohio, with her husband, Mel. She is the mother of four, which includes her first-born child Kimberly Hobbs of Women World Leaders, and is the grandmother of six and great-grandmother of seven.

My Paddle through the Pain

By Carol Ann Whipkey

We've all had times that have shaken us up. I want to share an experience that shook me to the core. I trust my story will show you the power of our living God when Satan tries to shake us off our foundation of faith. Even through pain, God has His always-present hands of help on us. He is our cornerstone: *Together, we are his houses, built on the foundation of the apostles and prophets. And the cornerstone is Christ Jesus himself* (Ephesians 2:20 NLT). God is our help in times of trouble. He is our unshakable, living God who never leaves us or forsakes us. He is our rock.

My story of being shaken took place over several months. My daughter and her husband were separated at the time, and knowing I was not accepting of what she was doing, my daughter and I became estranged. I did not know what would happen with our relationship or in her life or mine. I began keeping a journal of my feelings—speaking to the Lord and writing my prayers to Him. That was when a scary episode happened to me.

I was carrying a heavy load of wood and branches while working outside when suddenly, I could not take another step. A tiredness overcame my entire body, encapsulating me from my head to my toes. I knew something was wrong. My husband was at work at the time, so I called my son Michael and told him what was happening.

Knowing my late husband Mike had died from a massive heart attack years before, my son made me promise to see my doctor immediately. Reluctantly, I went. The doctor ordered me to go directly to the hospital. He said I could either go by ambulance or call my husband, Mel, to take me. It was that urgent! So, I quickly called my husband, and he rushed home from work to take me to the hospital.

The doctor who examined me told me I would need to have a stent put in because of the condition of my heart. He scheduled the procedure for a couple of days later. Here is what I wrote in my journal when I returned home:

"Today I go to the hospital again for my heart. So, I will write to You, Lord, and pray that You will give me more time here on this earth. I know whatever You have planned for me is for my good. Thank You for giving me a great life so far. You have been here for me in good times and especially in bad ones. I pray for my children. I know that this is harder on them than me. And I pray for my sweet husband, Mel. My life has been blessed. I pray for strength and courage to face tomorrow. Please let me be a good witness today to everyone I meet. I love you, Lord, in Jesus' name."

I returned to the hospital to get my stent. Wow, what was supposed to be a one-day visit turned into a week.

When I arrived, the doctors and nurses prepared me and started an IV, poking me several times to find a thin, buried vein. Then they took me into surgery, which was supposed to be at 7:00 AM. That turned into an 8-hour procedure because of an emergency. Little did any of us know at the time that I would face one of the biggest challenges of my life in that operating room.

The medical team administered a drug to "take the edge off" before putting in my stent. The procedure was not easy, but the team got in successfully, only to discover that an artery that had been fixed months earlier was now blocked in a different place. The doctor had no choice but to reopen it. I have very tiny veins that are so hard to find, let alone try to put a needle in, and when the doctor proceeded with the needle, my vein collapsed. He took the balloon out and tried four more times to get it placed.

Due to the type of drugs that had been administered for the initially intended procedure, I felt all of this! I was in severe pain. It was the most horrible pain I have EVER experienced, even worse than natural childbirth without medication. My chest and my arms were in agony. All I could do was cry aloud to the Lord!

My doctor heard me and kept saying, "I'm so sorry! You are going to be okay," but my pain only escalated. I was NOT okay. He sounded so remorseful that he had to put me through this. I felt and saw that he was in tears, but he kept trying to assure me I was going to be okay. The team kept calling out to give me more morphine, but it was not helping!

I remember thinking about how much pain Jesus must have been in when He was on the cross. That was one of the things that helped me. I believed if Jesus went through worse pain than me on the cross, I could make it through this. What they did not tell me was I was experiencing a heart attack! The doctor had caused it by trying to get the stent into my tiny vein so that I would not have to go through open-heart surgery!

While everyone was in the operating room running around frantically, I remember someone asking, "Should I get the paddles?"

All I could think of was, *Oh no, I'm dying. Paddles? What? Please, no paddles.* But my pain only intensified, and they scurried to save my life. I did not know they had gone out to ask my husband if he was okay with letting me have the heart attack under a controlled condition or if he wanted me to have surgery.

Mel asked the doctor point blank, "What would you do if it was your wife?" After receiving the answer, Mel agreed with the doctor's recommendation.

I am writing this to explain to you that I was in the most horrible pain I think anyone can feel. How is it possible for someone to endure such pain? It certainly was not by my own strength.

After this event in the operating room, they put me into a critical care unit and gave me morphine continuously. My sweet husband stayed with me the entire time I was there. I developed a morphine itch, which was relentless, and they gave me ice to put on it to try to ease the itch. My boys and my son-in-law came to see me. Later, my daughter-in-law Denise and my brother Ed visited. I was still in such horrible pain. I was getting calls from everyone, but the only one I did not get a call from was my daughter, Kimberly. It had been two years since we last talked. I longed to hear her voice.

I did not know what God was doing behind the scenes.

While I was lying in the critical care unit, my brother Ed leaned over to me and asked, "If Kimberly came in, would you see her?"

With all the strength I could muster, I said, "Of course I would."

At that moment, Ed got up, held his finger to my face to stop me from talking further, and left the room. So many things went racing through my head. I had not heard from my daughter for such a long time. Although I was hurting physically in that critical care unit, the ongoing void of our relationship in my heart was even more painful. As my brother left the room, my thoughts drifted to how I must look. With my messed-up hair, no makeup on my face, tubes coming out of my body everywhere, a sandbag to stop the bleeding, and riddled with so much pain, what a sight I surely was!

Suddenly, my daughter Kimberly walked into the intensive care unit. Her eyes met mine, and I just held my arms out the best I could for her to fill them. Kimberly fell into my arms, and all my pain just lifted off me. It was a miracle!

In that moment, I remember Kimberly looking into my eyes and saying, "Mom, you look so beautiful!"

I felt so good! I held on to my daughter like I never wanted to let go. We could not take our eyes off each other that day. I remember thinking we should NEVER allow anything to keep us apart ever again.

Although I was partly the cause of our separation since I did not condone what she had done, just holding her felt so good that I was able to release my thoughts of the incident and rest in the sweet moment. I knew God allowed this heart attack to bring her back to me. My life verse, Romans 8:28, says, *And we know that all things work together for good to those who love God, to those who are the called according to His purpose* (NKJV). Even though I could not see it as I was enduring my heart attack, God was working everything out for the good. I had been praying for my daughter to come back to God! He was giving me hope through the pain.

A couple of days went by. I did not need any more meds and began seeing how God had brought me through this. God was my rock. I was in the critical care unit with Him by my side, never doubting His miraculous power.

The hospital had sent a woman into my room to discuss what had happened to me and what was going to happen next. The first thing she said to me was, "You had a heart attack, and you will never be the same again. You cannot do ANYTHING for six weeks! NOTHING!"

What? I thought. She scared me half to death. She scared me so badly that I thought if I moved at all, even a muscle, I would die. She gave me no hope. I was so shot down. But I was not dead! God had saved me!

Then she told me she would be coming back the next day, and with that, I said to myself and God, "Lord, please spare me. Oh no, I can't endure her again."

After the depressing woman left, I was transferred to a step-down unit. Since I was no longer in the critical care unit, I felt like I was getting better. That gave me hope again.

As they wheeled me into my new room, I saw a beautiful elderly woman sitting on the edge of the bed, with the window behind her. She was glowing with a white light surrounding her! On the windowsill was the most beautiful bouquet of wildflowers. It was like God sent me an "angel" from above with wildflowers surrounding her. I said to her, "I love those flowers!"

The beautiful older woman reminded me of my mother, who had always loved flowers. The kind woman gently spoke, "My children call them weeds, and so does my husband."

I replied, "But God made them, and to me, they are some of the most precious, beautiful things of His creation!"

She agreed. Then she came over to my bed, gently cupped her hands to my cheeks, looked into my eyes, and said, "Honey, you are going to be fine!"

I believe she must have sensed deep inside that I was rattled by what I had been told previously.

Another miracle. God sent me an "angel" that day, and we bonded instantly. I felt wonderful!

This beautiful "angel" helped me endure my time in the hospital. It was like my mom was there with me. One day when we were alone, she said, "Come with me. I want to take you on a tour." She grabbed my arm, and off we went around the second floor. On our tour, we talked to doctors, nurses, and everyone in our path. We modeled our hospital gowns, getting applause and laughs as people who saw us said we put a fresh glow into that dreary place where we all were staying. One nurse even told us that we were the cutest couple of nuts they ever had on that floor.

My heart was light, and the rest of my stay was pleasant.

My "angel's" doctor came in to release her to go home. She just needed to call and have somebody come and pick her up. I got sad; I did not want her to go! She told me she would stay another day, just for me, if I wanted her to. But I could not let her do that. We exchanged phone numbers and addresses. She was 85 years old and ever so cute—just as spry as my mom had been!

As visiting hours approached, my husband came in, and my "angel's" friend's daughter came to pick her up. We all sat together and laughed and talked and had fun. Her family and mine were like a forever family! I know that it was God who sent her! God provided an "angel" to me in that state.

He knew exactly what I needed.

My special "angel" went home that day, but the next day, she came walking right back through the door to see me. She brought me a book titled A through Z of the Bible. She was indeed a real messenger from God! There is no doubt that God works in mysterious ways on our behalf. This dear sister reassured me that I was going to be all right. God allowed her to keep me solid in my unshakable faith, able to focus on HIM and not cave into fear.

Weeks went by, and I felt so good it was as if my heart attack never happened. When I got home, I wrote my prayer in my journal: "Lord, I do not want to sit around and do nothing. Lord, please help me, direct my life, and show me the plans You have for me. I want to be as unshakable as the 'angel' You sent into my room as an example of faith to others."

I knew God would answer my prayer because He has promised, *"For I know the plans I have for you," says the Lord. "They are plans for good and not for disaster, to give you a future and a hope"* (Jeremiah 20:11 NLT).

Although I knew God was with me through this event, I admit it was not easy. Through it all, I remained unshakable because God showed up to sustain me with His hope: My flesh and my heart may fail, but God is the strength of my heart and my portion forever (Psalm 73:26 ESV).

I would go through it all again if need be because I was given a chance to reunite with my daughter through this heart attack.

God gave me each of my children, and I hold them dear to my heart as I do each of my grandchildren and great-grandchildren. Although many disheartening things have happened in my family, God always uses every circumstance to work for good. This heart attack brought my daughter back to my side.

I hold all my kids up to God in every way. He is my loving Savior, and He knows what is best. He will work everything together and take care of it all when we trust Him for every outcome. GOD IS THE MOST UNSHAKABLE ONE OF ALL. He always knows what is best for us, even when we do not. As in my situation, I would never think that He caused my heart attack, but you can see how He made so much good out of something that was hard to endure, and through it, He gave me cause to rejoice in His love.

God sends His representatives—brothers and sisters in Christ—to guide us, just as He did with my "angel" in the hospital. She is gone now, but I am so absolutely in awe as I write this story and share how He sent her to me in my time of need!

If you have a situation in your life where you need any kind of help, please be assured that God is always aware of what is going on with you. All you must do is call on His Name, Jesus, and believe in your heart that He is Lord, and He will come to you. He will save you. God cares about what you go through in every circumstance. He will meet you where you are.

> *And my God will supply all your needs according to his riches in glory in Christ Jesus* (Philippians 4:19 CSB).

God's Word is a promise, and you, too, can become unshakable in God's kingdom work—no matter what you go through here on earth. You don't have to face pain alone. You don't have to fear and tremble, because God is with you.

> *For I, the Lord your God, hold your right hand; it is I who say to you, "Fear not, I am the one who helps you"* (Isaiah 41:13 ESV).

Unshakable Despite Circumstances

By Leecy Barnett

Years ago, I was working in a Christian ministry; one of my responsibilities was supervising our Guest House, where we welcomed missionaries, students, and other visitors from overseas. One weekend, the Guest House was unexpectedly full. As the only one on duty, I was overwhelmed with preparing the rooms so everyone would feel welcome. I was washing sheets in the basement laundry (which was not normally my job) on the verge of tears when one of the guests sought me out and quoted a Bible verse to me: *And we know that God causes all things to work together for good to those who love God, to those who are called according to His purpose* (Romans 8:28 NASB).

I didn't appreciate it at the moment, but as time has passed, I've learned to appreciate this verse as a reliable compass to help navigate the trying circumstances of life. Let's go through Romans 8:28 together, word for word, so we can better understand what it means and, just as importantly, what it does not mean.

"*We know*" means to see, perceive, recognize; a seeing that becomes knowing, a gateway to comprehending spiritual truth from physical experience. Paul, the author of The Letter to the Romans, knew from personal experience that God works everything together for good—he knew because he had seen God working out the intricacies of his many hardships. *Five times I have withstood thirty-nine lashes, three times I was battered with rods, once I was almost stoned to death, three times I was shipwrecked, and I spent one day and night adrift on the sea* (2 Corinthians 11:24-25 VOICE). Despite these turbulent times, Paul went on to say, *I am at peace and even take pleasure in any weaknesses, insults, hardships, persecutions, and afflictions for the sake of the Anointed [Jesus] because when I am at my weakest, He makes me strong* (2 Corinthians 12:10 VOICE). By remembering how God has come alongside to help us and others navigate difficult circumstances, we, too, can *know.*

"God causes" means that God is in control of the outcome of every circumstance. God is not the instigator of the bad things happening to us. Scripture tells us, *I know you [God] get no pleasure from wickedness and cannot tolerate the slightest sin* (Psalm 5:4 TLB). In His sovereignty over the universe, God permitted sin to enter the world when humans chose to disobey Him, so now we live in a world where bad things happen. But God is in control of outcomes; He miraculously *causes* every occurrence and circumstance to work together for our good over time.

"Good" implies intrinsically good—good in nature, good whether it is seen to be good or not. Remember as a child when your mother gave you medicine and said it was good for you? It tasted bad, but later, it made you feel better. This is what is meant by *good* here. Not everything we go through will be pleasant or enjoyable, but God ensures us that He will use everything we go through to shape our character and make us more like Jesus. That is SO *good!*

"To those who love God, to those who are called according to His purpose." These phrases tell us that this promise is conditional—it does not apply to every human being. God's promise to make all things work together for good is a specific promise for those who love and seek to obey Him. We must put our faith in Almighty God for this promise to apply to us. Our love for God is always a response to His love for us: *And we have come to know and to believe the love that God has for us. God is love. Whoever lives in love lives in God, and God in him.... We love Him because He first loved* us (1 John 4:16,19 MEV). The Bible teaches that God has a special purpose for followers of Jesus. God does not call us because of any good works we have accomplished, *So God can point to us in all future ages as examples of the incredible wealth of his grace and kindness toward us, as shown in all he has*

done for us who are united with Christ Jesus (Ephesians 2:7 NLT).

Because we know God is at work, because we know He has our welfare in mind, and because we know our ultimate purpose is to glorify Him, we can be unshakable in any circumstances that come our way.

I wish I had understood all this when I was about to cry in that basement laundry, but God was teaching me. In fact, He was using *that* situation for *my good*...because I love Him.

The next time circumstances don't go your way, instead of giving up, complaining, or even stoically pressing on, why not choose to operate in joy? Author and pastor's wife Kay Warren says, "Joy is the settled assurance that God is in control of all the details of my life, the quiet confidence that ultimately everything is going to be all right, and the determined choice to praise God in all things." That sounds a lot like unshakable joy to me!

Father, help me see You in the midst of my circumstances. I thank You that when bad things happen to me, You are at work to turn them around for my good. Remind me that You created me to bring You glory. Give me joy knowing that You have ultimate control over the details of my life.

Dee Mills

Dee Mills is a speaker and entrepreneur who [illegible]

[illegible]

Dee Miller

Dee Miller is a speaker and author who hosts a podcast titled "Picking Up the Pieces." Dee has been a disciple of Christ for 30-plus years, passionately following Him and still learning who she was created to be as a woman of God.

Dee is the Founder of MJM Ministry (mjmministry.org). When she left her home state to begin her transition to male, she cut off all communication with her family. MJM is dedicated to her parents, Mary and John Miller, who rushed back into her life at the precise moment the door was reopened. MJM was birthed to do the same for others. No judgments, just a hand up.

Dee is passionate about walking with others on their journey to discovering their identity in Christ. We all bear God's image and are created in His likeness. Dee supports parents and churches as they navigate the narratives that surround the teachings that tell us to follow our feelings over the Word of God.

Stay connected with Dee at Dee@mjmministry.org.

Who Was I Created To Be?

By Dee Miller

Being unshakable in the Lord despite life's circumstances requires trusting Him unconditionally. That was something I had to learn.

Although I was raised in a family that went to church every Sunday, I was never taught how to have a personal relationship with the Lord. As a child, I remember having to say I was unworthy of receiving communion. That fits with my experiences within my home. My mom was abusive and outspoken about not wanting a girl. My brothers followed her lead. By seventeen, I had decided God couldn't exist because of the traumas I had already faced. If He did exist, He must have made a mistake in making me a girl.

I was working in a rural hospital when my self-destructive lifestyle of drinking and painkillers caught up with me. This led to a rehab stint at the age of twenty-two. I now recognize I was feebly attempting to cope without God. Looking back on this time, I realize I always wanted to live, not just survive, but I didn't know how.

After rehab, clean from drinking and painkillers, I had to face life without anything blocking the pain of my past. All my childhood traumas tormented my mind. *How could I stop them? How would I get through life?* That was when an old coping behavior from childhood reappeared.

Dissociative behavior can be the result of trauma. It is an escape the victim uses to protect the mind from what is happening to the body. It was a trick, a coping mechanism I learned when I couldn't control what was happening to me as a child. It meant I could go anywhere I wanted and never leave home. As an adult, I dissociated in another way.

It all started simply enough. When I was alone, could no longer go drinking with friends at the bar, and longed to stop the memories of the past racing through my mind, I escaped by using dissociation and living as a man. I found I could create a person people were drawn to. He was comfortable in social situations, the life of the party! Most importantly, he flourished in everything he did. He was everything I wasn't as my female self; I created everything I wanted to be in that male person. Being him became a safe, happy, and extremely comfortable place to be.

In real life, I became ill, requiring admittance to the hospital where I worked. Once admitted, a nurse, Grace, came to my room with a painkilling shot. As much as a mind-altering drug sounded perfect, I wasn't sure this was the best idea. I hadn't met Grace before. She was new to the hospital and knew of my rehab stint. Grace made herself comfortable on my bed as she compassionately explained why I deserved to have my pain relieved. Her eyes stayed on mine, so full of concern that she convinced me to take the shot.

Once home, I learned that Grace was my upstairs neighbor. A friendship quickly bloomed. Her care and compassion continued, which led to her becoming my confidante. In quick succession, we became lovers. The more time we spent together, the more I craved living the way I knew I was meant to be. I finally confided my ultimate secret to her—I should have been born male. Sharing meant risking rejection, but I also knew I needed to correct God's mistake of making me a woman. Now, I laugh at how I could be angry at God, whom I didn't believe existed.

Grace was on board with my pursuit of changing my birth sex. I proposed marriage; she accepted, changing my life in an instant. To make this happen, we would need to relocate to another city. The process is different today than in 1986 when I was transitioning. One had to present as the gender they wanted to become for a minimum of two years before any medical intervention could be started.

Once we were settled into our new home, I legally changed my name and wardrobe to match the male identity of which I had dreamed. In today's language, I socially transitioned. Every aspect of my life now existed as male. My biological family was not on board with what I was doing, so I ceased all communication with them. I had everything I needed with Grace. Once married, we would have kids, and then I would finally be part of a loving family.

I'm grateful for the waiting period, as it gave God time to work on my hard heart. I was blind to how I was trying to build my own happiness and, more importantly, protection. Those periods of dissociation, creating stories, were fairytales that had set me up for failure. They might as well have been sandcastles on the beach with no foundation. When the storms of life came, I went crashing down. After four years of waiting, Grace left me and moved back to our former town. The leading medical institution for transgender surgery had stopped doing procedures. No physician in the city where I lived would work with me. I went into a deep depression that left me uncertain about where I should go next.

One Sunday morning, I visited a friend's church and filled out the visitor's card. I then received a phone call from a man named Mark from the church; he told me I needed to invite Jesus into my life. This made me chuckle because I was convinced Jesus wasn't real. Jesus was just the figure hanging on the cross in my childhood church, a character within a fairytale book.

Mark continued to call often to check in on me. As consistent as he was with his suggestion that I invite Jesus into my life, I was just as consistent with saying, "No." I needed a real solution in my life.

After a little over a year, we finally met in person for the first time. When Mark again made his usual request, to shut him up, I said, "Why not?"

I certainly was not expecting what happened next.

My hard, stony heart turned to flesh. Jesus was not dead. He is ALIVE! He made His presence known to me. I sat with Him, feeling the love of His presence and knowing He accepted me in every way. Did my troubles go away? No. But I felt hopeful for the first time in my life.

It only took minutes for the devil to show up with condemnation and accusations. "What is Mark going to do when he finds out you are just pretending to be a man?" My life had been full of rejection. Telling Mark the truth and handling whatever response followed was a risk I was willing to take.

When I told him, Mark was truly filled with godly wisdom. He went to His bookshelf and came back with a Bible for me. He said, "I won't tell you what to do. You need to pray and ask God what you should do."

In that moment, I was unhappy that Mark wouldn't tell me what to do. I didn't understand what it meant to pray or how to seek God for guidance. In hindsight, however, I will be forever grateful for his wisdom! He allowed me the space; no, he *forced* me to press in to find God and hear Him for the most critical decisions I needed to make in my Christian walk. *Who does God want me to be?* That was how I saw it. I was willing to accept who God created me to be, but I needed to hear directly from my Creator. And only from my Creator. No one else's thoughts would impact my decision. If any person had told me I needed to give up being a man, I would have doubled down on my efforts to become one! Even as miserable as I was, Mark leaving me in God's hands was the best place for me to be. It was the only place I should have been.

On the third day of my salvation, I brought my Bible to work. I asked a coworker who was very outspoken in his religious beliefs where I should start reading. But his dislike of me was evident. He stared at me, not seeing any evidence of change on the outside, handed the Bible back to me, and walked away. Frustrated, not understanding prayer nor where to start reading the Bible, I went into an office where I could be alone. I finally cried out to God, not really understanding that this was prayer.

"Do you want me to go back to being a woman?"

I heard the audible voice of God reply, "YES."

In response to this, I immediately went to resign from my job so that I could begin transitioning back to a woman.

When I read Romans 8:15 about being adopted into God's family, I knew that I was where I belonged.

> *For you did not receive the spirit of bondage again to fear, but you received the Spirit of adoption by whom we cry out, "Abba, Father"* (Romans 8:15 NKJV).

I understood what happened when Jesus came into my new heart of flesh. He filled that gaping void that I had been searching to fill. Changing my appearance back to looking female was a slow process. Accepting that God had created me to be female while allowing Him to heal my heart was an entirely different process.

I quickly learned that I was not like the other women in the church I attended. I had an androgynous appearance, meaning I could pass for either gender. I used to laugh if a child asked me if I was a boy or a girl. I'd smile while replying, "Yes." Now, wanting to look a little female, I didn't have a clue how to make that happen. I was trying to grow my hair out and find an appropriate wardrobe. I was trying so hard to be accepted by the women. *Why won't they let me join in?* My fears were great, and nobody was offering me a hand of fellowship. It wasn't long before I stopped attending church; it was clear I didn't belong there. 'My kind weren't welcome' was the message I walked away with.

I began telling God exactly how I felt. I was convinced He didn't want me. My biological family didn't want me, so why would He? I paced the hallways of my home trying to convince myself to take the point of a sharp knife and push it through my neck. I was convinced nobody would miss me or care if I were dead. Before long, I had a total mental collapse that resulted in a nervous breakdown. I was angry at everyone, especially Christians. I didn't understand the difference between God my Father and the people at the church yet. The people that attended that church were as broken as I was.

The risk of stepping back into a church building was too great to consider. Yet, I felt an unbelievable draw to do so. After two years, I gave in and visited a small church. I couldn't bring myself to be a weekly attendee or allow anyone to interact with me. The pastor eventually invited me to dinner at his home. My assumption was it would be my final meal before being shown the exit door. The dreaded question soon came about my past. The pastor's advice was that I should not ever tell anyone about my transgender history. I was welcome at the church, but my story wasn't. I didn't see the problem with this advice at the time. In hindsight, I wish I had been told to build trustworthy relationships with people I could share my story with.

Over the next year, I got involved in church activities while making friendships with women. While at church one night, thieves broke into my home, dumping every drawer and pulling everything out of my closet. The police officers commented that the thieves had to have known me; they had to be looking for something specific. Why else would it look like a complete disaster inside?

The church ladies heard about my plight and were quick to call with an offer to help restore order to my home. I can still feel the panic that went through my body as I tried to decide how to respond to this wonderful offer. There was no way I was letting those sweet women into my home! On the outside, I was dressing as a female. I was going through all the necessary actions of attending church, reading my Bible, and renewing my mind. But God was pushing me off the fence to make a decisive decision. *And do not be conformed to this world, but be transformed by the renewing of your mind, that you may prove what is that good and acceptable and perfect will of God* (Romans 12:2 NKJV).

If I were to let my church friends in my home, my secret would be exposed. I still had not shared that I had lived as a man in the past, and half of my bedroom was still male belongings. *What am I going to do now? Put everything back as it was? Continue to hang onto the male persona that gives me a sense of security?* I had to make a choice as I picked up each item. *Put it in a box to give away or put it back in the closet? Who will I serve—God or my desire to be male? Who will I choose to follow—God's voice, which is telling me He created me to be a woman, or my inner, still-scared self that wants to self-protect and live as a man?*

God was pushing me off the fence to make my choice.

> *But if you refuse to serve the LORD, then choose today whom you will serve* (Joshua 24:15 NLT).

As I sat staring at the mess, the phone rang. The woman's voice was trying to understand why I wouldn't accept the offered help. Tears were trickling down my face as I was being torn by her kindness and my tremendous expectation of rejection. The pastor had advised me not to share my past. To take her help meant exposing my hidden past male life within the walls of my home. God was asking me not only to share my home but to share what was deep within my heart. *Can I risk sharing with her? What will the consequences be if I do?*

When I was a child, going against the authority of my parents brought about unbearable consequences. Likewise, sharing my past would go against the pastor's authority.

There was an awkward silence as I debated how I should proceed. The caller could feel the weightiness of my struggle. Her perception was that perhaps I didn't know how to receive help, or maybe my home wasn't clean to begin with. She began to throw out these thoughts, which only drove me into a deeper silence. I wanted to tell her the truth, but how? Where do you start telling someone that you lived as the opposite sex for six years of your life? And that you still had everything from that part of your life in your home?

She finally got blunt, "What is it? What is preventing you from accepting our help?" She began to share things about her past. She created a deeper, more intimate bond that allowed me to understand there was a place of safety between us. It's hard to see someone else's past when you're not healed and can only see your own shame. Once I understood where she had once walked, I began to share pieces of my life with her.

We later laughed about it all as she admitted she was grateful that our discussion had been on the phone. It wasn't a surprise to her that I had a girlfriend; the surprise was that I had lived as a man. She didn't care, but the shock would not have been hidden from her face.

God knew I needed to expose my hidden secret to move into a greater place of healing.

It was easy to hang on to all my wounds and hurts, but to grow with God and become more Christ-like would require me to let go of past hurts. I needed to learn to forgive and understand that forgiveness is for my benefit, not necessarily for the benefit of those who hurt me. All my anger had held me captive in a prison. I later called it a graveyard, where each tomb was an event marked with a headstone highlighting the occurrence. I would walk among the tombs, lamenting over everything that happened to me, picking at the scabs, not allowing anything to heal. The problem with roaming the graveyard is that you are spending time with the dead and can't thrive there.

As I allowed God to heal me, my desire to be male was replaced by understanding who I was created to be as a female. Is the statement "Time heals all wounds" true? In my opinion, no, it is not a totally accurate statement. But time does give you distance from the event that caused the wound. I could have gone to the graveyard daily and picked the scab off, causing the wound to bleed all over again. So, I had to make a choice to be healed by inviting God into my pain. I believe Jesus came to me to heal me in my body, mind, and spirit. Most people can't understand the pain that I carry in my mind. The difference now is those memories no longer torment me. They are only events that happened in my past. They can no longer control me.

> *It is like a person building a house who digs deep and lays the foundation on solid rock. When the floodwaters rise and break against that house, it stands firm because it is well built* (Luke 6:48 NLT).

Now, because I've learned to listen to and trust my Creator as I stand on the solid rock of His Word, I know exactly who He made me to be. When the storms of life come and the water rises, I stand firmly unshakable because I am made in His image. I am perfectly built by the Master Creator.

Unshakable In Where I Belong

By Donna Whartenby

An acquaintance recently said she was struggling to know who she was because of the direction our society is going with its focus on money, sex, materialism, political affiliation, and education. Not knowing where she fit in or belonged, she decided to sit and wait for something to happen until she found her place.

This confusion, uncertainty, and hopelessness is no way to live.

Today, many people are harnessed by labels thrust on them by society that can shake their identity and value. Additionally, more and more people are socially isolated due to job relocations or sustained mobility, possibly causing them to become more vulnerable about where and even if they fit in.

But followers of Jesus Christ can know who they are and where they belong. Jesus Christ gives each of His children a valuable identity and an impactful purpose.

God joins His family together purposefully. He has created us to live as one body and, together, shine His light and love into this dark world. As Christians, we have a new identity and assurance secured in Christ. We belong in the family of Christ. God has identified and labeled us as His.

> *Now you are the body of Christ, and each one of you is a part of it* (1 Corinthians 12:27 NIV).

As His beloved child, God transforms your heart through faith and love in Him. We live a free life that is not bound by social expectations. He gives us hope and a purpose to love and serve others. He takes us from being lost, empty, and hopeless and gives us value, worth, and dignity through His grace and mercy. We are His new creation. 2 Corinthians 5:17 tells us: *If anyone is in Christ, the new creation has come. The old has gone, the new is here!* (NIV). Galatians 5:1 tells us, *Christ has set us free to live a free life. So take your stand! Never again let anyone put a harness of slavery on you,* (MSG). And Romans 8:1 asserts, *There is now no condemnation for those who are in Christ Jesus* (NIV). We are given a new way when we choose to live in Christ. We gain value in Christ's power, authority, and direction. Living the ways of God shapes our course in life forever.

As believers in God, our purpose is to glorify God and enjoy our relationship with Him. When we follow His direction, we are blessed. He will sustain us by teaching us the way, guiding, and directing us. In Psalm 32:8, God tells us, *I will instruct you and teach you in the way you should go* (NKJV). In Him, we have unshakable victory, as 1 Corinthians 15:57 claims, *Thanks be to God! He gives us the victory through our Lord Jesus Christ* (NIV). We have victory over our old ways as God gives us eternal life and assures us that we belong in His family.

Your life did not occur randomly or by accident. God is the creator of the universe, and He is your creator. He has a plan and purpose for everything He has created. He will accomplish everything He has planned (Isaiah 46:9-11). God's plan for you was established before you were born—you belong!

You have been chosen to be a part of the family of God; you have a place in His kingdom. God alone secures your identity, purpose, and value. Our unshakable destiny is eternal life with the perfect, loving creator, provider, and forgiver—the most high God.

If you haven't yet, you can join the family of God today. Pray this simple prayer with an open heart, asking Jesus to rescue you from a life without identity, purpose, or value. As God's child, you will be unshakable in where you belong!

Dear Jesus, without You, my life is a mess. I ask You to rescue me from this life of confused identity that has no worth or purpose. I believe You are Jesus, Son of God, and I believe You sacrificed Your life on the cross to save me from my unacceptable ways of living. I surrender my life to You, Jesus, as Savior and Lord. Thank You for giving me hope, purpose, and identity in You. Thank you for inviting me to belong to the family of God. In Your precious name. Amen.

Tawana Lowery

Tawana Lowery is a dynamic and inspiring figure in the world of women's leadership and personal growth. With over 25 years of experience, she has dedicated her career to empowering women through her roles as a women's leadership coach, author, YouTube content creator, international speaker, and founder of Miss Overcomer Global. As an inspirational speaker and workshop leader, Tawana specializes in keynote addresses, workshops, and team coaching, tailoring her sessions to meet the unique needs of her audience.

Tawana's journey is marked by her remarkable resilience in the face of daunting challenges, having overcome domestic abuse, date rape, poverty, loss of loved ones, bankruptcy, and divorce. Tawana Lowery is a trusted resource in personal growth and spiritual development. Her ability to connect with her audience and her deep understanding of the challenges women face makes her an invaluable asset for any event or workshop.

When asked to share her best advice, her response reflects her belief in the power of an Overcomer spirit: "If you quit when times are tough or give up too soon, you'll miss seeing how God works all things together for good."

Website: www.MissOvercomer.com
YouTube: Miss Overcomer Global
FBK & IG: @Miss Overcomer Global

Unshakable Identity

By Tawana Lowery

I have an unquenchable fire in my soul to help women overcome whatever is holding them back. This fire was ignited by an unexpected "burning bush" moment similar to the experience Moses had in Exodus 3. But unlike Moses, my life-changing encounter did not happen on the back side of a desert but on the back side of a thirty-year cycle of tragedy that culminated with a triple dose of heartbreak.

In the spring of 2013, my mother died suddenly from a stroke. Six months later, I discovered my second marriage was in the death throes of a painful conclusion. The following year, my father passed away from heart failure.

The day after my father's memorial, I was at home looking at family pictures in hopes of connecting with a happier time. As I placed the picture of my dad back among the other perfectly displayed photos on my living room credenza, a deep, nauseating sorrow swept over my mind. In that moment, I realized that the life and future I had hoped for was forever out of reach.

Family gone. Marriage gone. Plans and dreams were gone as well. And worst of all, it felt as if the tsunami of loss had also swept away my identity. It was like watching the sands of my life falling through my fingers. There was nothing I could do to bring it back.

Beneath the weight of overwhelming hopelessness and helplessness, I dropped to the floor in gut-wrenching pain. All I had left was a cry of despair as I screamed toward the heavens, "Look at all I've overcome. Look at all I've overcome." Through the intense tears of a wounded, rejected victim identity, I continued crying out to God, "Look at it! Look at all I've overcome!"

And I was not only thinking about the back-to-back loss of parents and marriage but also the thirty years of hardship that preceded it—hardships that included the childhood pain of domestic abuse and being date raped as a minor, with the added emotional trauma of having a forced abortion. Adding insult to injury, I also experienced homelessness, divorce in my twenties, living below the poverty level as a single mother, loss of businesses and homes, and two bankruptcies.

From my perspective, the back-to-back loss of parents and marriage was the final blow in the final round. I had no more strength or desire to overcome another hardship. Ring the bell. Game over! Although I was a Bible-believing follower of Yeshua, this was the last straw. It was time to wave the white flag and dive headlong into the abyss of a permanent victim.

While lying face down on the hardwood floor in complete exhaustion, I heard the kind, loving voice of God speak to my ravaged heart. He whispered, "Tawana, did you have to overcome it, or were you enabled to overcome it? Were you forced to overcome or empowered to overcome?" As if being grabbed by the coat tail before falling off the edge, His question rescued me from a spiraling black hole of despair.

Then He continued, "The truth is, you did, in fact, overcome every single event because I prepackaged you ahead of time to be an overcomer. But you have spent your life focused on the loss and pain rather than the victory. I know you're hurting, but this is not the end. Tawana, just look at all you've overcome!"

Psalm 3:3 says the Lord is the one who lifts my head high. Hearing the Lord's voice lifted my head off the floor and my spirit from the jaws of defeat. His words were undeniable. I had, in fact, overcome each and every hardship.

But there was more God wanted me to know concerning my true identity and why it mattered. He began speaking to the hidden place where false identity had taken root by saying, "I know everything you've been through. I know it very well. But you don't see it the way I do. You're thinking like a victim who only sees a list of liabilities. The hardships are not a list of liabilities. That is your resume. And you are not a victim. Tawana, you are an overcomer!"

Then the burning bush moment flamed even brighter when He asked, "What are you going to do with it?"

Immediately, I saw my catalog of despairing liabilities transform into a bright, glowing list of assets. In the twinkling of an eye, it became the powerful, valuable resume of a seasoned overcomer. Receiving the truth from the Spirit of Truth set me free, just as the scripture had promised.

In my mind's eye, I could see my self-protective armor of false identity fall into the abyss of lies where it belonged. As it dissipated, I saw a new wardrobe adorn my life. The old garments of false identity, the smelly robe of a rejected victim, was replaced with the royal cape of an empowered overcomer, with a 30-year resume to prove it.

No doubt the enemy had hit me over and over and over again with the hellish intention to dismantle my spirit with false identity. With trickery and deceit, he desired that I align my value with the transitory things of this world and circumstances that are frequently subject to change.

No doubt the God of Abraham, Isaac, and Jacob had another plan. His plan was to prosper me and rescue me from the lies of false identity. He gave me a new name so I could walk in my true identity that comes from Him alone. He desired that I align my identity with the things of His unshakable kingdom.

My transformative burning bush encounter reoriented me towards a focused determination to reap the full benefits of my unshakable identity. But in order to walk forward in perseverance, I knew I would need a supportive, faith-focused sisterhood for the journey.

So I began searching for a community that embodied three important areas of support. The first was a safe, judgment-free sisterhood where I could be transparent about my pain. The second was a team of women to help me reclaim lost courage. Thirdly, I wanted guidance on how to use my calling to advance the kingdom. Unfortunately, I came up short. I could not find what I was looking for in my time of need.

But the burning bush question had emboldened my determination. Not being able to find the resources I desired was no excuse to stop. Because I was committed to walking in true identity, my thoughts were higher. I asked better questions. I viewed the challenge as an opportunity to grow or develop new skills.

Rather than giving up, I chose to move forward in my true identity by asking, "What would an Overcomer do? How would a Princess Warrior Dragon Slayer approach this challenge?"

The answer came quickly. "An Overcomer would become what she cannot find in her time of need to help others overcome."

With that new insight, my first step was to write a blog about how to overcome common struggles of life. Within a few months, people from 90 countries were reading my overcomer messages.

In 2015, I wrote and published my first book with the purpose of helping others amplify God's voice through prayer. After all, God's voice had rescued me from the pit of lies. His voice propelled me forward. My desire was to help others connect with the Father's voice so they could walk in freedom and truth.

Several months later, God allowed me to launch a women's nonprofit to connect women of faith with the community and resources I was looking for during my overcomer journey. When a person knows their true identity, knowing what to do and how to do it becomes easier. The key is to stay connected with truth and renounce any lie the enemy might use to knock us off course.

Countless women of faith find themselves trapped in a false identity because of their experiences. Like me, they have assumed their identity comes from roles, titles, acceptance, or accomplishments. When those circumstances are shaken, they are shaken as well.

As disciples of Jesus, we are admonished to build our lives on that which can never be shaken. That means we must be secure in our true identity spoken over us from the foundation of the world by the King of the universe.

You might be thinking, *I am a child of God. That is my identity and all I need to know.* And you would be partially correct. You are indeed a child of God. But you also have a unique fingerprint, which means you also have a unique identity that is as unique as your fingerprint.

The Lord's desire is that we live and move and have our being in complete truth. We walk it out with others to advance His kingdom together, but also in our unique God-ordained selves.

Because we are God's divine offspring, He placed a component of Himself in each person. His breath fills our lungs. His blood redeems our souls. But His character has also been imparted to each of us in order to work in unison as one connected, cohesive body.

Sadly, many believers ask the same questions as non-believers, "Who am I, and why am I here?" They live in daily uncertainty and fear because they do not know who they truly are. As a result, they spend much of their lives hiding in the false rather than thriving in the truth. They mistakenly believe that being is determined by doing. But if we do not know who we are, how can we know why we are here and what our magnificent purpose is?

Perhaps you are curious about how a person can know their true identity. Maybe you are wondering what steps are needed to get there. If so, let me share a very simple process that has empowered hundreds of people to engage with their true identity and break free of the false narratives.

The following steps outline the same process I share in workshops and seminars. I call it "The Identity Reveal."

STEP 1: GET PREPARED

Find a quiet place where you can spend a few minutes alone with the loving presence of God. Grab a pen and journal.

STEP 2: BE OPEN

In order to receive truth from the Spirit of Truth, we must release the false. That includes any false identities we have believed about ourselves created from experiences or the false narratives of the world. We will begin by praying the following prayer.

"Heavenly Father, I give You all the false identities I have adopted as truth. I give You all the lies I have believed about myself based on my experiences with the world and people. I ask that they all be crucified on the cross of Jesus and made completely dead. Forgive me. I truly did not know what I was doing. Resurrect me in Messiah to receive my true identity that You spoke over me before time began. Amen."

STEP 3: BE HONEST

In the days following my burning bush experience, I wanted to go deeper and wider in receiving my true identity. That required honest confession about the false identity formed out of my experiences. However, because I had adopted many of them as truth, it was impossible for me to identify every lie without receiving revelation from God's Spirit.

In this step, we will confess the false identities by calling on the Spirit of Truth to reveal them to our hearts and minds.

To begin, it's important to relax your mind so you can receive. Next, be sure to journal everything you hear from God. Then, pray the following prayer as an act of faith.

"Heavenly Father, show me all the names and labels I have called myself that are not from You. Tell me what I am saying about myself that wounds my soul. Speak to my heart, Lord, and silence the voice of the enemy on my behalf so I can clearly hear what You want to say. I give You permission to speak truth to my mind about all the lies I am believing about myself. Amen."

Be sure to write down everything God speaks without any feelings of condemnation or judgment.

STEP 4: BE SET FREE

The scriptures tell us to cast all our cares on the Lord because He cares for us. That means giving God our burdens, griefs, and sorrows. Carrying a false identity definitely qualifies as a burdensome grief that can cause a great deal of sorrow.

In this step, we will intentionally cast away the burden of false identity. In other words, we will give God the list of lies we just wrote down in Step 3. First, close your eyes and visualize Jesus standing before you.

Next, see yourself giving Him your list of false identities. Visualize yourself placing it in His hands. Then, be sure to take note of what He does with your list of false identities. Journal what you think God wants you to know about the false identity.

STEP 5: THE BIG REVEAL

Now that you have released the false identity, it is time to receive your true identity. That means allowing the King of heaven to reveal His truth to your heart and mind.

Begin by relaxing your mind and be prepared to journal what you hear God speak to you. Try not to filter or dismiss what you hear. Simply write down every word He speaks, even if it sounds unusual or unorthodox. Let's pray the following prayer.

"Lord, what did You call me before the foundation of the earth? Lord Jesus, who do You say that I am?"

Journal everything you hear. Next, read each name out loud. Journal how it makes you feel.

STEP 6: ADD YOUR AGREEMENT

In chapter 1 of Luke, the angel addressed Mary, calling her *highly favored* (Luke 1:28 NIV). The angel called her by her true identity. Her response upon hearing it should be our response as well: *"I am the Lord's servant," Mary answered. "May your word to me be fulfilled"* (Luke 1:38 NIV). Review your new identity and then pray this prayer.

"Heavenly Father, thank You for speaking truth to my heart and soul concerning my true identity. And now I add my agreement by saying, 'May your word to me be fulfilled.' I also ask for wisdom and revelation for the days ahead. Amen."

STEP 7: OFFER FORGIVENESS

When we are free from the lies and shame of false identity, it fills our hearts with compassion for those who remain trapped in the false.

With this in mind, let's pray the following prayer for others who need to come to the saving truth of their true identity, especially those who have wounded us.

"Heavenly Father, I chose to forgive those who spoke false identity over my life. I ask that You forgive them and set them free to walk in the truth. As Your disciple, I ask that You would advance Your kingdom and salvation in all of us for the praise of Your glorious name. Amen."

Sister, God has not called us to walk in perfection but to walk in truth. He desires that we live and move and have our being in the true, authentic, appointed, anointed, assigned identity that is rightfully ours to possess. As we continually align our hearts and minds with the truth, we are set free of the lies that seek to consume us each day.

Our true, unshakable identity propels us forward with confidence. It empowers us to stand and step into the unknown with faith. Our true identity enables us to engage each person and each challenge in our true self without fear, without being shaken. This was the reality for Gideon, Esther, Peter, Moses, David, and countless others. It is the same for you and me.

True identity does not come from the things of this world. It does not come from relationships, possessions, titles, accomplishments, failures, religious affiliation, or the approval of others. All those sources are like the shifting sand. They are all subject to change. All can and will be shaken.

But our true identity comes from the one and only God of creation. And it is sourced in His unconditional love. It comes from the Father of light, from the Spirit who spoke the world into being. Because it comes from a kingdom that will never be shaken, we, too, can stand securely in our unshakable identity.

With regard to the women's nonprofit I launched, the name is *Miss Overcomer Global.* God allowed me to keep my promise to become what

I could not find in my time of need. The mission of Miss Overcomer is to provide a loving community of faith for women of destiny so they can lead with courage and calling in their true identity.

From the world's perspective, I should have been just another statistic. But God had another plan. His plan was to empower me with unshakable true identity. Although my hardships were multiplied, I was given an opportunity to multiply hope and lead others into their unshakable identity found in the unshakable love of Jesus, our Savior and King.

> *"If you abide in My word, you are My disciples indeed. And you shall know the truth, and the truth shall make you free"* (John 8:31-32 NKJV).

Unshakable When You Trust God

By Donna Whartenby

Some days, it isn't easy to know who to trust. In today's world, information is often stated inaccurately, truth is intentionally sidelined, and once-trusted sources have become unreliable. But God can be trusted; in Him, we can be unshakable. We can trust every outcome we put in God's hands. For believers in Jesus Christ and Yahweh, our Lord God, Romans 8:20 (ESV) tells us *all things work together for good.*

You can trust that God wants the best for you. God is omniscient, which means He knows everything. He knows your needs better than you do. Proverbs 3:5-7 (NLT) promises, *Trust in the Lord with all your heart; do not depend on your own understanding. Seek his will in all you do, and he will show you which path to take.* As His children, we can trust God completely—with all our hearts and minds. On the contrary, we cannot trust others—or even our own feelings—to tell us what is right or best for us. Ask God for His direction in your life—He knows your needs before you even ask. Then, listen to Him without fear or doubt, knowing He will guide your path in your life. The ESV version of Proverbs 3:7 tells us, *Be not wise in your own eyes; fear the Lord and turn away from evil.* Stand firm. Psalms tells us, *Trust in Him at all times...pour out your heart to Him, God is our refuge* (Psalm 62:7-8 NIV). Be unshakable in your trust in Almighty God.

Delight yourself in the Lord, and he will give you the desires of your heart. Commit your way to the Lord; trust in him, and He will act (Psalm 37:4-5 ESV).

Reading scripture will bring you joy, teaching you to trust and commit everything to Him—your life, family, job, and future. God promises to bless you in ways you cannot expect or imagine; He will protect and provide for your needs, fight for you, and never leave you. I've never counted all God's promises written in the Bible, but some sources say He gave us over 8,800 promises. He has already fulfilled some, and others are yet to be satisfied. But we can trust that what God has promised will surely come to be.

Prayer will set your mind on God, helping you become in tune with Him and reinforcing the fact that you can trust Him. You can communicate directly with God. He will communicate His will, plan, and purpose for you. Humbly present your requests to the Father so He can reveal His provision for you and guide you down the path He has planned for you. When you believe His promises and follow Him in obedience, you can trust that His will—which is better than we could ask or imagine—will be fulfilled. And He will bless you by allowing you to play an integral part in Yahweh's plan for eternity.

> *And this is the confidence that we have toward him, that if we ask anything according to his will he hears us. And if we know that he hears us in whatever we ask, we know that we have the requests that we have asked of him* (1 John 5:14-15 ESV).

Seeking to know God will solidify your trust in Him. My hope is that your heart's deepest yearning would be to know God—for when you know God, you will develop an unshakable trust in Him. You can discover God's attributes and promises by studying His Word. Jesus taught, *"If you abide in my word, you are truly my disciples, and you will know the truth, and the truth will set you free"* (John 8:32 ESV).

Fully trusting God will set you free in several ways. I'd like to highlight two of them.

When you trust God, He will renew your mind, replacing the thoughts, ideas, and desires that go against Him. Trusting and following God's truth will set you free from unacceptable living in God's eyes and break the bondage of sin, giving you unshakable freedom.

Trusting God allows you to look to Him for help (Micah 7:5-7). This can be so important, especially through difficult times of conflict, distrust, and disappointment with family, marriage, friends, and co-workers; it can be hard to know where to turn.

As Christians, we can trust that God wants the best for us and will fulfill every promise He has ever made. We can seek Him through Scripture and prayer, trusting He will reveal Himself to us. And when we do, He will renew our minds and give us the perfect wisdom only He can offer.

God loves you and cares about you more than you can know. He will faithfully guide and lead you—He alone deserves your trust. And when you fully rely on and trust Him, you will indeed be unshakable!

> *As for me, I look to the Lord for help. I wait confidently for God to save me, and my God will certainly hear me* (Micah 7:7 NLT).

Father, help me to fully accept Your truth by studying Your Word. Show me Your will for my life. Help me when my circumstances seem impossible and I do not know what to trust. Show me Your promises. Guide me to turn to You in complete and unshakable trust, knowing You hear my prayer. My hope and trust are in You, Lord, because You always keep Your promises. Thank you for loving me. I rejoice in Your love. AMEN.

Kimberly Ewell

Kimberly Ewell has been walking with the Lord for eleven years. During that time, she learned to walk in faith and obedience, which brought her to where she is today. After years of healing and training, Kimberly founded WildFire International Ministries in Orlando, Florida, and has become a bestselling published author sharing her experiences and the love of God that changed her life forever.

Because of Kimberly's personal experiences of childhood trauma, abuse, pain, grief, and loss, Kimberly has been given a powerful testimony of God's love and healing power.

As part of her journey, the Lord called Kimberly to Colorado Springs, CO., to learn ministry work at Focus on the Family. There, she gained experience of what it's like to be on the battlefield's front lines. The Lord opened Kimberly's eyes to the depths of the brokenness that runs rampant across the world. During her time at Focus on the Family, she ministered, counseled, and poured out the love of Jesus to many people across the nation.

Kimberly firmly believes that every person should be empowered to fulfill their God-given calling and destiny. She desires to see people healed and living in freedom.

Kimberly can be reached at wildfireintl.us@gmail.com

Unshakable Faith—A Gift from God

By Kimberly Ewell

Over the years, I've been asked countless times, "How do you do the things you do?"

"I couldn't do it!" I have always responded. "I don't know; I simply listen to the Holy Spirit and follow His lead. It's a journey that feels effortless, guided by Him."

As a baby Christian, I was still wet behind the ears and learning. I knew about having the faith of a mustard seed, but honestly, I didn't completely understand it. So, I believed in what the Holy Spirit told me, and I stepped out with the faith God had given me. Like a mustard seed, this faith has grown and transformed me, enabling me to do things I never thought possible.

My unshakable faith adventure began around Easter 2015. I lived in California, hadn't seen my family in Florida in a few years, and it was time for a well-overdue vacation I desperately needed. I looked forward to spending time with everyone and relaxing on the beach.

Just days after my arrival, my sister-in-law shared a dream she had about me. She said that the Lord showed her that I would be moving back to Florida.

I stood there looking at her as if she was insane, and I replied that there was no way I'd ever live in Florida again. She shook her head and said, "I dunno, I think you're moving back!" Little did she realize she had planted a seed that God would water later during that visit.

My sister-in-law, Tiffany, and I enjoy shopping at the local thrift stores. My family lived in a cute beach community with some of the best thrift store shopping in the area, where they sold some of our favorite surf-style clothing like what we had grown up with. So off we went!

While browsing through the clothes, I heard a woman with a British accent saying, "Hello!"

I turned to see an older lady with bright red hair, and I couldn't help but think of the movie character Nanny McPhee. Though I didn't want to take the time to chat with her, I politely replied, "Hello."

I continued going through the clothes as she began to spark a conversation with me. It was a simple chat about the weather and how much she loved thrift store shopping. She also mentioned that she couldn't drive, so her husband would drive her all over town to shop while he waited in the car, sometimes for hours, until she finished. I thought the poor man must be bored out of his mind sitting in a hot car for hours.

Our conversation ended, and I was about to enter the dressing room when she said, "Jesus loves you!"

Because I just wanted to be left alone, my prideful self replied with a smile, "I know." Then I turned and walked into the dressing room.

As I began to try on the clothes, I couldn't help but reflect on the encounter. The woman's simple words, "Jesus loves you," stirred something within me. I was confronted with my pride and rudeness, and I was convicted.

In that moment of conviction, I heard an urgent whisper in my spirit. It was a clear command: "Tell her you're sorry and appreciate her for telling you that Jesus loves you."

It was a command that required immediate action, and I knew I had to obey. However small, this act of obedience was a testament to my trust in God's guidance. It reassured me that when we listen and follow, even in the smallest things, God can use us for His purpose.

I immediately halted my activities and began frantically searching for the red-headed lady. I couldn't find her. *Where could she be?* I had to find her because the Lord had told me to do this. I was determined to be obedient and couldn't let her leave yet. Scanning the store, I spotted her by the window, attempting to engage a young man in conversation. As I observed her, she looked at him and said, "Jesus loves you."

The look on the man's face was heartbreaking to me. He ignored her and looked at her as if she was kooky. I watched her walk away with her head down, looking like she had been rejected again.

I rushed up to her and said, "Ma'am, I want to apologize to you; Jesus does love me! I know He does, and you reminded me that He does love me! I had forgotten just how much. Thank you!"

Her face lit up with a radiant smile, and her joy was palpable. I thanked God for her and that reminder as I watched "Nanny McPhee" leave the store. At that moment, It dawned on me that she hadn't purchased anything despite the hours she spent in the store. She wasn't there to buy clothes; she was on a mission to share a simple message, the love of Jesus, with strangers. The Lord sent "Nanny McPhee" for me, not for the man I saw her talking to. It was about God's love for me, my obedience, and whether He could trust me to go to the next step He had for me. This unexpected encounter was a reminder that God works in ways we can't imagine, often using the most unlikely people and situations to teach us His lessons.

Staring out the window on the Delta flight back to California, I was talking with Jesus and thinking about my sister-in-law's dream. I told Jesus I'd move to Florida if He wanted me to; however, I needed confirmation. Of course, that meant at least three confirmations, so I'd know for certain. I told Him my expectations of how I wanted it to go. He would provide financially for the move because I didn't have the money. He would relocate me to the beachside community where my family lived so my daughter and I would be near them. My list went on and on. My demands were reasonable and would make for an easy transition.

I learned later that my ways and God's ways are entirely different.

Have you done this as well? Have you given God your list of demands only to find out He had a different plan? God's ways are so much better than ours. If He did things our way, how could our faith grow to rely on Him when life's challenges arise or when He asks us to "Go"?

I worked at the corporate office of one of the largest Christian radio companies in the nation. I returned to work after my vacation the following day. My boss, the best I've ever had, approached me when I arrived. His first words were, "You can't leave me and move to Florida."

Okay, I thought.

Later, I saw my director—what do you think he said? LOL, "When are you moving to Florida?"

Toward the end of the day, the company's president showed up in my office, saying, "It looks like you had a great time in Florida. Have you thought about working at the radio station in Orlando?"

I thought to myself, *Lord, you're up to something. What's going on?*

David, the president, then suggested I contact the general manager of the Orlando station. So I immediately sent him an email, and within seconds, I had a response. "When are you coming to Orlando? Stop by, and I'll take you on a station tour."

Four weeks later, I was taking that tour and being offered a job. I left the station dumbfounded. "Lord, what is happening?! Am I moving?" I said as I drove away.

About a block from the station was a sizable sign in front of these vibrant, towering pine trees, lush green bushes, and rich, colorful flowers. The sign in front read Barrington at Mirror Lakes. As I passed this property, the Holy Spirit immediately answered my previous question. The words I heard were this, "That's where you will be living!"

I knew, without a doubt, that was where I would be living! I also knew I would be moving sooner rather than later.

When we are obedient to God and are in His will, things start to happen right before our eyes! It's mind-blowing to see God work. Especially when He's doing things we know we can't do alone. My faith grew as I watched Him make things happen—from breaking the news to my boss that I was transferring to Orlando to getting three transfer approvals from higher management—all completed in less than a week. Wow, only God!

Jesus, in His wisdom, used the analogy of a mustard seed to illustrate the power of faith.

> *So Jesus said to them, "Because of your unbelief; for assuredly, I say to you, if you have the faith of a mustard seed, you will say to this mountain, 'Move from here to there,' and it will move; and nothing will be impossible for you"* (Matthew 17:20 NKJV).

This analogy resonated with me deeply and mirrored my faith journey, which started small but grew into something powerful and transformative.

> *Now faith is the substance of things hoped for, the evidence of things not seen* (Hebrews 11:1 KJV).

It was only two months before moving day and the start of my new position in Orlando, and it was time to break the news to my daughter, Cheyanne, who prefers to be called Chey. I approached Chey with great excitement to tell her what the Lord had shown me and that we would be moving in two months. I assumed she would be just as excited about this new adventure. However, she was not. She wanted to stay in California with her dad as she had a community of good friends and was well-established there.

I was distraught and even tried pulling the authoritative "mom card" by putting my foot down to make her go, but that only worsened things. When I was her age, fourteen, I recalled my mother moving us away from our home, and I rebelled. It was the worst thing to happen to me then, and I knew Chey would feel the same way.

In my quiet time with the Lord, I cried to Him, "Help! What do I do?!"

The answer came quickly, "Let her stay. I will protect her, and she will return to you. I need to do things with you and can't if she is with you."

I knew I had to trust the Lord, walk in faith, and understand that He would protect my daughter. I didn't stop praying that the situation would change. However, I also chose to let my hope be in Him, even though I couldn't see what was behind the scenes.

The Holy Spirit told me to read about Abram. After reading this scripture, The LORD had said to Abram, *"Go from your country, your people and your father's household to the land I will show you"* (Genesis 12:1 NIV), I knew I was to "go." I knew I had to trust the Lord and walk in faith like Abram did. I had to surrender and say, "Yes, I will go." Once I did, I had peace. I knew everything would be okay. I was given a precious gift, a gift of faith.

Only the Lord can provide a faith that will enable us to move into something far beyond what we can do with human faith.

In preparation for my move, Chey moved to her father's home. Shortly after, I received a call from her. For some time, she had a massive cyst on her lower back, but she could no longer bear the pain as it continued to worsen. I instructed her to go to the nearest emergency room. She did so. They drained the fluid from the cyst, confirmed she had a blood infection, and admitted her right away. My baby girl was on the edge of death, and we didn't know it. I drove two hours to the hospital she was in, and as I pulled up, I realized this was the same hospital where my son Christopher had died. I was struck with an overwhelming urge to vomit! My nerves were shot as my mind replayed the death of my son over and over again.

I sat in the car for a few minutes, pulling myself together and praying. I asked for the Lord's peace and strength to help me, then took a deep breath and went to see my daughter. I approached her door and calmly walked into her room, unaware of what I would see. My Chey was lying in the bed with leads attached to her body and monitors beside her. She was alert and able to talk to me, but over the next twelve hours, she became feverish, and her blood pressure dropped significantly to the point of concern. The doctors gave her every antibiotic possible to fight the infection, but nothing worked. The following two days, Chey's health declined, and I knew if things got any worse, I may lose her. I cried to the Lord, "I don't know what to pray! Help!"

Sometimes, "Help!" is all we can say.

That night, as I slept, I woke up and heard my daughter talking to someone. She repeatedly told them she wasn't going with them. In the morning, I asked her who she had been talking to, and she told me someone in black was hovering over her bed and telling her she had to go with them. I knew right away it was the spirit of death. I prayed again to the Lord for help, and by that evening, Chey's blood pressure began to rise. Her face started to gain color. She was getting hungry and wanted to eat something. She was quickly recovering.

The following day, we walked around the hospital with her IV pole and spent time on the patio enjoying the mountain views and each other. We spent seven days in the hospital; seven days later, I would be moving to Florida. When she was discharged from the hospital, we said our goodbyes and embraced one another with tears, making promises to call and visit. We talked on the phone several times daily from that day forward, and I shared with her what God was doing in my life.

It took me five days to drive across the country to my new home. As I approached my destination, the familiar GPS voice said, "Turn left here." Halfway into the turn, at the entrance was the sign, *Welcome to Barrington at Mirror Lakes.* The place the Lord told me I'd be living. He had fulfilled His promise to me.

Just weeks after being in Florida, I flew back to California to visit Chey. And then I returned again a few weeks later for Christmas. We continued to talk throughout our days apart.

Shortly after Christmas, I had a moment when I no longer wanted to be in Florida due to spiritual warfare and missing my daughter. I was fighting a spiritual battle I knew nothing about. I knew something was wrong, and my only answer was to run back to California. Chey called me one evening, just when I had enough. She asked me what was wrong, and I told her I hated Florida and wanted to go home. I wanted to be with her; I was lonely. My daughter spoke up to me for the first time and said, "NO, Mama!! God took you to Florida for a reason, and I've been watching Him change your life for the better. I've seen what He's been doing. Hang in there, and do not give up!"

That conversation was a huge pivot point in my life. My daughter saw something happening I didn't: my transformation from the old me to the new creation God created me to be. Chey witnessed my belief and faith in the Lord. She saw me take a huge step to go into the unknown alone. Well, I wasn't alone; Jesus was with me every step of the way.

Though we were physically separated, God continued to grow us closer as mother and daughter.

Now twenty-four years old, Chey is on her journey with Jesus. She has grown into a beautiful young woman and will someday have her own God adventure. When she does, I hope she will remember mine and recognize she can trust God and step out in faith, knowing Jesus will be with her every step.

My adventure began with a seed that the Lord watered by bringing "Nanny McPhee" to remind me of His love for me. My faith grew each time I said, "Yes, Lord," and watched Him open doors I could never have opened myself. I left California with my move completely paid for. I had been in deep debt, but that was all paid in full two months before I left. I had a job waiting for me when I arrived. And I made my home in a stunning apartment, which I shouldn't have been able to qualify for. But God!

Nine years ago, I said "Yes" and went where God asked me to go. I have yet to stop. We—the Lord and I—traveled across the United States as He shaped me into the woman He called me to be. Because of my obedience, He now uses me to minister to others and share what He has done.

You, sweet sister, can also take the step to move forward. Whatever the Lord is calling you to do, do it! Just step! Trust Him, and the Holy Spirit will guide you. When you do, hold on tight because it will be the best adventure you will ever have.

Then people will ask *you,* "How do you do the things you do?"

And you, too, can share your Unshakable Faith, the gift God gave you.

Unshakable When You Need Guidance and Direction

By Donna Whartenby

Making decisions can be difficult; following someone else's guidance and direction can be even more challenging. We can be hesitant to follow God's guidance when we don't know Him well, but deciding to trust the Sovereign God, no matter what difficulties, trials, and challenges we deal with, will allow us to get to know Him intimately and bring us unshakable peace. Trust God, not out of fear, but in confidence that He is Creator of heaven and earth. He designed and created you in His image. He knows what He is doing because He is our Sovereign God. As a start, depend on God as your Sustainer, Provider, and Protector when needing guidance and direction.

God is a loving God. Hebrews 13:5 promises He will never leave you. His desire is for you to prosper; therefore, He will direct your steps into the correct path. Proverbs 20:24 tells us that the Lord directs a person's steps and asks, *How then can anyone understand their own way?* (NIV). If you choose to go on your own without God's direction, your success rate will undoubtedly be low. The prophet Jeremiah cried out to the Lord, *Lord, I know that people's lives are not their own; it is not for them to direct their steps* (Jeremiah 10:23 NIV). God's desire for you is always good. He is in control. The Lord promises He will make a way through the waves of life that come against us (Isaiah 43:16-19). He will clear your path. Proverb 16:3 promises, *Commit to the Lord whatever you do, and he will establish your plans* (NIV).

How can we commit to the Lord and become unshakable by harnessing His perfect guidance and direction? We can choose to.

Choose to have faith in God. God had a plan and purpose for your life designed *before* the foundation of the world! (Ephesians 1:4). You can choose to exercise faith, even when your faith is weak, through prayer, thanksgiving, worship, and living His ways. You have a purpose in His plan for eternity. God will not lead you astray. He is ready to show you the way that will keep you safe, protected, and going in the right direction.

Choose to focus on God. It is difficult to follow someone when you do not give them your full attention. Your unshakable focus on God will help you realize His direction and guidance. Keep your focus on Him through prayer, the study of His Word, listening for His voice, and being aware of His prompting within your spirit. God is pure wisdom and love. And He loves *you!*

Choose to trust and obey God. Luke chronicles a story about trusting God in Luke 5:1-6. After an unsuccessful night of fishing, Peter reluctantly obeyed Jesus and threw his nets back into the water. His boat became so filled with fish he needed help from another boat to take them all in. Peter learned that obeying Jesus's direction can result in a miracle! Miracles *do* happen even today.

Choose to wait on God. Sometimes, God's direction and guidance do not come immediately. We must learn to wait on the Lord. But we can trust that our God is unshakable, and when we wait on Him, our faith will be made unshakable.

> *Wait for the Lord; be strong and take heart and wait for the Lord* (Psalm 27:14 NIV).

Choose to follow God. Trust God with your future. Rely on the God who knows, directs, and guides His children. He will keep you safe and without fear. Proverb 1:33 teaches, *Whoever listens to me will live in safety and be at ease, without fear of harm* (NIV). God knows what tomorrow will bring. Allow Him to lead you down the path He has chosen for you, is beneficial for you, and is a part of His plan. In prayer, ask Him for greater understanding, peace, and strength to carry out His plan.

You can choose to follow God's guidance and direction in whatever you do. Seek His counsel for clarity; allow Him to confirm the direction He wants you to go and give you His peace.

> *Do not be anxious about anything, but in every situation, by prayer and petition, with thanksgiving, present your requests to God. And the peace of God, which transcends all understanding, will guard your hearts and your minds in Christ Jesus* (Philippians 4:6-7 NIV).

> *"For I know the plans I have for you," declares the Lord, "plans to prosper you and not to harm you, plans to give you hope and a future"* (Jeremiah 29:11 NIV).

You can become unshakable by following our perfect God's direction and guidance.

Heavenly Father, I trust Your guidance and direction in my life. I trust Your plans for my future. Thank You for being my Savior, Sustainer, Provider, and Protector. Thank You for making a way for my life and for Your plans that give me hope for my future. I trust You will never desert me and always be with me; strengthen and guide me and direct my steps. My unshakable hope and trust are in You, Lord, because You always keep Your promises. Thank you for loving me. I rejoice in Your love, Your peace, and Your promise of eternal life with You. AMEN.

Kat Pennington

Kat Pennington is family-oriented and loves spending time with her husband, three children, and seven grandchildren. They recently welcomed an addition to their family, Trooper, a mini-schnauzer with a big personality!

Kat is a retired Certified Professional Photographer with the PPA (Professional Photographers of America). During her 30+ years as a professional photographer, she lectured at several state conventions and two International PPA Conventions. She also taught graduate-level photography as an adjunct instructor at Northwestern State University.

As a Stephen Minister, Kat is trained to provide one-to-one care for people going through a difficult time. She and her husband currently lead their church's Marriage Mentoring Ministry, sharing their passion for living marriage—God's way.

A member of WWL (Women World Leaders), Kat was a chapter writer in *Miracle Mindset,* an International Amazon #1 Best Seller book. She was also a chapter writer in *Hope Alive,* a WWL 9x bestselling book.

The Decision Journey

By Kat Pennington

Sometimes making major decisions can be overwhelming. But, there is a process, inspired by Biblical scripture, that offers guidance for making a decision—*and* living in peace with what we decide. In my story, I share how my husband and I used this process at a significant crossroads in our lives, and the consequences of that decision.

CREATING MEMORIES

I married a military man, so we knew we would move a lot during his career. Since Lee and I were both planners, we created lists of things we wanted to collect, places to visit, and activities we wanted to experience.

We enjoyed seeing how things were made, so one of our priorities was to tour regional factories during each assignment. My job was to do the research and schedule our visits.

We also decided to collect postcards from places we visited. As a professional photographer, I realized local photographers knew the best places to shoot. So instead of hunting for interesting locations, we would buy a postcard, record our experiences on the back, and then add the card to a postcard album. This would give us extra time to explore and create a special travel journal.

Years passed, and with every assignment, we turned houses into homes using items we collected here and there. We acquired many meaningful things—a vase from a glass-blowing artisan, local pottery, sculptures, and unique kitchenware. At that time, we didn't realize our valued possessions may be temporary!

What we treasured much more than anything else was our relationships with our children, grandchildren, parents, siblings, extended family, and close friends. Laughter from around the dining room table, warm embraces, and trips together created cherished memories for everyone.

DUTY CALLS

One of Lee's assignments was to the U.S. Embassy in Paris, France. We were excited about our overseas venture and planned to discover romantic Paris together. But duty called, and we were separated within days of moving to Paris. Lee was sent on a six-month assignment to northern France, where I couldn't accompany him.

While Lee was gone, I adapted to Paris, from navigating the metro and bus systems to acclimating to French culture. I worked on my beginner-level French skills by shopping at local markets and spending time with my new and now lifelong Parisian friend who lived in our apartment building.

God was at work in Lee and me during our separation, as we both fell in love with the French people and their culture. To this day, whenever asked how we liked living in France, our answer is, "The United States is our country; Paris is our city."

EGLISE BIBLIQUE BAPTISTE de PARIS

As we learned about French culture, we discovered that France is seen as a post-Christian nation. Yet we still assumed it would be easy to find an English-speaking church to attend because Paris was the largest city in the country. Sadly, as with many countries today, most of France had given way to intellectualism, with New Age philosophies creeping in to dominate the beliefs of its people.

After visiting the only American church in Paris a few times, we realized they had very liberal beliefs, which were against many of our convictions. I was in tears at the thought of being "churchless" for our three-year assignment, so Lee and I asked God to please lead us to any Bible-based Christian community.

God's answer quickly came in the form of a little yellow sticky note, posted in the corner of a bulletin board at the embassy. It was an invitation to attend a French church called *Eglise Biblique Baptiste de Paris,* located across Paris from where we lived. The note said it was a Christian church, so off we went, hopeful but not fully knowing what to expect.

As we walked through the doors of the tiny church, we were warmly greeted by a small congregation of about 25 people. We sat through a sermon given in French by a French pastor. That day we met an American missionary who sat behind us, translating the message for us. No one in the congregation seemed to mind the sound of a quiet, soft voice coming from our new friend.

We were invited to stay for lunch that day and by the end of the meal, we knew we had found our church home. Despite the language barrier, we were united with fellow Christians by the Holy Spirit, who speaks a universal language! If I could picture the New Testament early church, I imagine it would be exactly like our experience was that day.

Eglise Biblique Baptiste de Paris was founded by Dr. Art Sommerville, an American pastor who established several Protestant Christian churches throughout France in the 1950s. The three of us became close friends; we didn't know how important our bond would become in the future.

Lee's Paris assignment passed quickly, and through our next several moves, we attended wonderful churches wherever we were stationed. Then one day, after 32 years of military service, it was time for Lee to retire and for us to finally settle down. Or was it?

RETIREMENT—OR NOT

When Lee retired, we bought a little condo in Florida, believing it would be our final home. We had moved many times and endured multiple, long separations from each other and our family, and we were looking forward to settling down in our forever home.

Just as we were beginning retired life, one day out of the blue, Lee received a phone call from our friend Art from Paris. After the call, Lee asked me a direct question. "Baby, how would you feel about 'taking' a church in northern France?"

My first thought was, *What did he just say?!?*

Lee related Art told him that every Sunday morning, Christians in the village would meet and ask God to send a pastor to lead them. Since Art was an American pastor who spoke fluent French, he offered to train Lee to perfect his French and become their pastor.

Yes! What an opportunity! This sounds wonderful, doesn't it? It certainly did to Lee.

But to me, *hmmm,* not so much.

Things were complicated. Emotions washed over me like a tsunami crashing onto the seashore. As a child, I wondered what it would be like to serve the Lord as a missionary, but to be the wife of a pastor in a French church in a small village in the north of France—where English wasn't spoken? That seemed overwhelming! The choice to go or not was ours.

Lee's pastoral position posed several challenges for me.

Lee spoke French very well but I spoke French like a child, with "Me go shopping yesterday" and "Me like cookie" sentences. I could make people understand me and knew my language skills would eventually improve, so I placed this concern at the bottom of my "challenge list."

As Americans, buying a house in France would be another challenge, but God took care of that. We wouldn't have to endure the ordeal of purchasing or even finding a home, as the congregation owned a furnished little house next door to the church that would be available for us to live in. So thankfully, house-hunting was off my list.

Another concern was the cost of shipping our possessions overseas. The expense was beyond our budget, meaning we could only bring what would fit in a suitcase. Not wanting to rent a long-term storage unit, we would need to sell our furniture and car and give most of our possessions away. We could store a few collected items at our children's homes.

Then came the most difficult challenge of all. Pastoring a church halfway around the world would prevent us from doing life with our children and grandchildren. Lee and I would be separated from our precious family, again! It was not just time together; in all practical terms, our life would be lived indefinitely without our family. This would *not* be a normal three-year military assignment.

With a move to France, we would miss the times we had been so looking forward to in retirement. At first, I thought, *Well, at least we can return for the holidays.* Then it occurred to me: holidays are when most congregations need their pastor to be there for them.

Leaving behind the embrace and fellowship of family and the comforting familiarity of accumulated possessions seemed an unthinkable act of sacrifice. We were on the *precipice of a choice* that could forever alter the course of many lives. My heart ached at the thought of being absent, again, from family. And my world was shaken to its foundation.

THE DECISION JOURNEY

Lee assured me he wouldn't force me to do anything I didn't feel called to do and that we needed to agree on this life-changing decision. We knew it was time for a *Decision Journey.*

When we attended *Eglise Biblique Baptiste de Paris,* Art introduced us to a simple method of making major decisions. We had used it several times, knew it worked, and had nicknamed it our *Decision Journey.* Simple yet powerful, it consisted of praying and fasting for three days while humbly listening for the Holy Spirit's direction. Fasting, or abstaining from food, and depending solely on God, is mentioned over 70 times in the Bible.

Our journey was based primarily on Acts 13:3, *Then after fasting and praying they laid their hands on them and sent them off* (ESV).

Scripture doesn't mention exactly how long one should fast and pray, but three days was Art's guidance, and it felt right for us. During our journey, Lee and I didn't discuss any concerns with each other, so we didn't know how the Lord was leading the other. The only counsel we sought was to read our Bibles. By the end of the journey, we were confident we would have the peace to make a decision.

As I started my journey, tears fell on my shirt during the day and my pillow at night. I felt selfish and guilty as emotions of "NO!" repeatedly ran through my head. I felt caught in a web of choosing between God and my family.

I wish I could say that my tears quickly dried up as I listened to God's calling during my *Decision Journey*, but I can't. Instead, tears turned into blubbering as I pleaded my case to the Lord, justifying why we shouldn't go. *We want to be with our family. We just bought a home. We've moved many times. It's time for us to settle down.* The list went on.

After three days, our *Decision Journey* was complete. God is always good! On the third day, waking up exhausted, my angst was supernaturally gone. It was almost scary how calm I was. I knew then that *if we served others for God, the sacrificed time with our kids would result in God's presence in our family relationships.*

With peace and surrender, I told the Lord I was ready to follow Him wherever He wanted me to go. It felt like I had passed a test. I now jokingly call it a "stress test," but I did pass! Lee also received confirmation about moving.

We began making lists right away. One of the essentials was to buy the largest suitcases the airlines would allow! Other lists divided our belongings between kids, grands, and close friends. As I made checklists, I thought of God's promise to Jacob after he left home to go to a completely foreign place. God appeared to Jacob and gave him this promise, *"I am with you and will keep you wherever you go"* (Genesis 28:15 ESV).

ANOTHER PHONE CALL

One never knows what the Lord knows!

That day, we planned to call Art to get details to tell our children. Then suddenly Lee received *another* out-of-the-blue phone call. It was from a pastor from a church we had previously attended in Alabama. The church planned to develop multiple sites and needed someone to set up those sites. Since Lee had a doctorate in Organizational Leadership, the pastor felt that Lee would be the right person for the job. He was asked to drive to Alabama for an interview.

After receiving the second call, Lee contacted Art to explain what happened. They prayed together, and Art encouraged Lee to follow God's lead. So, in peace and with an open mind, Lee left for the interview.

During the interview with the pastor and elders, Lee felt the Holy Spirit nudge his thoughts. He knew he was being called to serve God—but not as a pastor. Though he had been excited about pastoring the church in France, Lee knew God wanted him to help the Alabama church grow. The interviewers knew it too, as they offered the job to Lee that day.

It was a Proverbs 16:9 moment: *The heart of a man plans his way, but the LORD establishes his steps* (ESV).

I'm convinced that during our *Decision Journey,* we were prepared to accept God's guidance for anything. Lee came home and said, "Hey baby, start packing, but not for France."

Stunned at the news, a comfort washed through me as I sat and listened to Lee's heart and God's leading. And the bonus news was we would be relocating near our family! We called our kids and told them we were moving back to Alabama.

We put our Florida retirement home up for sale, and it sold within a week. Thanks to military assignments, we were moving pros, so we found and rented an apartment in Alabama, packed, moved, unpacked, and Lee was at work in less than a month. Everything fit together like a jigsaw puzzle only the Lord could have made.

At about that same time, the Christians in the village in northern France received an answer to their prayers, as God sent a French pastor to lead them. Lee and I knew the young man from our Paris church and couldn't imagine anyone better to shepherd the congregation. It was additional confirmation that God was moving with purpose in many lives.

UNFORESEEN CIRCUMSTANCES

During the time Lee worked in Alabama, we received unforeseen blessings from God, which included:

Grief comfort: One Sunday morning my nephew was killed in a horrible car accident. During the following days, I was able to be with my sister as she organized her only son's funeral service, closed his accounts, and picked up his college diploma, which he never had the chance to see. My sister grieved so deeply that she suffered a heart attack from Broken Heart Syndrome, and again, God granted me the opportunity to be with her while she recuperated.

Reconciliation: When my dad developed Alzheimer's, his wife put him into a nursing home. Because of God's direct intervention in our lives, I visited Dad almost daily. Though we had been estranged for many years, the Lord allowed us to reconcile everything during our precious time together in the nursing home. The past hurts between us were completely forgiven, and my anger from desertion and rejection melted away. God gave us those wonderful days together before Dad transitioned to heaven, and I was gifted with a seemingly impossible and unexpected blessing of healing in our relationship.

A newly found ministry: While Lee worked at the church, he and I were trained to become Marriage Mentors. The time we spent mentoring couples developed into a passion, and to this day, we continue to be honored and excited to help couples live strong, committed marriages God's way.

QUESTIONS AND ANSWERS

Sometimes I can't seem to wrap my head around the fact that God knows our tomorrow. Fleeting questions pop up, like, "Why?" and "God, are You (positively) sure You have the right person to do this?" When I'm trying to make a decision that's clouded with confusion, I implement a *Decision*

Journey, remembering that God already knows the answers and outcome, and no decision, one way or the other, will alter His divine plan.

In seeking God and honoring Him with all of my heart, I know He will take *whatever* I decide and weave it into the tapestry of His ultimate design. Even when I make my decision through whining and tears, He will use that decision for good, if *He* is honored. When Jesus was facing the most significant decision of His life, obeying God by going to the cross, He prayed, *"Father, if you are willing, remove this cup from me. Nevertheless, not my will, but yours, be done"* (Luke 22:42 ESV).

Although Lee was immediately willing to leave for France to serve God, I identified with Moses from the Bible. When God asked Moses to do something, he whined and gave reasons for not doing what God asked. But in the end, Moses was completely willing to serve the Lord. After completing my *Decision Journey,* I was completely ready to follow the Lord and found peace with my decision without the need to reconsider it.

UNSHAKABLE

I admit that some things upset me, especially when I face unforeseen circumstances or have to make an unexpected decision. I wish I were instantly unshakable, but I'm not. Yet, I do know where to find the *only* unshakable refuge—a refuge so solid that nothing can or will ever budge it.

This refuge is *God Himself.* He is always here for everyone, and anyone can turn to His living words in the Holy Bible to get to know Him, how He thinks, and what He expects.

God and I have a personal and unbreakable relationship. The great news is that this same relationship is available to anyone. God is consistently there, and we can truly face anything with Him. The Lord God has always been and always will be totally, absolutely, and unmistakably unshakable.

GOD is unshakable.

God IS unshakable.

God is UNSHAKABLE.

Unshakable When Called to Serve God

By Donna Whartenby

Have you ever felt God calling you to do something you have never done before? Or asking you to do something far beyond what you believed you were able to do? I have. I could not believe God was directing me to follow His will by teaching a Bible study. *Not me! Teach a Bible study? How can I teach a Bible study when I have not been to one? Why me?* But God turned my shakable doubts into unshakable service to others when He called me to serve Him.

In the Bible, Moses had a similar experience. In Exodus 4:10-12, Moses told God he could not speak to Pharoah. Scholars say Moses stammered. He knew he could not address Pharoah, the Egyptian ruler. God instructed Moses to demand Pharaoh release the enslaved Israelites, God's chosen people, and allow them to leave Egypt. Even though Moses made the demands, Pharoah was not willing to release hundreds of thousands of slaves.

The tasks God calls us to are not often easy; His assignments require us to depend on Him. We need His understanding and wisdom to accomplish what He asks us to do. Knowing we cannot accomplish the task alone, we must humble ourselves to serve our Lord. And by doing so, we learn to glorify and trust Him.

> *For it is God who works in you to will and to act in order to fulfill his good purpose* (Philippians 2:13 NIV).

God shows us His desire for us to do His will through the Holy Spirit, who dwells in each of His believers. The Holy Spirit is our Helper and Teacher (John 14:26). He guides and directs us in the way we are to serve God to accomplish our task. As believers, because of our love for God, the Holy Spirit transforms and teaches us God's ways as we read His Word and communicate with Him in prayer. *And this is love: that we walk in obedience to his commands. As you have heard from the beginning, his command is that you walk in love* (2 John 6:6 NIV). Our love for God gives us the desire to accomplish the tasks He assigns us. Because of my love and trust in God, I earnestly studied and learned the content, enabling me to teach that first Bible study and, unshakably, to teach dozens more since—because I am doing God's will by serving Him.

"For even the Son of Man did not come to be served, but to serve" (Mark 10:45 NIV). As we learn who Jesus was and understand His earthly ministry, we see Jesus instruct us how to be servants. As an example, in John 13:1-17, Jesus humbled Himself to wash the feet of His twelve disciples. He then taught them that if their leader/teacher/Lord washes their feet, then they are to wash the feet of others in service to God, too. Jesus said, *"If you love me, keep my commands"* (John 14:15). Jesus calls us to obey God in service.

Jesus shows us that as we serve others, we give of ourselves. Luke shared Paul's words in Acts 20:35, *"In everything I did, I showed you that by this kind of hard work we must help the weak, remembering the words the Lord Jesus himself said: 'It is more blessed to give than to receive'" (NIV).* And Paul teaches further, *For you have been called to live in freedom... don't use your freedom to satisfy your sinful nature. Instead, use your freedom to serve one another in love... For the whole law can be summed up in this one command: "Love your neighbor as yourself"* (Galatians 5:13-14 NLT).

But don't just listen to God's word. You must do what it says. Otherwise, you are only fooling yourselves. For if you listen to the word and don't obey, it is like glancing at your face in a mirror. You see yourself, walk away, and forget what you look like. But if you look carefully into the perfect law that sets you free, and if you do what it says and don't forget what you heard, then God will bless you for doing it (James 1:22-25 NLT).

God calls us each to serve in unique ways, but the underlying connecting component is that we are to love others as ourselves (Mark 12:31). We are called to serve by loving others in the same manner Jesus does—without regard to race, station in life, health, or location on a map.

> *Jesus replied, "But even more blessed are all who hear the word of God and put it into practice"* (Luke 11:28 NLT).

> *How joyful are those who fear [revere, honor, obey] the Lord—all who follow his ways!* (Psalm 128:1 NLT).

God blesses and rewards our obedience in serving Him.

Look for serving opportunities that help and serve others. Listen for the Holy Spirit to guide you into the task He has prepared for you. Pray for God's direction to serve in obedience. God can turn your shakable doubts into unshakable service to others, just as He did for me.

Lord, I will obey whatever you call me to do, no matter how hard I think it might be. I love and trust You. Thank You, Holy Spirit, for directing my path in service to the Lord. In Jesus' name. Amen.

Marli Brown

Marli Brown is a gifted speaker, author, and musician with a unique style of communication. A dynamic storyteller, Marli uses humor and everyday situations to describe the love, mercy, and grace of God. Her calling to *worship, witness, and write* is based on Psalm 96:1-3. Marli grew up in Brighton, Michigan, earned a BA in Psychology from William Tyndale College, and was ordained with the Evangelical Church Alliance, Chicago, IL, in 2006.

Marli is the author of *Ridin' Shotgun,* which recounts her family's journey of living on the road in an RV for eight years. Marli and Randy have been married for 36 years and serve together in a full-time worship concert and speaking ministry, *Randy & Marli Ministries,* which takes them throughout the United States. Randy & Marli focus on encouraging the body of Christ through concerts and women's ministry events. Their mission is *"to see the lost saved and the saved made stronger."*

They live in Grand Rapids, Michigan. For more information on Marli Brown or *Randy & Marli Ministries,* visit their website at www.randyandmarli.com.

Unshakable Provision

By Marli Brown

"Lord, what if we've made a colossal mistake?"

I could barely squeak out the words as my throat hurt from the muffled cries. I was confused, frustrated and broke. Yet, I was determined to follow the Lord like the disciples did when Jesus told them to preach the gospel in distant cities without taking along a walking stick, a change of clothes, or money for travel expenses.

I thought of what the Bible says in Matthew 10:9-10: *"Don't take any money in your money belts—no gold, silver, or even copper coins. Don't carry a traveler's bag with a change of clothes and sandals or even a walking stick. Don't hesitate to accept hospitality, because those who work deserve to be fed"* (NLT).

Jesus sent His disciples on a mission without the necessary supplies to sustain them. That created quite the dilemma for them as travelers. And just like the disciples, the Lord took my family of four on a journey without the means to get across the country or even to the next state. But we went because we were certain of our mission, convinced of our calling, and trusted His character. Most of all, we had to learn the countercultural lesson that money is never our source of power.

But at that moment, I was shaking. Everything familiar was gone, and I was a mess. I questioned every decision that led us to that place. Answering my question, God's voice was clear, "Marli, with Me, what is a colossal mistake? What can you do that I cannot redeem?" His *unshakable* confidence brought instant peace.

Early in our full-time worship, concert, and speaking ministry, my husband, Randy, and I (along with our two young children) went to Florida for two months of ministry. We helped a small church develop a worship team. They gave us a weekly paycheck, which, although generous considering the size of the congregation, was only half the amount needed to make our weekly budget. We owned a house in Michigan but needed housing in Florida. With no money, no surplus, and no support, we found a small rental house for January and February. Miraculously, two separate parties paid the rent.

Our plan was to schedule concerts on Wednesday and Sunday evenings and use the CD sales and love offerings to offset the shortage. However, other than three concerts, Randy was unable to book our open evenings. Doors continually shut. Hindsight reveals that the Lord designated that season as training. At the time, we were discouraged and scared; we couldn't pay our bills and we were spiraling further into debt. I tried my best to trust beyond what I could see, but sometimes, my emotions got the best of me. As the bookkeeper of our ministry and household, I kept track of the numbers, and everything looked bleak.

A few weeks into the tour, Randy said, "I think the Lord wants us to give away half of our salary."

"What? Honey, I know the numbers, and we have a stack of bills. You realize we're going down, right?"

All he said was, "I know. Wanna go down giving?"

That was an interesting idea, and silently, I revisited Malachi chapter 3. God said to test Him with our giving.

"Okay, let's do it. We tithe first, cut everything in half, and give the rest to whomever God tells us to."

At the end of two months, we were almost thirty days late on our mortgage payment, but we were still giving. It seemed irresponsible and futile. It wasn't. It was obedience. It was a test—no, it was an *exam.*

Pulling out of the church parking lot after our final concert in Florida, I opened the envelope that held the love offering. I knew it would be the mother lode of all offerings, and the Lord would use it to fix our money problems in one fell swoop.

It wasn't, and it didn't. The offering was only ninety-eight dollars.

What were we thinking, giving half our salary away? I asked myself and instantly relinquished everything I knew to be true. Again, I was shaking. I turned on God and my husband. I looked at Randy and said, "I cannot believe we are in this situation after obeying God. *What* is He doing?"

Unlike me, Randy is a steady soul, rarely rocked by circumstances. I, however, can be laughing one minute but crying the next. "Reel it in babe, reel it in," he often says to remind me of my passion that often leads to roller-coaster emotions.

After counting the crumpled tens, fives, and single dollar bills, I said, "We are hundreds short of what we need. Hundreds." I explained that I had saved a little money from some CD sales and told him of the measly amount in our bank account. When added to that day's love offering, we were still hundreds short.

Now, I'm no math whiz, but it wasn't that hard to figure out—especially because the numbers didn't have that many zeros. If more goes out than comes in, you'll have a shortage. We started the tour short, so why was I surprised we were still behind?

"Count it again," said Randy.

I did and got the same amount. We were hundreds short. It was quiet in the SUV as we drove. Randy looked at me with peace and confidence.

"Count it again."

I did, and to my amazement, when I added it up the third time, it was all there! We had enough to pay the outstanding bills. It wasn't enough to make a life-changing investment, but it was enough to write a check for our mortgage payment.

I can't explain what happened in the car that day because I really don't know. Maybe God hid the extra money from my eyes on the first two counts, or maybe He physically multiplied the money in my hand. I have no idea. But I do know that what happened was miraculous, and no one will ever convince me otherwise. Since I kept track of the numbers, I knew the totals.

God did the impossible with our finances and provided for us in a way I could not foresee. In that moment, I pictured Jesus—eyes fixed on me, arms folded, grinning ear to ear, elbowing the angel next to Him, saying, "Watch this. Watch what I'm going to do for Randy and Marli."

I'll never forget feeling His faithfulness: relief, thankfulness, and indescribable glee. It was downright *fun*. But I also felt regret. I had been so quick to judge the Lord as a failure, and I lacked the patience and stability it took to keep trusting Him.

Even with a small offering, God was not limited. He doesn't fail. He *can't*. With limited perspective, we evaluate God's decisions, and usually what we deem a failure, He proves a success. With compassion and mercy, He continues to develop godly characteristics in me that I need to walk in faith. He uses situations like that to stretch me, and even though it's hard, it's always for my benefit.

I apologized to the Lord for having such a strong opinion about how *He* should answer *my* prayer. Even now, years later, when we're in a bind, we name that miracle, and then—we rest.

I think that's one reason Jesus sent the disciples without money. He grew them in confidence and trust so they would serve Him faithfully even when all seemed hopeless. The tests and trials God designs for each of us are not random. He designs each one with a very specific purpose in mind. Our response reveals the depth of our trust in Him.

The end of those two months in Florida found us reeling from God's miraculous provision. We'd been flying high for about fifteen minutes when we realized we had to drive from Florida to Southern California for our next set of concerts. Since the Florida church had run out of money and was unable to pay us for our last week of service, we had no money for travel expenses. We had plenty of work scheduled in California, but no way to get there.

Just like the Israelites, we were fickle. We decided to go home. We told the Lord, "Unless You show up, we're throwing in the towel, heading north, and crawling home with our tails between our legs."

Not even two hours later, the pastor from Pasadena who'd hired us to teach a marriage seminar called with God's answer: "We decided we're not paying you enough to come all the way to California. We are adding an extra three hundred dollars. It'll be waiting for you when you get here."

What? Who does this?! We've been in ministry a long time, and I assure you, that's extremely rare. Budgets are tight, tithing is down, and the economy is fragile. We never want to hurt a church budget, which is why we prefer love offerings. But that day, the pastor was God's voice saying, *I am calling you on a journey without an extra cloak or bag of money. Wanna go?*

Since we didn't have that money in hand, the question still gnawed at me: *How are we going to get to California with no money?* Nonetheless, we knew where God wanted us to go and decided that if He could part the Red Sea, He could get us to California.

We spent the last night in Florida with friends from the church. After a great breakfast, we packed the car. The kids were tucked safely in the backseat, but I was shaking. I couldn't believe we were about to get on the expressway and start the twenty-five-hundred-mile trek across the country with hardly any money. I thought we were not only crazy but irresponsible. I kept looking at the kids, thinking, *I am so sorry. I promise to pay for your therapy when you're older.*

As Randy started the engine, we heard a car horn beeping frantically behind us. Looking in the rearview mirror, we saw our friend, who had already left for work, running up to Randy's window. He handed him a stack of cash.

Out of breath, he managed to explain: "I was in my office, and the Lord said, 'Hurry! Go to the ATM and get five hundred dollars for Randy and Marli.'" Then he added, "That's so crazy. I've never heard the Lord speak like that before."

He was excited, and we were relieved. I doubt our friends realized how God used them to spur us on to deeper faith. They literally paid our way to the West Coast. Their obedience made all the difference on our journey. Because they yielded to the Spirit, we were able to go. They sent us. It was a much bigger deal than just getting us to California for a marriage conference—that test molded our faith. I think that's another reason Jesus sent the disciples without money. It gave others an opportunity to support their ministry and provide for God's servants. It stretched and challenged more than just the disciples.

One person's obedience, in the hands of God, can change the world.

We were careful with the gift. Even with that amount of money, it was hard to eat well. So we ate at gas stations. Two hot dogs for a dollar could feed all of us for five bucks, including drinks and nachos. But as you know, even the biggest junk food eater gets sick of a constant diet like that.

"What in the world am I feeding my family?" I asked Randy as we drove through New Mexico. With all of that time on our hands (and sick of playing the alphabet game), I posed a question to get everybody laughing: "If you could eat anything right now, what would it be?"

The kids started shouting, "Pizza, pizza!"

But I wanted healthy food—fresh vegetables and protein. Something substantial to eat, something your body will thank you for. I said, "How about a Japanese steakhouse?" (The tables are built around a large, steaming hot hibachi grill and the chef cooks right in front of you. It's dinner and a show!) We started salivating over the thought of ginger dressing drizzled over a crisp lettuce salad and an appetizer of grilled shrimp. But it simply wasn't an option because of *money.* It was just a silly game to pass the time.

Approaching the outskirts of Albuquerque, New Mexico, Randy said, "We have to stop at the next exit for gas. If there's a Japanese steakhouse, we'll go."

Minutes later, we ramped off the highway. The only billboard at the end of the exit ramp said, *THE JAPANESE STEAKHOUSE* with an arrow. Randy and I burst out laughing. Then he got quiet.

"Oh no, Randy, it was just a joke. You didn't really mean it." He asked me what I thought, and I told him what he already knew: "It is irresponsible to spend our money like this. God didn't give us that money to go to an expensive restaurant. Besides, it would use most of our remaining gas money, and then what will we do?"

He nodded in agreement and said, "I know it was just a joke, but God was in the car when I said it. He heard it, and He wants us to go. Everybody out."

I was thrilled and scared to death at the same time.

The seating hostess escorted us to a table with a family of six seated at the other end. The cooking style of a Japanese steakhouse makes for a unique seating arrangement, and unless you have a large party, you end up sitting with strangers. The idea is to fill up each table so the chef is cooking everyone's meal at the same time.

The family we were seated with had four children, all younger than ours. Instantly, I was irritated. I silently said to the Lord, *Father, in the past two months we've driven from Michigan to Florida and then Florida to New Mexico with two kids in the backseat—all without a TV! The last thing I want right now is to sit with four more kids.*

I could tell Randy was thinking the same thing as he let out a little groan. We smiled politely and greeted the couple as we gave our drink orders. Then the show began. Our kids loved every minute of it. The fresh food was fantastic, and we ate our fill. I tried to focus on the fact that I was caring for my family by feeding them something other than junk food. I kept my mind busy instead of wondering how we were going to make it the rest of the way to California. But inside, I was *shaking.*

We finished our meal, thankful that all six children were very well-behaved. Everything went well, and we didn't even have time to talk with the family at the opposite end of the table. They were busy with their kids, and we were busy with ours.

"We're ready for our bill," I said to the waitress.

She replied in a very thick Japanese accent, "It's taken care of."

Obviously, we had a language barrier problem, so I spoke louder. "Oh, I mean, our bill. The check. So we can pay."

She looked irritated and matched my volume. "It's taken care of—they pay for you." She flippantly waved her hand toward the other end of the table. The young couple was busy wiping four little mouths and collecting their belongings.

We sat, stunned, and finally said, "You paid for our meal?"

They smiled and nodded as if it was no big deal. For me, the restaurant fell silent, and I no longer needed to breathe. In the spirit realm, God pushed the pause button and let me take in the moment.

I quickly thanked them and told them our story. "We're missionaries to the United States, traveling from Michigan to Florida...California...hot dogs... a billboard sign..." I was in such shock that I mumbled incoherent details. Little of what I said made sense. Assuming this young couple had heard straight from God, directing them to buy our meal, I recounted the recent events that brought us to a Japanese steakhouse in Albuquerque, New Mexico.

The woman simply looked at me and said, "Pardon me, what's a missionary?"

In that moment, the Lord taught me a priceless lesson. He can provide for me anytime, anywhere, and through *anyone* He chooses.

With tears, I said, "I feel like God reached down and kissed me on the forehead."

God was teaching us, *I can provide for My children whenever and through whomever I want—even through people who don't know Me.*

We basked in the blessing of that experience for miles. Granted, it was just one meal, one day on a journey far from home. But the lesson we learned has changed us forever.

That day, God drove us to a restaurant and bought our dinner. What about that season? Well, He planned that season with incredible intentionality to convince us of His promise to always provide for us. He took us on a journey that wasn't fun or easy to understand. In fact, it was hard-really hard. It was a *shaking* of all we had known in an unfamiliar territory He wanted us to experience. He wanted us to experience His strength in our weakness, His provision in our lack and His steadiness in our *shaking.* We did and we found Him utterly unshakable. And then we realized He wants us to be the same.

The decades of ministry we were headed towards needed us to be *unshakable.*

Our family needed us to be *unshakable.*

The world needs us to be *unshakable.*

So, now I know...to become *unshakable* I must be shaken.

Unshakable With Your Finances

By Leecy Barnett

If I said the whole world is in debt, I would hardly be exaggerating. According to Wikipedia, you would have to move to Liechtenstein or Niue (an island country off of New Zealand) to live in a country without debt.[1] Debt is only one of the many, many reasons why it is so hard to be unshakable with your finances. Personally, I have always been frugal (read "cheap"), so debt has not been a big problem for me. Despite this, money is the area in which I have struggled to trust God most. I need to remind myself continuously of a few principles I have learned over the years that have helped me remain on relatively steady ground financially.

1. *Everything I have belongs to God.*

There used to be a program that aired on a local radio station called "God's Money." I loved listening to this program because I needed the daily reminder that everything I have is on loan; everything I have belongs to God. We like to think we deserve our money because, after all, we worked hard for it. But God's Word says: *What do you have that God hasn't given you? And if everything you have is from God, why boast as though it were not a gift?* (1 Corinthians 4:7 NLT). My mind, my body, my life, my health, my job—simply everything I am or ever will be comes from God.

2. *How I use money shows what is important to me.*

Jesus said, *"Wherever your treasure is, there the desires of your heart will also be"* (Matthew 6:21 NLT). I don't know who first said that there is a direct line that runs from your heart to your wallet, but I have found it to be true. The Apostle Paul taught, *You can be sure that no immoral, impure, or greedy person will inherit the Kingdom of Christ and of God. For a greedy person is an idolater, worshiping the things of this world* (Ephesians 5:5 NLT). I love what Timothy Keller, pastor and Bible teacher, had to say about greed: "Jesus warns people far more often about greed than about sex, yet almost no one thinks they are guilty of it. Therefore, we should all begin with a working hypothesis that 'this could easily be a problem for me.'"[2]

3. *God will supply my needs.*

The ancient Bible history tells us the children of Israel saw miracle after miracle yet were constantly grumbling and doubting God would come through for them. I have seen God supply my needs in many miraculous ways. Yet when finances are tight, my condo fees go way up, or the air conditioning or the refrigerator dies, I begin to worry if I will have enough money to make it. It seems Jesus was speaking directly to me when He said,

> *"So don't worry at all about having enough food and clothing. Why be like the heathen? For they take pride in all these things and are deeply concerned about them. But your heavenly Father already knows perfectly well that you need them, and he will give them to you if you give him first place in your life and live as he wants you to"* (Matthew 6:31-33 TLB).

Paul also reminds us: My God will use his wonderful riches in Christ Jesus to give you everything you need (Philippians 4:19 NCV). Everything we need! Just when we need it!

4. *I can't outgive God.*

God gave us a gift beyond compare: *Since he did not spare even his own Son but gave him up for us all, won't he also give us everything else?* (Romans 8:32

NLT). That most famous Bible verse says, *For God so loved the world that He gave* (John 3:16 KJV).

You can't love without giving. If we want to show God that we love Him, we will give generously to His work in the world and to the people He created in His image. When we give, Jesus says God will outgive us: *"Give, and you will receive. Your gift will return to you in full—pressed down, shaken together to make room for more, running over, and poured into your lap"* (Luke 6:38 NLT).

I am not perfect with my finances. But remembering those four principles—everything I have belongs to God, how I use money showcases what is important to me, God will always provide, and I can't outgive God—allows me to stand firm even when it seems I am on shaky financial ground.

Father, I acknowledge You are my Provider, and You have more important things for me to do than worry about my finances. Help me trust You, focus on the work You have called me to do, and become generous like You are. Thank You for giving me everything I need.

---

[1]*List of countries by external debt.* (2023). Wikipedia. Retrieved October 21,2023 from https://en.wikipedia.org/wiki/List_of_countries_by_external_debt

[2]Keller, T. (2009). *Counterfeit gods: The empty promises of money, sex, and power, and the only hope that matters.* Penguin, p. 53.

Kelly Williams Hale

Kelly Williams Hale is a speaker, author, and life coach. She is passionate about Jesus and encourages others to deepen their personal relationship with Him. Her teaching and online courses help Christian women walk in their unique calling to bring God glory.

Partnering with the Holy Spirit, Kelly teaches women how to be courageous and confident in Christ. Her speaking topics include spiritual growth, emotional resilience, and leadership.

Kelly is happily married (third time's a charm!) and a mom of three—each born a decade apart—delivering her youngest at 44 years old. Kelly is living proof that our mess truly becomes our message and past mistakes don't define future success.

To connect with Kelly, you're invited to join her Facebook group, *Sisters Who Shine,* or visit thebebravelife.com.

God's Faithfulness Never Fails

By Kelly Williams Hale

> *"For if you remain completely silent at this time, relief and deliverance will arise for the Jews from another place, but you and your father's house will perish. Yet who knows whether you have come to the kingdom for such a time as this?"* (Esther 4:14 NKJV).

Why do we beat ourselves up so much when we mess up? When I used to make a mistake or get caught up in something I knew wasn't in God's will, I remember thinking, *Why am I so stupid? How could God love me after what I just did?* There have been so many times I felt such disappointment in myself and unworthy to call myself a Christian. It's no secret the enemy comes to steal, kill, and destroy. He will do anything to keep us from our full potential. And when he can get us thinking that we're not good enough, well then, he's won.

The truth is we are ALL going to make mistakes. But, friend, there is literally NOTHING that will keep us from the love of God. The

Bible says it plainly: *No power in the sky above or in the earth below—indeed, NOTHING IN ALL CREATION WILL EVER BE ABLE TO SEPARATE US FROM THE LOVE OF GOD that is revealed in Christ Jesus our Lord* (Romans 8:39 NLT, emphasis mine).

Growing up, I learned to be a good girl to receive praise. When I did something right, I was rewarded. So when I thought of God as my Father, I felt like I had to "be good" for Him to bless me. When I made mistakes, I thought, *There's no way that God could love me.* But based on Romans 8:39, we know God loves us no matter what. Okay, got it. But knowing what we know and all the ways we've fallen short, how many of us still wonder, *Can God REALLY use me?*

I had a very superficial relationship with God when I was in my 20s. I knew I needed to be in church, but it was a struggle to survive most days. Primarily due to financial turmoil. Which then made me feel unworthy and ashamed of the choices I made. I spent more time focused on what I didn't have rather than trusting the One who created everything. I was a single mom who was worrying about the future rather than walking each day by faith. I didn't yet understand grace.

> *God's law was given so that all people could see how sinful they were. But as people sinned more and more, God's wonderful grace became more abundant* (Romans 5:20-21 NLT).

As I reflect on my past, I realize that I am who I am today *because* of the mistakes I made and the obstacles I overcame. I have so many regrets about the choices I made, especially how they impacted my daughter. However, as I sought a deeper relationship with Jesus, I started to believe that God *could* use me—despite my mistakes. God has shown me how the trials in our lives become our testimony *for* His glory.

Before we go any further, let's take a trip down memory lane. I'd like to paint a picture of where I was when I began my journey to where I am now. My prayer is that you will see *God's faithfulness* in my story. And recognize Him as He writes your story.

Let us hold unswervingly to the hope we profess, for he who promised is faithful (Hebrews 10:23 NIV).

I remember the day so clearly, thinking to myself, *I can't breathe.* My second husband was an avid deer hunter, and we were driving through the woods near our home in the country. My son was 18 months old and bouncing on my lap as he peered out the window. A typical Sunday afternoon. I was trying to simply convey how I felt and share what I was thinking. Nothing terribly serious. But as I tried to speak, my husband would cut me off. I had a physical response that day to what had become a common occurrence in our marriage. My voice didn't matter.

My relationship with my husband was not healthy. And I realized that day that something had to change. I am a peace lover by nature and not one to initiate confrontation. I was the one who "took it"—being treated badly—to avoid conflict. Through counseling, I learned that my avoidance was a tactic I used to control situations. If I didn't react or argue, the discussion wouldn't (or couldn't) go any further. Since I "knew" how my husband would react, I made the choice NOT to engage, thereby "controlling" the situation. As someone who adapts easily to most situations, I was the last person anyone would describe as "controlling." Something stirred in my spirit, however, when my counselor introduced this concept to me.

My friends would often comment about the way my husband talked to me. Degrading. Belittling. When I expressed how I felt (hurt), he quickly said, "Oh, I'm just pickin'" (teasing), which I was super familiar with since that's how my entire family communicated. It turns out it was a form of verbal abuse that I was unaware of. My counselor recommended a few books that were pivotal in providing insight into my own behavior.

I began to seek the Lord. He revealed to me that divorce was necessary. I was in an emotionally abusive relationship, my husband was unfaithful, and God did not expect me to stay if it would be harmful. The days were difficult, and it seemed like my faith was the only thing that sustained me—my faith and God's promises.

For we walk by faith, not by sight (2 Corinthians 5:7 NKJV).

Prior to my divorce, my church attendance was sporadic at best. Tithing was unheard of. I had no money for groceries, much less any to give to the church. However, this is exactly *when* we should give! This simple act of faith turned out to be one of the most tangible examples of God's faithfulness. I remember reading Malachi 3:10, where God says, *"Bring the full tithe into the storehouse, that there may be food in my house. And thereby put me to the test, says the Lord of hosts, if I will not open the windows of heaven for you and pour down for you a blessing until there is no more need"* (ESV). I definitely tested Him! And I saw His hand in my finances. My faith became the evidence of Jeremiah 29:11 as I began to *believe* that God had a plan for me—plans to prosper me and not harm me. Plans for hope and a future.

As I dug into God's Word, scripture spoke to me in a fresh new way. I started to understand who I was in Christ. The Bible says *we are the light of the world. A city set on a hill* (Matthew 5:14 ESV), that He has called us (2 Peter 1:3), and we are chosen (Revelation 17:14). My thoughts slowly changed from fear and doubt to grace and acceptance. My self-talk went from *Why is this happening?* to *What is God teaching me?* Life did not become perfect, but I began to trust God more fully in my circumstances.

The faithful love of the Lord never ends! His mercies never cease. Great is his faithfulness; his mercies begin afresh each morning (Lamentations 3:22-23 NLT).

During this time, I was invited to a jewelry party hosted by my sister-in-law, Leigh Ann, at her friend's house. I was now a single mom and decisions around money usually boiled down to one thing: *I can't afford that.* There was certainly no extra money for jewelry! But I went to the party to support my sister.

Oh boy, the setup was so pretty; the jewelry sparkled and shined and seemed to call to me. Before I knew it, I placed an order! Little did I know that evening would change the trajectory of my life. To make a long story short, I became a jewelry lady myself. It was the best decision I ever made.

I became part of a community of women who supported and encouraged each other. I learned so much about myself. Here I was—the intimidated, insecure girl who was terrified of public speaking—now giving presentations to random strangers in other women's homes! The company was founded on biblical principles, so I was able to share my faith in a way that was very easy and natural. I was uncomfortable in the beginning, but as my business grew, so did my confidence; my friends and family noticed the difference in me. Despite having no experience (and no money!), I took a leap of faith to start my home business, and God blessed my action. Looking back, I can see that God was preparing me for His plan.

But even if we are faithless, he will still be full of faith, for he never wavers in his faithfulness to us! (2 Timothy 2:13 TPT).

Friend, the devil wants to limit us and our potential by reminding us of the mistakes we've made. His lies sound like, *How can God use you? Remember what you did? Don't even try that new thing.* When we *make a decision* to trust—and obey—we are choosing to live the life that Jesus promises. John 10:10 records Jesus as saying, *"I have come so that they may have life, and have it to the full"* (NIV).

I've messed up so many times and have learned something new each time. About myself. About God. About life. Failure often brings new opportunities to get it right. Or at least try again. If we're not careful, however, we can assume what we do should be perfect. But we aren't called to be perfect. We are imperfect humans saved by the sacrifice Jesus made on the cross. He paid the price for our sin.

> *For it is by grace you have been saved through faith—and this is not yourselves, it is the gift of God—not by works, so that no one may boast. For we are God's handiwork, created in Christ Jesus to do good works, which God prepared in advance for us to do* (Ephesians 2:8-10 NIV).

One of my favorite scriptures teaches that God makes a way where there is no way (Isaiah 43:19). He makes a way through our mess. He is *for* us. He wants us to succeed. Our confidence comes from the assurance that He's got our back, which means we can confidently pursue the dreams He's placed in our hearts, knowing He is with us. He is a good, good Father.

Back to my story. It is now 2004, and God is about to plant a seed—a dream—in my heart. I am now a Wednesday night Bible study girl. AND a consistent Sunday School attendee! I remember reading Matthew 6:33—*But seek first the kingdom of God and his righteousness, and all these things will be added to you* (ESV), and realizing that to claim my blessings, I needed to seek God *first.* This was such a revelation at the time. As a single mom, I had many responsibilities and items "to do." God wasn't always at the top of the list.

In addition to the Bible, I devoured Christian non-fiction books. I discovered story after story of God's grace.

One book that really stood out to me during this time was *When I Lay My Isaac Down* by Christian author and speaker Carol Kent. It's a story of faith, perseverance, and hope during unimaginable tragedy and despair—how God sustained her as she navigated the impossible reality that her only son killed a man in cold blood. Her son, Jason, now shares the gospel in prison to men who may have never heard the Good News of Jesus. I thought, *If God can use a man who committed murder, then maybe he could use little ol' me: a twice-divorced single mom.*

> *The one who CALLS you is faithful, and HE will do it* (1 Thessalonians 5:24 NIV, emphasis mine).

There are moments in our lives that we can mark as "before" and "after." When it's impossible to go back to what was because you've had a glimpse of what's next—my moment happened at a business event when I heard my first motivational speaker. He stood in front of the room and shared his story. It was a powerful message of forgiveness, and I was mesmerized. I thought to myself, *Omigoodness, I want to do that!* I felt a quickening in my soul that came directly from the Holy Spirit.

> *May he work perfection into every part of you giving you all that you need to fulfill your destiny* (Hebrews 13:21 TPT).

Another seed was planted when I was asked to co-lead my first Bible Study, *The Purpose-Driven Life.* This was notable because I was learning that God DID have a purpose for me, despite my past.

Two years later, I would hear about a Christian women's conference called

She Speaks. The conference was nearly 400 miles away, and the registration cost was $350. I didn't know how God would provide, but I. Was. Going.

Well, God did it. I attended the *She Speaks* conference in August of 2006. And it was there God spoke to me. I was startled from a sound sleep on the first night, hearing that still, small voice that we *know* is the Lord. He said, "*My grace is sufficient* (2 Corinthian 12:9). My grace is enough. You are enough. You can do all things through me. I will give you strength."

I was more certain than ever that God had given me a gift to speak and share hope with my voice and with my words. It's no surprise to look back and see how Satan tried to silence me. I left that weekend changed. At the time, I couldn't articulate what had occurred, but I now understand the concept of transformation. And that's what happened. I was on the cusp of defining the "after" version of myself.

The definition of faith is *complete trust or confidence in someone or something.*[1] I was trusting in God, fully submitting to His will and His ways. As my faith grew, I discovered it kept the chaos at bay, meaning I could depend on Jesus. If you're in a season of struggle or hopelessness, please remember this: God has a plan. During difficult circumstances, may I encourage you to lean on the hope and faith found in Jesus Christ. I love The Passion Translation of 2 Timothy 2:13—B*ut even if we are faithless, he will still be full of faith, for he never wavers in his faithfulness to us!* When I finally got out of my toxic relationship, my hope was renewed. I was excited about who I was becoming and looking forward to my 40th birthday in just five short months.

Sweet friend, the enemy will use shame, doubt, and fear to keep us from our destiny in Christ. It takes courage to step out on faith. We can live a life full of impact, purpose, and meaning. The life that God knew before we were formed in our mother's womb (Psalm 139:13). HE KNOWS YOU and the plan He has for you. Life is too short for just "okay." We were created for purpose—to make a difference while we're here. Serving others. Using the gifts and talents that God has blessed us with. Leaving a legacy. Some of us think we have disqualified ourselves from the work God has planned for us because of the mistakes we've made. But, friend, your past doesn't define your future.

> *For the gifts and the calling of God are irrevocable* (Romans 11:29 ESV).

Our calling doesn't have an expiration date, but we could delay God's plan if we don't obey. God's given us free will, so we get to choose. Each day. We decide to step out in faith... or not. Our job is obedience. God's job is the results. We don't have to know HOW things will work out. Or honestly even WHAT we're supposed to do. We just move forward, asking the Holy Spirit to guide us each day, for that day's work.

> *Since we live by the Spirit, let us keep in step with the Spirit* (Galatians 5:25 NIV).

God is faithful. But He also requires us to stretch our faith. When we believe the lies of the enemy and say, "I just can't," we are essentially saying God is not big enough. Our doubt will limit our progress. When we speak out "I can" and partner with God, all things are possible (Matthew 19:26). Proverbs 18:21 says, *Death and life are in the power of the tongue* (ESV).

God has a plan for every single one of us. I am convinced that He allows the tests in our lives because He knows they will become our testimonies—*if* we choose to share them. Our experiences, choices, mistakes, and sin are no surprise to God. He *knows* the plans He has for us. When we find ourselves on the other side of impossible circumstances and faith-shaking hard times, we are becoming uniquely qualified to serve other people. We've been there. We've done that. AND we have the T-shirt! Going through the pain of divorce, which led me to the truth—God's Word—provided me with wisdom and compassion that I now pass on to others.

> *But without faith it is impossible to please Him, for he who comes to God must believe that He is, and that He is a rewarder of those who diligently seek Him* (Hebrews 11:6 NKJV).

I felt unworthy of God's love for many years, but I now know—and *believe*—that I am God's precious daughter. I pray my story will help you see your value, too. I pray the hope you carry will shine the light of God's love into someone else's burden-filled life.

> *"You are the light of the world. A town built on a hill cannot be hidden. Neither do people light a lamp and put it under a bowl. Instead, they put it on its stand, and it gives light to everyone in the house. In the same way, let your light shine before others, that they may see your good deeds and glorify your Father in heaven"* (Matthew 5:14-16 NIV).

When we share our story with others, we get to be the bridge that leads people to hope. Unshakable faith is built on the power of our testimony. Our pain becomes the portal to our purpose. God loves you, just like He loves me, and He is calling us all *for such a time as this* (Esther 4:14 NKJV).

---

[1]Oxford Languages, Google

Unshakable Because of God's Unfailing Love

By Leecy Barnett

Have you heard the expression something is "lost in translation"? This refers to the difficulty in understanding the true meaning of a word or a custom when it is taken from one language or culture to another. At the time the Bible was written, there was a custom practiced all over the Near East called cutting a covenant. In its full biblical meaning, a covenant was a binding agreement between two parties who committed to unbreakable friendship and mutual protection. Covenants were sealed by cutting a blood sacrifice, symbolizing that death awaited the one who would break the covenant. No contract or agreement in modern culture matches the significance and seriousness of the ancient covenants. That practice has been "lost in translation."

Likewise, "chesed" is a word in the Hebrew Bible that is very difficult to understand. Bible versions have sought to convey the meaning of chesed by translating it in many ways—lovingkindness, kindness, mercy, favor, unfailing love, steadfast love, loving devotion, and faithful love—none of which completely envelop the word's true meaning. We have a hard time understanding chesed because it is related to the foreign concept of covenant.

Throughout the Bible, God made covenants with His people. Chesed is the love that motivated God to choose us and pledge Himself to protect us. Chesed is covenant love in action: the consistent, ever-faithful, relentless, constantly-pursuing, lavish, extravagant, unrestrained, furious love of our Father God! Chesed is strength, steadfastness, love---the loyal love between partners in a covenant relationship. Over and over again, God promises this loyal love to us:

> *Know this: GOD, your God, is God indeed, a God you can depend upon. He keeps his covenant of loyal love with those who love him and observe his commandments for a thousand generations* (Deuteronomy 7:9 MSG).

> *O GOD, God of Israel, there is no God like you in the skies above or on the earth below who unswervingly keeps covenant with his servants and relentlessly loves them as they sincerely live in obedience to your way* (1 Kings 8:23 MSG).

> *(to His reclaimed bride) I'm going to marry you, and this time it'll be forever in righteousness and justice. Our covenant will reflect a loyal love and great mercy; our marriage will be honest and truthful, and you'll understand who I really am—the Eternal One* (Hosea 2:19 VOICE).

So how do God's promises to love those He pledged Himself to in covenant relate to us today? In the ultimate expression of His loyal love, Jesus pledged His life for us in a new covenant. The night before His death, Jesus joined his disciples in celebrating the Passover. *After supper he gave them another glass of wine, saying, "This wine is the token of God's new agreement to save you—an agreement sealed with the blood I shall pour out to purchase back your souls"* (Luke 22:20 TLB). The wine Jesus shared that evening was a symbol of the death He was about to undergo. Jesus' death not only provided forgiveness for our sins, but it also was a demonstration of the depth of God's love. *But think about this: while we were wasting our lives in sin, God revealed His powerful love to us in a tangible display—the Anointed One [Jesus] died for us* (Romans 5:8 VOICE).

Because God loves us with an eternal, unconditional, all-encompassing love, we can be unshakable, knowing He is always with us, always on our side. *"Though the mountains be shaken, and the hills be removed, yet my unfailing love for you will not be shaken nor my covenant of peace be removed," says the LORD, who has compassion on you* (Isaiah 54:10 NIV).

The Bible instructs us to build our lives on God's unshakable love: *You, however, should stand firm in the love of God, constructing a life within the holy faith, praying the Spirit's prayer, as you wait eagerly for the mercy of our Lord Jesus the Anointed, which leads to eternal life* (Jude 20-21 VOICE).

Christian, you can face anything that comes your way because, *Surely [God's] goodness and unfailing love will pursue me all the days of my life, and I will live in the house of the Lord forever* (Psalm 23:6 NLT).

Dear God, I thank You for your unfailing love. Jesus, I am so glad You gave Your life for me and have included me in Your new covenant. You have promised that nothing will separate me from Your love. Remind me every day that Your goodness and unfailing love are seeking me out.

Diane Lawbaugh

Born in Canada, Diane met and married a handsome American who is still her favorite human after four-plus decades. She is an international best-selling author, a graduate of Westervelt College, a professional administrator, an event planner, a singer, and a lover of all things purple.

Diane's joy is connecting people with hope, one another, and a better quality of life. To support this passion, she achieved her facilitator certification with Theotherapy, Sozo, and Heart Sync. Most recently, she added her Mastery and Certification training with PAX Programs Inc., investing over 1,300 hours in research, training, and teaching that helps men and women appreciate their differences rather than see them as obstacles.

In 2020, Diane published her first book *Connecting…the present to the past to find hope for your future.* It is available on Amazon. Currently, she's writing a book that helps women and men dismantle misunderstandings and create better responses, results, and relationships.

Her ideas of fun are long walks, couch picnics with her husband, romantic comedies, and all things NFL—especially cheering for her Tennessee Titans.

You can reach her at diane@hopewithoutlimits.com .

Chronically Ill–Does God Love Me?

By Diane Lawbaugh

Squealing brakes pealed. I was thrown forward and then abruptly snapped forcefully backward. Flames of burning pain licked down and around my spine. My world was literally rocking as the energy from the impact dissipated out of our car.

Suddenly, my husband and I saw two people standing in front of our car. They asked us if we needed help. We answered yes. Within a couple of minutes, an ambulance arrived. When my husband tried to thank these people, they were simply gone. No one else had seen them. We both believe these were angels sent to our aid. It was 1996, and cell phones were not yet a part of everyday life.

I had no idea that a life-changing journey would begin for me that day or that many more God interventions lay ahead.

For the next eighteen months, I experienced gradual healing from the whiplash. Then, my recovery took a 180-degree turn for the worse. Pain and weakness in both my arms increased at an alarming rate. Anything that required using or raising my hands caused a burning fire in my neck, shoulders, arms, and back. A feeling like shards of glass scraping over my muscles began rotating through my body, manifesting in different locations each day. I couldn't sleep for more than ninety minutes at a time. I went to multiple specialists, but no one had an answer. I was beginning to believe I was crazy because no one could explain my myriad of symptoms.

Holy Spirit guided me off the merry-go-round of doctors and back to my family practitioner. His kindness brought me to tears. Having known me for twenty years, he assured me I was not imagining my pain. He promised to work with me to find an answer. And he did.

On October 8, 1998, I received a diagnosis and prognosis. I wept as the doctor told me, "I have good news and bad news. The good news is you are not crazy. The bad news is you have Fibromyalgia, a disorder you will need to learn to live with." He put me on medical leave for seven weeks to rest and begin to build a new way of living.

My relief from having a diagnosis was short-lived; I was quickly drowned in a flood of shame and fear. *How would I be able to please everyone in my life, including God, if I could not perform for them the way I always had?* Little did I know that burning question within me was my heavenly Father already at work, dismantling what the enemy had purposed for evil and preparing to use it for His good purpose (Genesis 50:20). The accuser was seeking to destroy me. In contrast, God sought to pour life (abundant life—John 10:10) into me by dismantling layers and layers of perceptions I had built up that told me that being loved is a result of our performance.

God kick-started our journey together by showing me a vision of a closet stuffed so full that there was no room for anything else in it. The door was about to burst open from the pressure of everything behind it. I heard Holy Spirit tell me, "This is your soul. It's up to you to look at what's in here. You have to decide what to throw away and what to keep."

I was stunned at how such a simple vision could tell me so much about myself. My method of coping had always been to "stuff" pain, grief, disappointment, and fear. I certainly felt I was about to explode. At that point in my life, when I read, *For I can do everything through Christ, who gives me strength* (Philippians 4:13 NLT), what I heard was, "Don't be a wimp. Grit this out. Get this done." I was sure God was disappointed in me when I had to ask for help. After all, there were many people with problems much bigger than mine. Can you relate?

One day, I was face down on my living room floor, crying out to God to help me. I was in so much pain, physically and emotionally. I had no clue how to live with this disorder and felt completely depleted of any strength. I had no words to express what I needed—I didn't know what I needed. But Jesus and Holy Spirit were praying for me.

> *And the Holy Spirit helps us in our weakness. For example, we don't know what God wants us to pray for. But the Holy Spirit prays for us with groanings that cannot be expressed in words. And the Father who knows all hearts knows what the Spirit is saying, for the Spirit pleads for us believers in harmony with God's own will. And we know that God causes everything to work together for the good of those who love God and are called according to his purpose for them* (Romans 8:26-28 NLT).

Some of the ways God answered the intercession of Jesus and Holy Spirit from 1998 through 2014 were:

- He provided a personal "watchdog" in the form of my husband. Then and now, my husband constantly researches ways to help me. More importantly, he is always on the lookout to protect me from pushing myself too hard or judging myself as a burden or inconvenience.
- God provided a connection, time, and finances to help me see myself

and be set free from the lies the enemy had sewn into my belief system by allowing me to study Theotherapy: "A modality of Christian counseling that utilizes biblical psychological principles to bring about the integration of human beings through a spiritual, psychological, and physical integration."[1]

- When I was feeling suicidal as a result of pain and the side effects of the medications, God connected me with a coach who completely revamped my diet, taking my pain levels from 86 out of 100 (100 being the worst pain) to 12 out of 100 in only three weeks.
- He provided a physical therapist who specialized in treating Fibromyalgia with myofascial release. The therapy helped relax my contracted muscles, improved blood and lymphatic circulation, and stimulated the stretch reflex in my muscles.
- When I was desperate from a twelve-week migraine and asked my husband to pray for me because I would "do anything" to get rid of the pain, God prompted my best friend to call me within minutes and connect me with a Christian acupuncturist. Once again, my heavenly Father provided what I didn't even know I needed. I believed that as a "good Christian," I should protect myself from any form of Eastern medicine. Reaching the point of being willing to do anything opened the way for me to receive God's supply. He reminded me that there is nothing He didn't create (John 1:3). Being authentic, my response to the relief I experienced was, "Why didn't You lead me to acupuncture sooner, God?" I was angry—why had God made me wait? His answer stunned me. He showed me that I hadn't been ready to receive that provision until that particular moment. Without God transforming my mind, I would have used the relief and energy to push myself harder and beat myself up more. That was not the life my heavenly Father wanted for me.

My journey reached a major turning point one night in 2014. I was lying in bed after a particularly long and painful day. I heard God ask me if I would still love Him if I was never healed from Fibromyalgia. The question surprised me. I had to think about my response. I mean, God is my healer. Why wouldn't He heal me? As I was still, clarity came that God's real question was, "Will you love me unconditionally?"

My mind reeled. Could this be true—God wants to be loved unconditionally? My thoughts turned to why our heavenly Father would risk creating something as volatile as free will, providing us with a choice. The answer became apparent: Just as we want to be loved unconditionally, God wants us to love Him unconditionally. He wants to be our choice. Without free choice, there would not be love.

Confronting me with that question opened a pathway for God to shine His light deep within me, revealing the real question burning in me: *Does God really love me if I am chronically ill?*

My head knew the truth of Psalm 71:15-16. *I couldn't begin to count the times you've been there for me. With the skill of a poet I'll never run out of things to say of how you faithfully kept me from danger. I will come forth in your mighty strength, O my Lord God* (TPT). However, my heart still had doubts.

Around this time, I told my physical therapist how disappointed I was in myself. I shared, "Everyone deals with some kind of pain. Why can't I just dig deep and move on? I'm doing everything I've been told to do to be well. I must be failing at something, or I wouldn't be feeling this way."

She was quiet for a couple of moments and then replied, "If a child was savagely ravaged and raped, would you blame the child?"

I lay there trying to take in what she had just said. *What did she mean? Of course, I wouldn't blame the child, but what did that have to do with me? Wait. Did she mean I was the child and what my body was experiencing from Fibromyalgia was equivalent to the trauma of a child who was brutally raped???? Was she saying I was being attacked by this disease and it was not my fault?*

With my head spinning, I blurted out what had been whirling around in my thoughts.

She gently responded, "That's exactly what I meant."

Driving home, I was trying to take in all we had discussed when my heavenly Father showed me an image of England being repeatedly bombed during World War II. He asked me, "If someone continues to be attacked by an enemy—does that make them a failure?"

My response: "Uh, no, it doesn't, Father."

His reply: "So, are you a failure?"

My response: "Well, I guess that would be no, too."

My heart was able to break off agreement with the lie that because the Fibromyalgia persisted, I was a failure and unlovable. I came into agreement with the truth that, indeed, I do have an enemy who is seeking to devour me (1 Peter 5:8). Still, God was telling me these things so that in Him I may have perfect peace and confidence (John 14:27). Holy Spirit reminded me that in the world I will have tribulation, trials, distress, and frustration; but I can be of good cheer, take courage, and be confident, certain, and undaunted! He has overcome the world! My heavenly Father has deprived the enemy and the world of the power to harm me; He has conquered evil for me (John 16:33).

The enemy was trying to crush my spirit through self-hatred, knowing that would disable me. *A healthy spirit conquers adversity, but what can you do when the spirit is crushed?* (Proverbs 18:14 MSG).

Prior to this revelation, I had been living captive to Fibromyalgia. There was a time when I felt like everything in the world was a threat to me—food, environment, stress—and there was no way I could be safe. I believed this was my reality, and I had no choice but to suffer.

Powerful change in the quality of my life started to flow once I became sure that the presence of Fibromyalgia did not define God's love for me. Now, I choose daily whether I will walk through the door of faith—believing God is who He says He is; I can trust Him; and He is my provision (1 Peter 1:3-7). Or, will I walk through the door of fear? Fear that is fueled by letting my circumstances—what I see around me and experience in my body—tell me whether or not I am safe and loved. Is the choice easy? No, it is not. But it is real.

By God's hand, my health has improved, though it has taken time—lots of time. Through all of it, God's unshakable patience has not wavered. He continues to answer my every question (James 1:5), catch every tear (Psalm 56:8), and exchange my strength for His (Isaiah 40:31).

Holy Spirit is my remembrancer; I have the choice to rely on God's faithfulness or my ability to gut it out.

Why would I even consider relying on my willpower? Two reasons: It feels familiar. And in some ways, it feels safer—I control my willpower, but I can't control God.

I've had moments of being tremendously afraid as I lay on treatment tables, believing if I truly surrendered my will, I would be destroyed. A part of me was utterly convinced it was up to me to protect myself using my willpower so I could continue to exist—that was a lie sewn into my life by the enemy. The truth is that pushing myself that hard was destroying me. I finally realized that trying to "be strong" was actually putting a barrier between me—my heart and my essence—and my Lord.

In conclusion, be strong in the Lord [be empowered through your union with Him]; draw your strength from Him [that strength which His boundless might provides]. Put on God's whole armor [the armor of a heavy-armed soldier which God supplies], that you may be able successfully to stand up against [all] the strategies and the deceits of the devil (Ephesians 6:10-11 AMPC).

Did you catch it? It's GOD'S armor. I don't create it by my willpower. Even wrapping myself in the shield of faith (Ephesians 6:16) is sourced by His faithfulness (Psalm 91:4). My part is living by this reality.

An unshakable quality to my faith sprouted when I read John 6:38, 40 (TPT). Jesus explains He did not come from heaven for His own desires but for the *satisfaction* of His Father. Now and always, reconciliation and spending eternity with me is what satisfies and delights my God!

My capacity to draw on what our Lord has always planned continues to grow. He sees our deficiencies as points of connection to provide what we need (2 Corinthians 12:9). We have a daily choice to surrender our willpower and depend on Christ's power. To depend on the fact God has already made peace with us (Romans 5:1). I've learned the purpose of surrender is creating space within me where I can receive God's provision of all He is!! Surrender is exchanging my capabilities for His. Such a deal!

Through hang gliding, a transformational experience that was a birthday gift from my heavenly Father, I gained a deep and personal understanding of what it means to soar high on wings like eagles (Isaiah 40:31NLT). We were at an altitude of 2,000 feet when my guide told me he was about to release the tug line connected to the ultra-light that had pulled us to this height. Until that moment, I had no clue how much I was depending on what I could see. When the rope released and dropped away, an incredible, invisible power from beneath lifted us another 200 feet higher. There was nothing I did to create that power; I only had to submit to that strength, rely on it, and let it carry me. It was a lot of fun! I needed guidance and help to make the most of that blessing, which was a lesson in and of itself.

God's unshakable presence has not changed during my journey. I have experienced the reality that *Jesus Christ is the same yesterday and today and forever* (Hebrews 13:8 NIV).

What has changed is me. As I experienced His mercy, graciousness, abundant loving kindness, and powerful truth (Exodus 34:6), my heart was set free from the captivity that told me I needed to perform to be loved (Isaiah 61:1). The reality of my heavenly Father's love has replaced my fear with freedom (1 John 4:18) that expands my capacity to receive His unconditional, unshakable love.

> *And I am convinced that nothing can ever separate us from God's love. Neither death nor life, neither angels nor demons, neither our fears for today nor our worries about tomorrow—not even the powers of hell can separate us from God's love. No power in the sky above or in the earth below—indeed, nothing in all creation will ever be able to separate us from the love of God that is revealed in Christ Jesus our Lord* (Romans 8:38-39 NLT).

I continue cleaning out the closet of my soul with His ever-present, unshakable help (Psalm 46:1). I now know without a doubt that when I encounter a problem, my biggest challenge is not the problem itself but rather it is what I choose to believe about my heavenly Father and myself. My prayer to navigate these times is, "What do I need to know about You, God? This fear? Myself?"

Back to my original question: *Despite my chronic illness—does God love me?* I KNOW the answer is YES. He has created each of us to be unique, living expressions of His glory (Isaiah 43:7). That's who I am—who you are.

So it is impossible for God to lie for we know that his promise and his vow will never change! And now we have run into his heart to hide ourselves in his faithfulness. This is where we find his strength and comfort, for he empowers us to seize what has already been established ahead of time—an unshakeable hope! We have this certain hope like a strong, unbreakable anchor holding our souls to God himself. Our anchor of hope is fastened to the mercy seat which sits in the heavenly realm beyond the sacred threshold, and where Jesus our forerunner has gone in before us. He is now and forever our royal Priest like Melchizedek (Hebrews 6:18-20 TPT).

Hallelujah!

---

[1]Christian Counseling International, (Calif.), Copyright © 1998 *Theotherapy Counseling Modality* [White Paper] https://www.angelfire.com/biz/isct/TTWP.html

Unshakable in His Waiting Room

By Donna Whartenby

We take our car to the auto repair shop when we have a problem. After explaining our concerns and issues, we are directed to the waiting room, where we wait for answers to the problem— information about what to do next or to find out there is no longer hope.

When we have problems in life, we pray to our living God, asking Him for answers—what to do next and how to proceed. And then, we wait for His response with faith that He will give us the answer. Thank goodness, God, unlike the auto mechanic, will never tell us there is no longer hope! We can trust in God's answered prayer—the hope and assurance of God's perfect love for His children is unshakable.

> *The Lord is far from the sinful, but He hears the prayer of those who are right with Him* (Proverbs 15:29 NLV).

When Philip said, *"Lord, show us the Father and that will be enough for us." Jesus answered, "Don't you know me...Anyone who has seen me has seen the Father...I will do whatever you ask in my name, so that the Father may be glorified* (John 14:8-9, 13 NIV). Jesus' answer reveals His true nature: He is always present and loving, sees all, is the giver of gifts, all-sufficient, our deliverer, our Redeemer, and so much more. Jesus hears our whispers from the heart and the thoughts in our minds; still, He wants us to come to Him with our requests.

Psalm 62:5 teaches us, *My soul is quiet and waits for God alone. My hope comes from Him* (NLV). Prayer is our way to connect with our God, who always hears us—He heals, mends hearts, forgives, teaches lessons, and desires us to follow His ways. Being connected to Him humbles us and strengthens our faith. James 1:17 says, *Every good and perfect gift is from above, coming down from the Father* (NIV). God knows what we need before we even ask because He is omniscient—all-knowing. And we rejoice when His answer is what we expect or desire.

But there are times when we must wait on His answer. Wait for Him to move in our lives. Wait for His direction.

Even Moses, David, Paul, and Jesus had to wait on God's perfect timing for their prayers to be answered. Times of waiting for God to answer our prayer teach us to put our hope in Him. He will be patient with us as He prepares to meet our real needs while aligning our desires with His. In John 14:27, Jesus tells us, *"I am leaving you with a gift—peace of mind and heart. And the peace I give is a gift the world cannot give. So don't be troubled or afraid"* (NLT). We can have peace of mind in every aspect of our life when we trust in our Creator God, Elohim.

Waiting in God's waiting room is not easy, particularly in our culture of instant gratification. And though you may be tempted to fight a battle of "my will versus God's will," thinking, *I can take back control to get what I want regardless of His silence,* I encourage you to seek God's will in the waiting.

Perhaps God has designed the perfect time and place to answer your prayer. Or maybe He has a better plan that you do not yet understand. Or could God possibly be waiting on you? Perhaps you have not forgiven someone, or He is helping you to build patience, grow knowledge and understanding, be obedient to His will, or love and trust Him more. If you seek His will in the waiting, you will gain so much more than you can even imagine.

When we wait on our sovereign Lord and trust in His will, He will grow unshakable peace within us. There is comfort in knowing God is in control and will always answer our prayers. As Christians, we can ask God to replace our fear with unshakable faith and trust in Him, His will, and His eternal plan.

Never give up! If you have been sitting in God's waiting room for a while, ask God to tell you His will and make His desire your desire. Ask Him: "What do You want me to do for You today?"

God delights in answering our prayers and longs to guide us into His will. He assures us, His children, that He will make all things work together for the good of those who love Him. That is solid, *unshakable* ground we can stand firm on—even as we wait.

Dear Heavenly Father, thank You for Your desire as Lord of Lords to hear my prayer. Thank You for answered prayer. I understand Your timing is not my timing, and my plans are not Your plans, so I spend time in Your waiting room. I believe You will provide an answer; therefore, I will not be shaken as I wait. As I seek Your response, I know 'Your will be done.' You are wise, kind, loving, and You will bless me in Your own way. I will wait for Your answer. In the name of Jesus, I ask. Amen.

Sandra Gonzalez

Sandra Gonzalez is a mom, wife, coach, public speaker, financial expert, and Senior National Sales Director Partner in financial services.

With 20+ Years as a partner and co-CEO with her husband, Eddie Gonzalez, they own and operate the No Boss™ Hierarchy. As Senior National Sales Directors, they have 16 Regional Vice Presidents in their organization. Born and raised in New York, Sandra has worked on Wall Street, NYC, Brickell Avenue, Florida, and currently has a financial services business with state & federal licensed representatives in 15+ states.

Sandra serves as the Senior Advisor for The (HALC) Hispanic Women's Committee—a nationwide organization of Hispanic women from diverse backgrounds who are committed to promoting the participation of women in leadership, finance, and business.

Sandra and Eddie have been married for 21 years. They live between Westchester County, New York, and Wellington, Florida. They have two amazing children, Gabriel and Alyssa, of whom they are immensely proud.

Sandra can be contacted at nobosspink@gmail.com

My Faith and Family Filled Journey

By Sandra Gonzalez

My faith journey has been filled with some sad, scary, and challenging days, along with blessings of family and faith-filled opportunities. Every day, I give glory to God for all He gives me, including my family and an unshakable life that has come from walking with Him.

On December 7, 2002, I experienced the saddest day of my life. It was by far the most difficult goodbye. I was heartbroken when my sister called to tell me our father passed away from lymphoma cancer. It was devastating for all of us. I felt such a deep sadness that, at times, I thought I was not going to be able to move forward. Remembering it today still brings tears to my eyes.

I will never forget my father's influence. He was a strong and brave man. My dad did what it took to love, guide, protect, and provide for my mother and his five children. He tutored me, "You will rise again, even when you fall. If anything is trying to hold you back, give no attention to it. Get your hopes up, get your faith up, and get ready to rise again. Rise up, rise up, and always rise up as you begin by putting your faith in God." My father had a personal relationship with God and taught me the importance of having such a relationship with our Creator. He taught me to look to and know God. He instructed us to know God's Word because "everything else was someone's opinion of how they viewed things." He taught us to have faith and trust in God.

Since his passing, I still experience times when adversity presents itself. In these moments, I would hear my father's voice saying, "Rise up." And then, I put my unshakable faith in God by praying to Him and spending time in His presence as He sustains me.

The Bible instructs us, *Let us then approach God's throne of grace with confidence, so that we may receive mercy and find grace to help us in our time of need* (Hebrews 4:16 NIV). Whenever I do not know what to do or say, I confidently spend time with God in my quiet place to get His answer. Often, when things are out of our control, the best thing to do is to let go of the problems and, with unshakable faith, allow God to take control. God wants us to tell Him our problems, but He already knows what we need. Surrender your problems and challenges to Him in faith.

My mom always had a huge Bible lying open on her dresser, which she read daily. She told us she had it there to "fortify" her. In other words, to protect her and us against attacks of evil. Its accessibility helped her go through life's challenges and adversities, including when something went wrong with the epidural as she gave birth to her fourth child, leaving her unable to walk; because of her unshakable faith, she was able to walk again in less than one year. She taught us to "read the Bible when you have issues so you can reap the rewards of what you read in God's Word." As kids, we were raised to be faithful to God by reading and knowing God's Word as it was taught in our home.

Not only did Mom read the Bible and pray, but she also instructed me to do the same. She would say, "Go to the Lord. Learn through reading His Word." And, "Pray to God because, in our house, we will serve the Lord, and if you pray to God, He will help you." She also cautioned me, especially when I was backed into a corner or in physical danger, to scream the name of Jesus. And keep screaming it! When I really needed Him to protect me, I screamed "Jesus!" exactly as she had taught me. And He protected me.

> *Submit yourselves, then, to God. Resist the devil, and he will flee from you* (James 4:7 NIV).

We should always stay close to God by submitting ourselves unconditionally to Him and calling on His protection against evil advances. We must not let our guard down in times of adversity, challenges, or struggles but keep our focus on God's love and protection. Because of my and my family's constant prayer life, miraculously, I believe that nothing happened to my children. I prayed and knew God was watching over them.

When I was ten years old, my favorite uncle was killed by a drunk driver. It was so devastating to me. My mom said, "Pray to God for understanding. If you pray to ask for help, He will help you." I began to pray a prayer that was familiar to me. It is known as the Lord's prayer, a prayer Jesus taught, found in Matthew 6:9-13 (NIV):

Our Father in heaven, hallowed be your name,
your kingdom come, your will be done,
on earth as it is in heaven.
Give us today our daily bread.
And forgive us our debts, as we also have forgiven our debtors.
And lead us not into temptation but deliver us from the evil one.

This prayer begins with praises to God for who He is. It encourages us to ask Him in faith for daily help and provisions for basic needs. It includes asking God for His forgiveness for our debts—our sinful behavior. By praying these words, we also vow our forgiveness for those who have sinned against us. This prayer ends by asking for God's protection against Satan, the evil one.

It's OK to scream the name of Jesus when you need help.

God has a plan for every person; we can each live with the purpose He has willed for us. *"For I know the plans I have for you," declares the Lord, "plans to prosper you and not to harm you, plans to give you hope and a future"* (Jeremiah 29:11 NIV). Discovering and living that purpose begins with prayer—we are each to ask Jesus for a personal relationship with Him. When you do, He will meet you with joy! You can trust God's plan for you. *God works for the good of those who love him, who have been called according to his purpose* (Romans 8:28 NIV). When we follow Christ, we can be confident in our hope and future.

In 1995, I was a trainer of physician recruiters. I was making an excellent income. However, the organization was not set up to empower women and promote them to higher leadership levels. I felt I had reached the "glass ceiling"—no other promotions were available to me. Yet, I was compelled to focus on my job 24/7, which resulted in working fifty to sixty hours a week, taking time away from my family. I also had a small jewelry business that required additional hours away. My son, Gabriel, was just five years old at the time. These conditions made it difficult to balance my career and family so we could enjoy a healthy quality of life. The extended time at work became an expensive price to pay for me and my family. Women in this situation often feel left without the option of balance and are compelled to choose between family and career. So they leave the corporate workforce and the excellent income they have been earning because it does not support their personal values and family priorities. I was one of those women. So, I did what my mom taught me: I turned to God for direction.

I also experienced challenges and turbulent times when I went through a divorce. These were some of my saddest and darkest moments. I often reminded myself that God's will is always good and that He can bring beauty from ashes. One of my favorite Bible verses is: *Teach me to do your will, for you are my God; may your good Spirit lead me on level ground* (Psalm 143:10 NIV). Through persistent prayer, God's Holy Spirit was at work, giving me a greater understanding and direction for my life. It was time to set new goals for my life. These goals helped me remove the apathy and indifference I had developed. I was being set free from feelings of inadequacy, creating new enthusiasm, and regenerating an inner power in my spirit as I allowed God to speak new life into me every day.

As Christians, we do not need to worry about problems or future because we have faith in an unshakable God. No matter what challenge or situation comes your way, know you do not have to face it alone; you can surrender every difficulty to God. Then, there's no reason to worry about those things any longer. Why? Because God created us. He's the Creator of the universe and the author of our faith. And God does everything for a reason; He has a plan. If we learn to turn our struggles over to Him, we can live doing what He created us for, according to His plan. You can know for certain He has a beautiful plan for your life.

God has filled my life with blessings. In 2000, I was introduced to a financial service company. To my surprise, the financial analysis report showed me how I could reach total financial independence using their financial strategies and principles. I realized a new-found financial independence that would allow me to build a legacy for my family. Most importantly, I could balance my family life and business life as I increased my income through my financial service business.

I met Eddie, who was a Regional Vice President at that time. With his leadership and direction, within a short timeframe, I was able to become a fully licensed Regional Vice President, obtain full ownership of a real business, and achieve many leadership goals. It has been a dream come true. Now, Eddie is not only my business partner who inspires me, but he also has become my loving husband.

When I first met Eddie, he was Catholic, as my family was, but he didn't read the Bible and did not have a personal relationship with Jesus. He lived an honest life and would never do anything unethical. In some way, he knew

God was watching him. One day, I asked him if he wanted to accept Jesus into his life. I suggested we pray together; Eddie accepted Jesus as His Lord and Savior and now walks closely with Jesus.

God has blessed our financial partnership in many ways. Luke 11:9 instructs us to ask God and that when we do, He will respond. So, we continually ask God to put a covering of protection over our business. We pray for our entire financial service team—sometimes finding an empty meeting room, kneeling down, and praying together. We ask God for wisdom to cover our business. God protects and sustains us by leading the right people into our business centers and removing those He does not want in our lives or business. We pray about everything. Unshakably, Eddie and I walk together in life and in faith with God. We are now blessed even more with our son and daughter joining this financial journey as our second-generation partners. Our first and foremost goal is to make a difference in the lives of others. Galatians 6:9 reminds us, *Let us not become weary in doing good, for at the proper time we will reap a harvest if we do not give up* (NIV).

Once we realized the importance of knowing and understanding the biblical financial principles we learned at church, Eddie and I began recruiting other Christians so they could teach their church friends what God's Word says about finances and the biblical principle for handling money. They started teaching others how to integrate financial and biblical principles to handle their money using God's principles. Life is about helping other people. It has been powerful to be able to build a mega financial services business with the goal of leaving a legacy for our kids and providing an opportunity for others to leave their own legacy. I am reminded of Ephesians 2:10, which tells us, *For we are God's handiwork, created in Christ Jesus to do good works, which God prepared in advance for us to do* (NIV).

The delight of my life has been watching my son and daughter grow up. God sustains me by allowing me to provide them the very best quality of life and be their example of what an exceptional life can look like. I am so happy I was able to replace a dead-end job with owning a rewarding business that allows me to spend more time with my husband and kids. So many people live their short lives filled with regret. I am thankful I had the unshakable courage to take the risk that enabled me to reach my goals and live out my dreams with our kids. With God, anything is possible.

When our children were young, our son, Gabriel, and daughter, Alyssa, helped teach us about faith in God. Our children loved the pastors and nuns at their school. With their innocence, the love and values poured into them in school and at home allowed these attributes to come out in the activities they were involved in, especially the school plays. It became clear that our children understood the importance of these values as they shared their knowledge with us. They also learned biblical values from their grandmothers, who I had also learned from, reinforcing what they learned in school. They developed strong faith because of their schooling and grandmother's influence, so they poured this learning into my husband and me, strengthening our faith in God. Eddie and I didn't attend church regularly until our children would not let us forget that we needed to go to church. They stressed to us the importance of our faith in God and being with other believers. Our family helped each other stay on the path God was leading us. Life values and faith in God should be passed from parents to children to grandchildren. We must teach our own children to embrace God's values and love, empowering future generations.

Family is sacred to us. I taught my family that quality family time together is essential. Our family eats dinner together, praying before the meal for God's blessing on the food. When any of our children's friends come to visit, family time still stands. Some of their friends call me "prophet mom" because of our focus and influence on family and biblical values.

Now that our children are older, when things go wrong, Alyssa will begin to pray. People around her say, "She sounds like her mother." I give thanks to the Lord because our kids don't do drugs and don't drink alcohol. I give God all the glory!

Family is important because we love, support, pray for, and teach each other. Family values must be instilled in every family member—children and adults. We need to pass family values from generation to generation. Quality family time is crucial for sharing our thoughts, problems, dreams, and fun times.

Praying—spending time in God's presence, talking and listening to Him—is vital. Prayer is based on a personal relationship with God. It's a time of praise, worship, and surrender to God of the universe. It's a time to ask Him for direction in your life, listen for His answers, and surrender your problems—giving them over to God. In prayer, you can confess your sins, ask for protection, call for help, or simply meet with God in love. Prayer can give you peace. In prayer, you learn to recognize and receive God's grace.

Praying together corporately as a family is powerful—whether it is a simple meal blessing of thanks, a prayer of praise, a bedtime prayer to say good night, or seeking God's provision for needs, safety, support, and love. Teach your kids to pray, and then let them instigate prayer time. Together, you will spur each other on to continually rely on God. And you will be blessed.

I shared my unshakable journey to show how life can be filled with family relationships, love, faith, and blessings from God. Your journey may be different—God's path for each of us is unique. But you can be assured that His will for you is purposeful. As you trust in God's provision and path, may your journey be unshakable as you praise and thank Him for the remarkable wonders in *your* life.

Unshakable in Forgiving Others

By Leecy Barnett

Have you ever thought, *I just can't forgive that person? Or, After what that person did, they don't deserve to be forgiven?* If so, I have news for you. You are stunting your own spiritual growth while the other person is going merrily on their way. Unforgiveness backfires every time.

When Jesus taught His disciples to pray, He told them to say: *Forgive us our sins, as we have forgiven those who sin against us* (Matthew 6:12 NLT). In case the disciples didn't understand this part of the prayer, Jesus gave this explanation: *"If you forgive those who sin against you, your heavenly Father will forgive you. But if you refuse to forgive others, your Father will not forgive your sins"* (Matthew 6:14-15 NLT). Refusing to forgive is not an option for a follower of Jesus. Jesus is known for His mercy and forgiveness, so anyone who claims to be His disciple must also forgive.

"Ok," you may say, "I forgave that person once, but they hurt me the same way again. Do I really need to forgive them once more?"

Jesus said, *"If another believer sins, rebuke that person; then if there is repentance, forgive. Even if that person wrongs you seven times a day and each time turns again and asks forgiveness, you must forgive"* (Luke 17:3-4 NLT).

Peter, the leader of the early church, had the same question for Jesus.

Then Peter came to him and asked, "Lord, how often should I forgive someone who sins against me? Seven times?" "No, not seven times," Jesus replied, "but seventy times seven!" (Matthew 18:21-22 NLT).

Don't think you can count up to 490 offenses and then quit forgiving. The expression seventy times seven is meant to represent an infinite amount of forgiveness. We are called to love one another, and love *is not irritable, and it keeps no record of being wronged* (1 Corinthians 13:5 NLT).

We don't need to wait until we feel like forgiving someone to forgive them. Forgiveness is a matter of our will. We choose to let go of bitterness and resentment. We choose to release the other person from the impossible demand to make it right. We can overlook everyday slights and shortcomings, but when we are intentionally hurt or wounded, we must choose to forgive. Colossians 3:13 (NIV) says, *Bear with each other and forgive one another if any of you has a grievance against someone. Forgive as the Lord forgave you.*

How did the Lord forgive us? In Pastor Todd Mullins' words: "He forgave us completely. He freely forgave us without reservation or hesitation."[1] Jesus forgave at great expense—He paid with His life. Forgiveness like this is humanly impossible. We must choose to allow the Holy Spirit, whom Jesus sent to live within His followers, to empower us to forgive. It is something we can never do on our own.

We can be unshakable in forgiving only when we acknowledge our inability to forgive in our own strength and rely upon God's mercy and grace to enable us to forgive the offender.

Father, I no longer want to hold on to bitterness in my heart. I want to forgive ______________________________, who hurt me so badly, but I can't do it in my own strength. Holy Spirit, I need You to give me Jesus' love and mercy for ___________________________ and enable me to forgive them just as Jesus forgave me.

[1]Mullins, T. & Mullins, J. (2024, April 21). *Overcoming unforgiveness.* https://youtu.be/eUKVe_hRhXg?si=OlyEmkwvafvad351

Betz Fishbein

Betz Fishbein grew up in Allen Park (Detroit), Michigan. She spent several years in different business fields, which, combined with her innate love for people, prepared her for her true passion: massage therapy. In 1996, Betz moved to South Florida, as her parents were snowbirds. A couple of years later, they both became ill, and she spent the next seven years taking care of them. During this season of her life, Betz grew closer to the Lord.

After surrendering the dream of having her own children, Betz realized that God still had an amazing purpose for her life. She invested everything into her career of helping people feel better physically, emotionally, and spiritually. Through having a God-centered business, her life has flourished in every way.

At age 60, Betz is now enjoying her best life ever with many blessings, from an amazing husband, family, and grandchildren to a loving church community. Walking through daily life is her opportunity to live life to the fullest, whether at work or with family or friends. Her heart is full of God's love and His purpose for her life.

A Persistent, Relentless Heart

By Betz Fishbein

It was 2001 when I drove past the church on the way to my parents' home. Every time I passed it, I got an unusual stabbing pain in my heart, so I attended Christmas service there. God knew what was coming my way. I would need a savior to help me through the years ahead. Tears ran down my face the entire service. The music was beautiful, and the sermon was just what I needed to hear. I continued attending as it brought me comfort I never knew existed.

In 2002, my mom's cancer returned after twenty years. She had been diagnosed with breast cancer at the age of forty-two, and now it was in her bones and in her brain. My mom and I were like best friends, and I could not bear losing her.

Then, my dog became sick, too. He was like a baby to me.

Adding more turmoil, I had been on fertility drugs for ten years trying to have children. Many miscarriages later, I became very sick. We tried adoption, and after multiple attempts and much struggle, we gave up the dream.

The Lord is close to the brokenhearted and saves those who are crushed in spirit (Psalm 34:18 NIV).

I had to be the strong one when everyone around me was falling apart. I kept going to church, where I could be my true self. Trying to help all my loved ones and keep my life together was a struggle. I felt like I was at a crossroad, and God wanted to direct me to leave certain parts of me behind,

So I say, walk by the Spirit, and you will not gratify the desires of the flesh. For the flesh desires what is contrary to the Spirit, and the Spirit what is contrary to the flesh. They are in conflict with each other, so that you are not to do whatever you want. But if you are led by the Spirit, you are not under the law (Galatians 5:16-18 NIV).

I sure felt a tugging at my heart and a new strength I had never known before. I knew God was right with me through these next few years. As Philippians 4:13 teaches, *I can do all this through him who gives me strength* (NIV).

My mom was in and out of the hospital. She wanted to return to church, so when she wasn't in the hospital, she attended my new church with me. She seemed to love it.

As we were leaving that first time, I noticed she was crying. I asked her, "Are you okay?"

She said, "Yes. But I can't go back to my church. What will I tell my relatives? Do you know what? I am not changing my religion. I am changing my relationship!"

Together, we started a study with the women in the church. We had the sweetest time. The ladies laid hands on my mom for healing. They prayed for her brain cancer to be totally gone, and praise God, it was no longer there! We saw miracle after miracle!

> *Stretch out your hand to heal and perform signs and wonders through the name of your holy servant Jesus* (Acts 4:30 NIV).

During this same time, my dad was diagnosed with lymphoma and congestive heart disease. He was in a lot of pain. It was very difficult taking care of two parents, but God was my strength through this seven-year storm. I could feel Him holding me up and directing me.

My husband was in and out of recovery for alcoholism. And my sweet dog had to be put down—my heart was broken. I felt like I had lost my child. This created a big scar in my life, but I had to keep going. We adopted another puppy a couple of months after the last one died. Amazingly, when we received her papers, she had been born the same day our other dog went to heaven. Wow, God really works in mysterious ways and brings peace to every storm!

Palm Sunday 2003 arrived. Palm Sunday is a very special time in our church; during service, we write down our sins on a piece of paper and then nail the paper to the cross. By this point, my mom was paralyzed and in a wheelchair. She could not write, so I wrote for her, positioned her paper and the nail, and handed her the hammer. My mom nailed her sins to the cross as we both wept. It was such an emotional experience.

The next week, my mom took a turn for the worse and ended up with sepsis, a condition where the body's infection-fighting ability goes awry throughout the body. She begged me to take her out of the hospital so she could attend church on Easter. I knew they would not release her. When I arrived at her bedside after service, my mom was in a coma. I didn't want to believe I was losing her.

The following morning, the doctor called to advise that my mom would not live for much longer and that we had better hurry to say our goodbyes. My dad and I rushed to the hospital, but we did not make it in time. The compassionate nurse told me she whispered in my mom's ear as she took her last breath, "Jesus, Jesus," and she went peacefully to be with Him.

My life was shattered. My best friend, the one I could tell anything to, was gone. I was crushed. But my dad still needed me, so I put my grief and emotions aside to move forward. I could feel God's peace holding me up.

My life totally changed after my mom died. My dad moved in with me and my husband in between his hospital stays due to his many health issues. My dad went to his eternal home three and a half years after my mom did. I knew they were reunited. They both had given their lives to Jesus and now had eternal life with Almighty God. I can rejoice knowing I will be with them someday—knowing that truth was the ONLY THING that made losing them bearable.

I pray that you know our Lord and Savior. If you do not, please take the time to reach out to Him today.

The scripture says, *Whoever calls upon the name of the Lord will be saved* (Romans 10:13 NKJV). If you want to know Christ, pray to receive His free gift of salvation.

With sincerity, say aloud: "Lord Jesus, I repent of my sins and surrender my life. Wash me clean. I believe that You, Jesus, are the Son of God. I believe You died on the cross for my sins and rose again. I believe in my heart and confess with my mouth that You are my Savior and Lord. I receive eternal life. In Jesus' name. Amen."

If you want someone to walk through this time of rebirth or just celebrate with you, ask one of your friends who knows Jesus. Or reach out to us at Women World Leaders by emailing prayer@womenworldleaders.com.

Giving your life to God does not mean you will not have trials or troubles, but it will be the best decision of your life.

John 16:33 records Jesus' words, *"I have told you these things, so that in me you may have peace. In this world you will have trouble. But take heart! I have overcome the world"* (NIV).

Through many prayers and confirmations, I knew God wanted more for my life. I now had no children or parents, and my husband and I had become just roommates. He told me he could not change; he was comfortable in his skin. I attended co-dependency classes. I had to change my ways so I would not continue the pattern I had been in—I wanted my choices to be God's choices. We were divorced after many years of counseling and trying to make it work. I remained single for thirteen years. I dated a few times, but discovered red flag warnings each time. Praise God, He showed me them. At times, it took me longer to notice His warning than it should have.

> *"For I know the plans I have for you," declares the LORD, "plans to prosper you and not to harm you, plans to give you hope and a future. Then you will call on me and come and pray to me, and I will listen to you. You will seek me and find me when you seek me with all your heart. I will be found by you," declares the LORD, "and will bring you back from captivity. I will gather you from all the nations and places where I have banished you." declares the LORD, "and will bring you back to the place from which I carried you into exile"* (Jeremiah 29:11-14 NIV).

God had great plans for my life. I knew He had planted hopes and desires in my heart that He would bring me in His perfect timing. I was lonely, though never alone. I poured myself into my friendships and work, sometimes working seven days a week. I participated in Bible studies, attended church every week, and grew in my faith. Previously, I had not dug deep into any study, using the excuse that I did not have enough time. But I began trusting

God more and letting go of old habits.

> *Blessed is the one who does not walk in step with the wicked or stand in the way that sinners take or sit in the company of mockers, but whose delight is in the law of the LORD, and who meditates on his law day and night. That person is like a tree planted by streams of water, which yields its fruit in season and whose leaf does not wither—whatever they do prospers* (Psalm 1:1-4 NIV).

As a new year started, I lost both of my dogs ten weeks apart. I became scared at night for the first time in my life because I was alone! I would hear all kinds of noises and cry myself to sleep. One night. I was crying out to God, "Why did you take my protection away?"

It felt like He crawled into bed with me, wrapped His arms around me, and explained that my pets were never my protection. He said He was always there and would never leave me. I cried as I felt such a warm comfort like never before. I didn't have a hard time falling asleep after that.

> *The LORD himself goes before you and will be with you; he will never leave you nor forsake you. Do not be afraid, do not be discouraged* (Deuteronomy 31:8 NIV).

There was a study in the church I knew God had wanted me to take, though I always had an excuse—I was too busy! One weekend, the church was doing sign-ups for group classes; the class I had avoided for so long was being offered again. A couple of people I knew were taking it, and they asked me if I was going to take it. I said, "I'm in a busy season as a massage therapist and do not have time."

Eight different people asked me! Then, a friend asked me to hold her books, saying she would be right back. I looked down, and I was holding the study

I had been avoiding.

Finally, I said, "Okay, Lord. I will take this class called *Triumph Over Suffering.*"

I made a commitment to myself and God that I would put Him first and do the work needed to help heal my heart. I stopped running from God. I took the time to grieve the loss of my parents and the loss of my dreams of a happy marriage and motherhood. I learned how to surrender and how to forgive. I was even freed from an addiction to cigarette smoking through this class. I realized I was holding on to something that I thought brought me comfort. Praise God, the stronghold of this was released forever! All this work and all these heartaches were so hard to process, but I completely surrendered my will to God's will.

The next thing God wanted me to revisit was the most uncomfortable yet! My little brother had been diagnosed with bipolar disorder. At the age of 49, he was very depressed and died tragically from suicide. A few weeks before he died, he shared with me that he had been sexually abused at a very young age. I knew how important it was to forgive others, but forgiveness, in this case, seemed impossible.

For several years, I held onto anger and bitterness toward my brother's abusers. I had a hard time forgiving them for taking my brother's life. After hard work and a lot of wrestling with God, I finally found it in my heart to forgive these men. I would not forget what they did or ever say what they did was okay, but I was able to release the anger and bitterness from my heart into God's precious hands.

Still, I dealt with remorse for not saving my brother. When the Holy Spirit revealed this unrelenting feeling, I broke down crying. My friend prayed with me, and I was able to ask God for forgiveness. I felt an immediate release and relief in my heart. God was able to heal my deepest of heart wounds and the grief and pain I had been holding on to. I finally felt freed. I was able to let go of many hurts and disappointments because of this class, which God had used to change me from the inside out. I felt closer to God than ever before. The time I spent with Him was so precious and full of healing tears. My faith and relationship with Jesus grew stronger because of this time with Him. I would never be the same. He never left my side, not for even a moment.

Proverbs 3:5-6 teaches us to *Trust in the LORD with all your heart and lean not on your own understanding; in all your ways submit to him, and he will make your paths straight* (NIV).

God taught me unshakable faith.

As my life moved forward, a new massage client who was referred to me was on my schedule. After the massage, the receptionist said, "Betz, you know that Bob-guy that was here? He said he has not looked at a woman like you since his wife died, that God told him you were the one."

I sarcastically replied, "WHATEVER!"

The next day, I received a book in the mail he had written. He asked me if he could take me for a cup of coffee.

I replied, "I'm too busy."

He continued to be very persistent. A couple of weeks later, I called him and told him I could meet him at a cafe for lunch. When we met, as we talked, we both had tears rolling down our eyes. I felt such love coming from this man, and I had so much love in my heart.

He told me a story about an accident he had been in. The officer told him he should not be alive and had prayed for him, saying he was a born-again Christian. I felt the Holy Spirit say, "Tell him that is what you are, too."

So, I followed the Holy Spirit's urging and asked him, "Do you even know what that means?"

Bob responded that he was Jewish.

My first thought was, *This will never work.*

But then Bob told me he wanted to go to church with me, and the next evening, we went to a Christian concert. He did not understand what he was feeling.

Then, COVID-19 hit, and everything shut down, including my business. Bob kept telling me nothing was off the table for us. He wanted to know more about my Jesus. We began doing relationship studies and talked every evening, revealing our answers. Bob wanted to know more. I suggested a couple of other Bible studies, and he jumped in with both feet. I feel like God gave me the time to spend to get to know Bob, and I got to know him well.

When I asked God about my relationship with Bob, He said, "What didn't I give you?"

I broke down crying. I waited for the red flags, but this time, it was different.

As we became closer, we decided we wanted to get married. Bob got baptized exactly seventeen years after I had. Six months later, we were married.

I told Bob from the beginning that Jesus would always be my #1. His response was, "That's okay. Can I be your #1A?"

I have an amazing husband who goes to church with me every week, is in a men's group, serves the teenagers, and prays with me daily. We have a beautiful family. I prayed for a godly man who had kids or grandchildren or loved to work with kids, and God gave me all three. We have three grown children; two are married and have given us four precious grandsons! God sure brings us the desires of our hearts as we surrender our hearts completely to Him. It reminds me of scripture.

> *Take delight in the LORD, and he will give you the desires of your heart* (Psalm 37:4 NIV).

> *"Ask and it will be given to you; seek and you will find; knock and the door will be opened to you. For everyone who asks receives; the one who seeks finds; and to the one who knocks the door will be opened"* (Matthew 7:7-8 NIV).

Keep praying and believing in our Almighty God as you hold on to your unshakable faith, continually surrendering to His perfect plan through a persistent, relentless heart.

God is faithful as we continue to surrender our hearts to His. My life is so precious, and I thank God daily for His faithfulness.

Unshakable in Grief

By Donna Whartenby

Walking through times of grief is inevitable in this life. I am sure you have endured the sorrow that comes from experiencing a loss, possibly even the loss of a loved one. It can be excruciating to watch a loved one suffer from affliction or disease, and it certainly is not easy to take that late-night phone call informing you that a loved one has taken their last breath. The range of human suffering from loss is broad. But the good news is that, for those who know and trust God, He will always be our refuge and strength, even when we are grieving.

> *The Lord is my rock and my fortress and my deliverer; My God, my strength, in whom I will trust; My shield and the horn of my salvation, my stronghold* (Psalm 18:2 NKJV).

Years ago, my sister-in-law battled cancer. During the ten years of her illness, she fought several types of cancers, endured surgeries, chemotherapy, and radiation treatments, and struggled for strength to stay alive to watch her young son grow up. We held her hand through the pain, prayed over her suffering, read scripture to her for comfort and peace, and sat with her so she was not alone. It was hard to watch life drain from her body.

God sustained us through our suffering and grief. In Joshua, the Lord tells us, *"Be strong and courageous. Do not be afraid or discouraged. For the Lord your God is with you wherever you go"* (Joshua 1:9 NLT). And in Isaiah, He tells us, *"Don't be afraid, for I am with you. Don't be discouraged, for I am your God. I will strengthen you and help you. I will hold you up with my victorious right hand"* (Isaiah 41:10 NLT).

We remained strong for my sister-in-law. Our family trusted God, and we knew He was in control.

> *Trust in the Lord with all your heart; do not depend on your own understanding* (Proverbs 3:5 NLT).

The Apostle Paul teaches us *God is our merciful Father and the source of all comfort* (2 Corinthians 1:3 NLT), and God certainly sustained us with His love, compassion, and mercy in my sister-in-law's presence, even as she took her last breath on her wedding anniversary. Our God is always good. The ending was not our desire, but He gave us comfort.

Scripture teaches that, for those following God, death is only the beginning. They will not vanish or turn to dust when they leave this earthly place. Jesus, God's Son, has prepared a place for His children in eternity. However, we must meet a condition to go to this heavenly place: we must believe Jesus is God's Son, that He died on the cross to rescue us from our sinful life, and we must accept God's gift of forgiveness and commit to follow His truth and ways (John 14:6).

We are all born unrighteous. Adam and Eve, the first humans, turned from God in the Garden of Eden, sinning against Him. And we have all followed in their footsteps. Sin is a serious matter; it separates us from our holy God. But God created a path for our sin to be wiped away. Jesus came to earth and lived a sinless life, and because the price of sin is death, the sinless, perfect Son of God should have never died. But Jesus willingly gave up His perfect life, dying on the cross and paying the penalty for sin that we each owe. Then He rose from the dead, overcoming death, and now lives eternally with God in heaven. When a believer in Jesus dies, Jesus will usher them into heaven's gates to spend eternity with our Sovereign God. However, those who die not believing in Jesus, having not accepted Jesus' payment for their sins, will themselves experience God's consequences and punishment:

death and eternal separation from God.

Although the future is bright for the one who has passed into Jesus' arms, when we are in the position of losing someone, our grief can be palpable. Queen Elizabeth II is quoted saying, "Grief is the price we pay for love." When someone special dies, it is ok to grieve. Grieving is human. The grief we feel upon losing someone we love may be profound. And with it can come deep sorrow and pain. When you experience this and do not know where to turn, you can find comfort, help, and hope in God's Word. Those who seek God and His Word grieve differently than the world because we have hope.

> *We want you to know what will happen to the believers who have died so you will not grieve like people who have no hope. For since we believe that Jesus died and was raised to life again, we also believe that when Jesus returns, God will bring back with him (to heaven) the believers who have died* (1 Thessalonians 4:13-14 NLT).

Decades later, we still miss our beloved sister. We reminisce over memories we shared, but God, in His goodness, left us with more than memories, comforting us with a joy only He could have provided. After her death, my husband and I were given the gift of raising her son, who blessed us with three delightful grandchildren who call us Grandmom and Grandpop.

Despite any loss we endure, as Christians, we can look forward expectantly to an incredible future. If we go to Him, our faithful God will provide comfort from others, from His Holy Spirit, and through the promises in His Word. And, as Christians, we can be most thankful for the abundant blessing of our eternal life in Christ, which He has already prepared. HALLELUJAH! We can be unshakable despite our grief!

Dear Lord, thank You for Your love and comfort when we are grieving. Help us face each day with comfort, hope, and joy. Thank You for the time we've shared with our loved ones. Let their memories bring us joy and comfort. Fill our hearts with peace that surpasses all understanding when we grieve, knowing that You are in control. Most importantly, thank You for the promise You give your followers for our everlasting life with You in heaven. Amen.

Da'Quanya Hanson

Da'Quanya Hanson is a disciple of Jesus Christ. She has a heart for God, His people, and His creation.

Da'Quanya was born and raised in Riviera Beach, Florida. She was brought up in a Christian home with a single mother, Deidra, and her younger brother De'Vario, both of whom have gone home to be with the Lord. Through grief and pain, the Lord healed her heart and gave her a vision to nurture "What's Your Seed Ministries," a ministry dedicated to serving inner city kids.

Da'Quanya teamed up with Women World Leaders, which has impacted her love for writing and telling her story with other women. Her mission is to share the Gospel through creative outlets, expressing the love of Jesus by providing meals, clothing, and words of encouragement to the homeless, whom she calls "future homeowners."

She enjoys drives near the beaches in her camper van, evangelizing, painting, and sharing hope, joy, and laughs with the broken and forgotten. Being sensitive to Holy Spirit, every day is an adventure for her. Da'Quanya is always ready to let her light shine.

God Is on My Side

By Da'Quanya Hanson

As I walked into the hospital room, my heart began to beat fast. It was 2005, and I was 14 years old. My family's faces were filled with concern, worry, and dread. Except my mom's. As she lay in the hospital bed, she seemed calm and relaxed, as if there was nothing to worry about.

Earlier that day, my mom had called me, my cousins, aunts, and uncles to visit her at the hospital so she could share some important news. Standing next to the hospital bed, I made eye contact with my mom as she gazed back at me with a slight grin on her face. I stared intensely at her, feeling my eyes stretching wider, my heart pumping faster than before, my mind wondering what important news she needed to share with everyone.

Weeks before, my mom had stayed in bed longer than usual, which was never her thing. It was difficult for her to breathe. Her body had become so weak that she began passing out frequently. We lived in South Florida, where it gets really hot in the summertime, so I first assumed that her body just needed to rest. My mother was always very active; her work kept her outside in the sun all day, but that had never stopped her from reaching her daily goals before. The illness landed her in the hospital.

When she called us in, I knew something was wrong. I wanted to hear the verse that I used to hear in church as a kid that gave me peace: *Let not your heart be troubled; ye believe in God, believe also in me* (John 14:1 KJV). Instead, that day I heard words that I never imagined I would hear my mom say. My life was about to change forever.

We all gathered around the hospital bed as my mom began to speak.

"I called everyone here today to say that I am HIV positive, and I may not have much time to live."

My family and I were all shocked. My heart sank as tears began to run down my face, and my stomach tightened as if someone had just punched me in the gut. With the thought of her leaving me at the age of 14 and my brother at the age of 9, my entire body became gripped with fear and anxiety. I ran into the restroom and slammed the door behind me. I cried, screamed, and felt so confused. *How could this have happened to her?*

Then I heard a knock at the door and my cousin shout, "Open the door, Sweetie. Everything will be okay, don't worry."

I looked into the mirror, took a deep breath, and began to feel at ease hearing her words. In moments of uncertainty, we can acknowledge God by shifting our thoughts to Him so He can speak to us and give us hope. I love how Psalm 94:19 tells us, *Whenever my busy thoughts were out of control, the soothing comfort of your presence calmed me down and overwhelmed me with delight* (TPT).

I opened the door, and my cousin gave me a tight hug. I could feel the pain releasing from my body as if it transferred to her. I wiped the tears from my eyes and walked back to the hospital bed. My mom still looked calm and peaceful. She smiled and said, "It's going to be okay, Baby." With her lying in a hospital bed, I could not understand why she would say that. But anytime my mom said it would be okay, I believed her. Before she got sick, she was so strong and independent. She was vibrant, beautiful, wise, ambitious, and funny. Even as a single mother, she took great care of my brother and me. She loved God, raised us in the church, and was always willing to help anyone she could. Nothing at all was making sense to me.

The doctor walked into the room and began to explain my mom's condition. I learned that HIV/AIDS is Human Immunodeficiency Virus/Acquired Immunodeficiency Syndrome. The virus can multiply and destroy someone's immune cells. Some people can have signs of fever, fatigue, night sweats, and swollen lymph nodes. Most people with the virus can have it for years and still live a healthy life. We found out that my mom had HIV for some time; she received the virus from a man she dated in the past, before she had given her life to Christ. She kept her diagnosis a secret from some of the family because she did not want to be judged. She had been able to live a healthy life until the process became too exhausting for her. For her to have a healthy immune system and live longer, she needed to take her HIV medication consistently. But sometimes the pills would not digest properly, which caused her to vomit to the point she had no energy.

February 2007 arrived; my mom's condition had gotten much worse. Her body could no longer fight off the virus, and she was admitted into Hospice, where those with a serious illness who are approaching death receive care, comfort, and a quality life. Before my mom got too ill, knowing the time would come for her to leave this earth, she made arrangements for my brother and me to have a place to live and be taken care of. I began to notice her praying more to God, asking Him to protect my brother and me. She often read the Bible, prayed over us, and played gospel music. Those things kept her going and at peace. At times, she shared with me about having faith, making sure that I would take care of my brother when she left and do whatever I needed to do to keep God first.

It was heart-wrenching to see her transform from a vibrant woman into someone who couldn't speak properly. She could no longer dress herself, dance, drive, or do fun things with us. She was no longer her beautiful self. For our sake, especially for my brother, I began to pray to God that she wouldn't die. I felt my brother needed her more because he was less prepared for what was happening to her than I was. He never wanted to see her when she was sick in the hospital or Hospice, so he didn't visit her. My mom understood his reason and never forced him to come to see her. She knew that it was painful and traumatic for him. It was hard for me to bear, but I understood as well.

I started journaling and writing letters to God day after day to share my thoughts. And I began to feel His love and peace.

> *And the peace of God, which passeth all understanding, shall keep your hearts and minds through Christ Jesus* (Philippians 4:7 KJV).

My family commented about how strong I was because I seemed at peace with everything happening to my mom. Experiencing a sick and dying parent was by no means easy. On the outside, they saw me calm and laughing, just being my normal self. But on the inside, I was hurting and sad as I processed with Jesus what was happening. The more time I spent communicating with God through journaling and praying, the stronger an unshakable faith was growing in me. I know God was listening to my prayers because peace, love, and joy became so real to me. I was gaining an unshakable faith even with the circumstances that were set before me.

I have discovered that the best remedy when we face hard times is to pray to God for His strength and direction. The world will tell you to run to artificial peace and comfort. But God's peace is everlasting; He is the God of all comfort. He is faithful to His children. When the situation seems impossible, we can remember that God is our Father who makes the impossible possible. Jesus is our peace. When we feel overwhelmed, we can call out to Him, the Prince of Peace. The Holy Spirit is our counselor in all circumstances. He will counsel and guide us into all truth. I learned to draw my strength from my unshakable God. Moments with my mom became more precious, allowing me to see God's hand over the circumstances and enjoy the moments I had left with her.

I was now in high school and was able to understand more than when I first found out about my mom's condition. I visited her every other day after school. My mom's sister, Aunt Moochie, stayed by my mom's side every day. I felt grateful that my mom didn't have to go through her illness alone. The virus irritated her skin often; my aunt would put Vaseline over her skin and rub her body down with praying oil as she prayed and sang over my mom. Although it was hard to see my mom battling her illness, having Aunt Moochie there made it so much easier. When my aunt ministered to my mom, I would feel the presence of God in the room.

One day as I was visiting, my aunt was praising and praying to Jesus and reading Psalm 103:2-4, *Bless and affectionately praise the Lord, O my soul, and do not forget any of His benefits, who forgives all your sins, who heals all your diseases* (AMP). Jesus was honoring those prayers and praises, revealing Himself to us in a tangible way. I experienced the Father of heaven and earth like never before. Fears and worry about the future began to leave me. I noticed a glow surrounding my mom as my aunt read the Bible and worshipped. She was so beautiful and filled with joy. When we send praises up to God, He inhabits our praises. Not because we deserve it but because He loves us. The Lord can reveal Himself to us at any time, and He visited us that day; it is something I will never forget. It was an unshakable feeling.

In the next few days came the reality I did not want to face. The virus eventually took complete control of my mom's body, and she passed away and went to be with the Lord three months before my high school graduation. This was very hard for my brother and me. I was 17 years old, and he was 11. She was the best mom anyone could ask for, and we would miss her very much.

On my high school graduation day, it was difficult not having her there to celebrate with me. I managed to press on and step up to what was next for me and my brother's life. I began the process of becoming my brother's legal guardian. My mom left us in a situation to have our own home to start a life together without her. We settled closer to the beach, which was a benefit growing up near the ocean, my mom's favorite place. The Blue Heron Bridge in Riviera Beach was one place she took us often. My brother and I would go to the beach to remember her, doing the things she did with us, from swimming to fishing, just reminiscing.

A new life without our mom was challenging. I started a new job, paid the bills, and tried to parent my brother as his guardian. We couldn't figure out how to deal with our emotions and began fighting over everything. The good relationship we had before my mother's passing became toxic. He did not want me telling him what to do, and I wanted him to do what I wanted him to do. It left us both frustrated and resentful. My family tried to step in to help, but that didn't help. I just wanted to be left alone, thinking I was an adult now with all the responsibilities. We were both grieving in our own ways, leaving us broken and confused. Aunt Moochie would pray for guidance for us and told me to pray to God. But asking God for help was no longer a thought because I became prideful and resentful. Deep down inside, I knew God could help me get through my situation, but a spirit of rebellion entered me. I began to resent my mom leaving us, causing me to set aside my dreams to take care of my brother. Even the thought of the man who gave HIV to my mom made me hate men. I soon would step into a whole new lifestyle that I never thought I would live.

As time passed, there was not much my family could do for me or my brother. My brother started hanging out with his friends every day, which gave me space to do things I didn't want him to know about. I started hanging around a new crowd of people and began to smoke, drink alcohol, attend wild parties, and sleep around with men. The spirit of rebellion became stronger and led me into a deep hole of prostitution and living a lifestyle of sexual immorality. I began sleeping with millionaires or anyone wealthy. That lifestyle was contrary to how I was raised, but I no longer cared about my values or morals. Money became an idol to me because it made me forget my circumstances.

I smoked and drank every day to forget who I was sleeping with. I wanted to numb myself of any feeling, connection, or emotion. I was introduced to Xanax, which became my everyday drug. Life seemed unlivable, and my hate for men increased. I manipulated them every chance I got.

When I needed to vent, I would call my cousin Audrei, who was well aware of the lifestyle I was living. When I told her about my wild experiences, she would just listen to me and then pray for me to be careful. She asked God to draw me back to Him. We were very close growing up; I was always able to tell her anything without her judging me. We partied together for some time before she gave her life to Jesus; after, she didn't treat me any differently.

One night, as I was preparing to meet a guy in Miami, I got a phone call from Audrei. She said, "Hey? I have to tell you something. As I was praying, I heard God tell me to tell you that if you don't stop doing what you're doing, you're going to die."

That caught me by surprise. With the lifestyle I was living, I thought God was mad at me and didn't want anything to do with me any longer. I love how it says in the Bible, *But God clearly shows and proves His own love for us, by the fact that while we were still sinners, Christ died for us* (Romans 5:8 AMP). As I continued listening to what my cousin was saying, I began to feel convicted. Audrei prayed for me, and we hung up the phone. I canceled the date with the guy, got on my knees, and began to cry out to God. Deep down, I was tired of living a sinful lifestyle. I was just too embarrassed to even pray to God for help.

As I cried out to God for deliverance, I could feel the same presence in my living room I felt at the hospital with my mom and aunt. The presence of God was so thick that it was as if His face was right before mine. Before that encounter with God, I had been depressed and full of shame, anxiety, anger, suicidal thoughts, lust, pride, and resentment. I was often strung out on alcohol and drugs, and I didn't want to face life. Money was my god; I thought it was the cure for my pain. My life was full of darkness, making me feel hopeless.

That night, I experienced the love of God. I felt His forgiveness and received total peace that money could never buy. At that moment, I was delivered from every evil spirit by my God who sees and knows all things. The God of mercy and kindness forgave me.

No matter how far I felt from God, He had never left or forsaken me, just as He promises in His Word. I turned my back on Him, but with His unshakable love, He gave me another chance.

My life completely changed after that night. I repented of my sins, got baptized, was delivered from demons, and was filled with the Holy Spirit. Drugs and alcohol were no longer a temptation for me. Men and money were no longer gods or answers to my situation.

My relationship with my brother became healthier and stronger than ever; we started attending church again. God was answering my mother's prayers to protect and keep us.

My desire for God increased so much that I attended a discipleship school, learning how to be a disciple and make disciples. I became the founder of "What's Your Seed," a youth ministry for inner-city kids who struggle in life that points them to God through the love of Jesus. After returning from ministry school, I had the privilege of baptizing my brother. Life became even more amazing as God continued to move in our lives.

Through my entire experience of losing my mother, raising my brother at a young age, and living a lifestyle of sin, the Lord was always by my side. He caused everything to work out for my good, making me stronger.

And I say with confidence, no matter what trial or temptation comes your way, you too can be fearlessly unshakable when you hold firmly to God.

Unshakable in God's Forgiveness

By Leecy Barnett

Years ago, I loved reading C. S. Lewis' *The Screwtape Letters* because it gave me a totally different perspective on myself. Using his amazing creativity, Lewis imagines a series of letters written by Screwtape, an experienced demon, to his apprentice, Wormwood, teaching him how to get Christians off course.

> *Whenever they [believers] are attending to the Enemy Himself [God, from the demon's perspective] we are defeated, but there are ways of preventing them from doing so. The simplest is to turn their gaze away from Him towards themselves. Keep them watching their own minds and trying to produce feelings there by the action of their own wills.... When they say they are praying for forgiveness, let them be trying to feel forgiven. Teach them to estimate the value of each prayer by their success in producing the desired feeling.*[1]

Satan wants us to keep our focus away from God and on ourselves. One way he tries to accomplish that is by encouraging us to measure God's forgiveness by how we feel instead of what God says. The devil wants us to believe that our feelings are more accurate than God's truth; after all, if we don't *feel* forgiven, how can we say God has forgiven us? Satan takes advantage of our uncertainty and uses our doubts to turn us away from God.

With such a formidable enemy, how can we be unshakable when it comes to receiving God's forgiveness?

As believers, we can be unshakable by deciding to take God at His Word!

So, what does God's Word say about forgiveness?

First, Scripture tells us God has complete authority to forgive our sins. The teachers of religious law in Jesus' day rarely got things right, but they did get one thing right. When Jesus told the paralyzed man, *"My child, your sins are forgiven," the religious teachers were horrified and replied, "What is he saying? This is blasphemy! Only God can forgive sins!"* (Mark 2:5,7 NLT). They were right! God is the only one who can forgive sins. But what they did not realize was that Jesus was and is God in the flesh. Therefore, when Jesus forgave sin, it was not a sacrilege. Being God gave Jesus the power and authority to forgive sin.

Secondly, the Bible teaches that Jesus' death made forgiveness possible. While dying on the cross, Jesus said, *"It is finished"* (John 19:30 ESV). What was finished? It seemed apparent that Jesus' life was finished—although He did rise from the dead. Jesus' suffering and agony were also finished. But He meant more than that. The word Jesus used for "finished" also means to complete or fulfill—He had fulfilled the prophecy made more than 700 years before His birth, making a way for forgiveness:

> *The Lord decided his servant [Jesus] would suffer as a sacrifice to take away the sin and guilt of others. Now the servant will live to see his own descendants. He did everything the Lord had planned. By suffering, the servant will learn the true meaning of obeying the Lord. Although he is innocent, he will take the punishment for the sins of others, so that many of them will no longer be guilty. The Lord will reward him with honor and power for sacrificing his life. Others thought he was a sinner, but he suffered for our sins and asked God to forgive us* (Isaiah 53:10-12 CEV).

Thirdly, the Word tells us that forgiveness is eternally complete for those who have submitted to God. Christ's death supplies forgiveness for all our sins for all time.

Think of it! All sins forgiven, the slate wiped clean, that old arrest warrant canceled and nailed to Christ's cross (Colossians 2: 13b-14 MSG).

For God's will was for us to be made holy by the sacrifice of the body of Jesus Christ, once for all time (Hebrews 10:10 NLT).

I used to think that Jesus died for the sins I committed *before* I trusted Him as my Savior. But I wasn't so sure about my disobedience in following God's Word *after* I became a Christ follower. How could those sins be forgiven? Then I realized that when Christ died, *all* my sins were in the future, and He died for all of it. Good news: *Therefore, there is now no condemnation for those who are in Christ Jesus* (Romans 8:1 NIV).

Finally, the Bible tells us how to experience God's forgiveness. *Now repent of your sins and turn to God, so that your sins may be wiped away* (Acts 3:19 NLT). We only need to repent—which means confessing our sin with an attitude of remorse, turning away from our sin, and turning toward God—to experience the forgiveness that Jesus bought with His blood.

God's Word tells us that sin started when Adam and Eve stopped believing what God said, and sin will stop being held against you when you put your faith in God. God has the authority to completely and eternally forgive all your sins through His Son, Jesus, who died on the cross for you.

Start believing what God says rather than how you feel. If you have submitted to God, stand unshakable in His forgiveness!

If you haven't given your life to Christ, or if you have turned away from Him, take a step right now and acknowledge Jesus is the Son of the living God. Invite Him to direct your life, setting you on the path to establishing a right relationship with Him and ushering His authoritative and eternal forgiveness into your life! Will you pray with me?

Thank you, Jesus, for dying on the cross to forgive my sin. Jesus, I trust You as Lord of my life. I believe You when You say I am loved, completely forgiven, and free for eternity. Help me to follow Your path in my life today.

....

[1]Lewis, C. S. (1961). *The Screwtape letters.* Barbour, pp. 25-26.

Denise Martin

Denise Martin, originally from New Jersey, now lives in South Florida with her husband, Michael. She recently retired from a twenty-five-year career in education. Dee has a Master's Degree in Reading and a Doctorate in Curriculum and Instruction. After being in the classroom for ten years, she worked at the District Level writing Math Curriculum and supporting teachers delivering math instruction throughout the District. Denise also served as a school administrator in the District.

When she is not reading, Dee is playing pickleball or golf. Her favorite thing to do is spend time with her granddaughter, Gabby. Denise loves the Lord and being with family.

Freedom from Silence

By Denise Martin

Little did I know the pain and suffering I would endure for the rest of my life because of the unspeakable decision made for me. It was the beginning of my silence, my guilt, and my shame. It was when I lost my voice.

My appointment was made by someone else. There was no discussion—I had no choice. I was to be driven to the clinic by my cousin. Because I was so far along, this couldn't wait another day. The next morning came; I woke up, got dressed, kissed my baby girl good-bye, and went out the door.

My cousin arrived right on time; not a word was said on the ride there. There was silence. The kind of silence that is so heavy you can feel it in the air. This was so unlike us. Whenever we were together, you could hear us laughing a mile away.

But not that morning. That morning was different. It was the kind of silence that is beyond uncomfortable.

We arrived at the clinic, I walked in, and there in the waiting room, were girls like me—some younger, some older, some holding a young child on their laps, but all pregnant; all of them here for the same purpose, to rid themselves of their unborn child. I remember thinking, *How is this even possible? How can there be a place on this earth like this?* I had this overwhelming sense of fear—that crushing fear, a paralyzing fear. I wasn't even allowed to sit down. I was quickly ushered into another room by a nurse waiting at the door. The next few hours would forever change my life.

Uncontrollable tears were pouring down my face. All I could think was, *This is it.* That and Isaiah 43:2, *When you go through the deep waters, I will be with you* (NLT).

Lord, these waters are way over my head, I thought. As I began to feel the effects of the drugs, I felt as if I was in deep, dark water all alone.

I was 22 years old, in a very abusive marriage, and had a beautiful 3-month-old baby girl. I knew my marriage was ending, and my world was about to come crashing down on me. I was told to either have an abortion or me and my babies would be out on the street. There was no other option. For the first time in my life, I realized I was shakable.

As the years went by, I felt worthless and guilty, becoming consumed with the lies Satan told me over and over again. I remained under his influence, distant from the life God intended me to live and the intimacy He wanted me to share with Him.

I had a wound so deep, caused by my belief that God had abandoned me because of my abortion. I was in agreement with Satan, who told me that the deep, dark, silent place I was in was all I deserved. He repeated those lies so often that I believed and accepted them as truth. I believed I would never find peace or forgiveness again. My thoughts had become so distorted about who I was that I no longer knew my true self. My feelings of insecurity and low self-esteem left me feeling undeserving of opportunities in my career and personal life. Satan was ever-present, whispering in my ear, "Not you. You had an abortion. You made an unforgivable choice. So no, not you." I had very little self-confidence. I hesitated to move forward in my career or speak up for myself when I knew I should have. I felt like everyone knew what I had done. I lived in isolation and had difficulty having relationships with others.

Along with having low self-esteem and self-confidence, I struggled to believe in Christ's forgiveness. That act of having an abortion hurt me beyond words. Satan kept telling me that my abortion was unforgivable and would always be with me. Emotions like guilt and shame blocked me from asking God for forgiveness and moving on. I lived with deep regret and lived it over and over, which kept me from moving forward; I finally began to work to break those thought patterns. When Satan told me lies, I'd stop him immediately. It took a great deal of practice. I had to be aware when the lies bombarded me so I could stand guard and stop them. I would write scriptures on cards and stick them on my mirror, carry them on post-it notes, and keep them available on my phone.

Ephesians 4:31-32 tells us we are to let *all bitterness, wrath, anger, clamor, and evil speaking be put away from you, with all malice. And be kind to one another, tenderhearted, forgiving one another, even as God in Christ forgave you* (NKJV). This instruction includes turning from the anger and bitterness I had toward myself. Meditating on these scriptures constantly, I began to learn to accept Jesus' forgiveness. I reminded myself that the child I aborted lives in the love and mercy of God beyond earthly malice. My child does not condemn me, and I knew I must stop condemning myself. I repeated this truth over and over until I began to believe it.

Over the years, I went to several counselors. I would explain my experience, reliving it again and again. I'd cry; sometimes, they'd cry. They would listen patiently and empathetically. I would leave feeling better, but it was temporary. There was still a void not being filled. It wasn't until I began spending more time with the Lord that I was able to turn my pain over to Him. I prayed and journaled in the morning and in the evening. I read books about healing. I felt like a breakthrough was coming. In retrospect, I don't think the breakthrough came from any one thing I did but from the combination of several. The counseling sessions did help, and looking back, I am glad I went, as none were ever wasted, but they also made me realize there were a few more things I needed to do.

Now, I enjoy reading back through my journals and seeing my progress. Some pages are stained with my tears, and that's ok—I don't ever want to forget what I went through during my healing process. Rereading my words allowed me to see just how far I have come. Sometimes when I felt my emotions overwhelming me, writing helped me gain control. When the enemy whispered those lies, keeping a journal helped me to create order. Journaling also allowed me to get to know myself by revealing my most private fears. Especially the fear of others finding out I had an abortion. Even though I was silent about my abortion, writing was very beneficial because it was a way for me to express what I was feeling inside—feelings I was too afraid to share with anyone else.

I began to learn that acknowledging the trauma of abortion and committing to the healing process did not mean I had to live broken and wounded. But I realized I needed to do more to heal. I attended a Bible study at a nearby church filled with women just like me—living in silence and unworthiness after aborting their child. We shared our stories, from the experience of the actual abortion procedure to the years that followed; there was one thing we all had in common: we were all crying out to God for forgiveness. Through months of praying together, crying together, and sharing our deepest pain together, I began to feel a breakthrough. You see, I had never told anyone about what I had done. I just lived with it. One night at the study, I began to feel a release. I had been holding onto this for so long, so tight, that it had become a part of me. Nearly 35 years had gone by, and I hadn't told anyone other than a counselor. I was always afraid of what others might say or how they would judge me. I just could not face sharing this with anyone.

Towards the end of the study, we were asked to write our unborn babies a letter. This is what I said to mine.

> *Dear Annie,*
>
> *I call you Annie because Gina, your sister, had a best friend named Annie, and I loved hearing her say "Annie" in that adorable,*

childlike voice. I know you are a little girl because Gina always spoke of having a little sister.

Baby girl, I would hold you in my arms and protect you from the world. I would love you and care for you. You would have the best older sister, Gina. You would love her, and she would love you! So often, I've imagined the two of you together and how our lives would have been so different. I wondered if Gina knew you should have been there. I've wondered what you would have grown up to be. A teacher? A doctor? A nurse? Would you have had the cure for cancer? I will never know these things. I do know you would have had a kind and gentle heart. I've always imagined you with big brown eyes and long brown hair.

We will meet each other one day, but until then, I love you. You are ever-present in my heart.

With love,
Mommy

We were also asked to write a letter to ourselves from God. This is what I hope He'd say to me.

Dear Beautiful Daughter,

I love you. I forgive you. I was with you during that most horrible, frightening, scary time of your life. I was there with you on the car ride and in the waiting room with you. And I collected every tear you cried on the table that day. Please let go, and let me put my arms around you for comfort, forgiveness, and peace. I died on the cross for you—do not tell me that was not enough. Accept my forgiveness, dear sweet child, and live the life I have intended for you to live. Free from bondage, free from the enemy holding you captive. Love me as I have loved you. Be free.

With great love,
Your Father

We were also asked to sign a letter acknowledging that we were releasing our child into the loving care of our Lord Jesus Christ. It was that day I thought how much it must have hurt my Father that I did not trust Him to care for my unborn baby. I was reminded of 2 Corinthians 1:3-4, *Praise be to the God and Father our Lord Jesus Christ, the Father of compassion and the God of all comfort, who comforts us in all our troubles, so that we can comfort those in any trouble with the comfort we ourselves have received from God* (NIV). God was there with me all along, comforting me, and I didn't even realize it.

On the final night of the study, we had a funeral for our unborn babies. So many tears were shed as we placed a flower on the infant-size coffin. I did not realize how important saying good-bye was to my healing. I had never taken the time to grieve my loss. Or adjust to living my life without my baby. Grieving an unborn child is unlike any other loss. It isn't something we do openly by preparing a funeral, mourning, or celebrating their life. For years, I had ignored this tremendous loss and tried to forget about it. That added to the darkness and pain. But that evening, I finally laid my baby to rest. I gave my unborn child over to God, knowing that she is fully loved, happy, and well cared for in heaven. I had worked hard at trying to let go of my unborn baby, knowing the memory was prolonging my grief. Now, I choose to hold onto my child by remembering her happiness in heaven.

After this three-month-long journey, I was at a crossroads. I could accept God's forgiveness and live the life He intended for me, or I could continue to believe the lies Satan was whispering in my ear. It wasn't until after I heard the stories from other women who were hurting as badly as I was that I decided to live the life God intended for me. I was not alone. I decided to live a life of unshakable faith in Him.

As a result of my decision, I noticed my time with God changed. My prayer life became bolder. My relationship with Him changed, and my prayer life became more meaningful. *For freedom Christ has set us free; stand firm therefore and do not submit to a yoke of slavery* (Galatians 5:1 ESV). God frees us to live in the power of His Spirit, not in ourselves. I prayed and meditated over Galatians 5:1 for countless hours. It was like I was in a tug-of-war with my shame and guilt; one day I would give it to the Lord, leave it at His feet, then the next day, I would take it right back. It was exhausting. Meditating on this scripture reminded me that we are not to be slaves to our sin; we are not to be slaves to the law or our own attempts to obey the law in our flesh. We are free. Acknowledging the trauma of abortion and committing to the healing process did not mean I had to live broken and wounded.

Then one day at work, I realized that my story of healing could be used to reach and comfort others. A young teacher came to me and asked if she could speak with me. I knew by the tears in her eyes and the expression on her face that she was in pain. We made time to meet, and she began to tell me her story. I knew she had been in an abusive marriage in the past, but what I did not know was she had an abortion. That day, the Lord allowed her to come to me and trust me with her deepest, darkest, and most painful experience. I realized that by refusing to listen to Satan and standing firmly planted in my unshakable faith, I could help a hurting sister. By releasing my pain and accepting Christ's forgiveness, I had the power to help someone else. We cried. I spoke, and she listened. She spoke, and I listened. And her healing began.

I reminded her of several scriptures.

> *Therefore, confess your sins to one another and pray for one another, that you may be healed. The prayer of a righteous person has a great power as it is working* (James 5:16 ESV).

> *In my distress, I called to the Lord, and cried out to my God: he heard my voice out of His temple* (Psalm 18:6 KJV).

I told her I cried out to God openly and loudly, and the Bible says He hears me. God is not far away; He is ever so present in the midst of our suffering.

Over time, the healing began; I could visibly see a change. Years, even months earlier, I would never have been able to help or comfort someone else because I was so attached to my own pain. But as soon as I took my focus off things on earth and began focusing on God above, I started to experience the life God had for me. As a result, the woman who came to me saw an amazing, faith-filled, unshakable woman, and I was able to speak into her life.

After forty-plus years, the Lord has strengthened me to share this experience with my precious daughter. I always felt that I needed to explain to her why I made the decisions I made and sometimes why I did what I did. I needed to explain to her about this past mistake and how it affected me for the rest of my life. The Lord gave me that opportunity one Sunday afternoon as we sat in my car about to go into the store. I began telling her about my past and how that one event affected my life—the life God intended me to live. With great compassion, my daughter cried and prayed with me. My experience and transparency allowed her to see that we can always return to living as God has intended us to by trusting Him, submitting to Him, and having unshakable faith despite anything we have done or anything that has come against us.

Now after many years have passed, the experience of my abortion is still with me, but I no longer allow the enemy to whisper lies to me, telling me I am unworthy, unforgiven, or undeserving. Instead, I live a life of unshakable faith. In Christ I am completely accepted. *Yet to all who did receive him, to those who believed in his name, he gave the right to become children of God* (John 1:12 NIV).

I know that by faith, I have been born again into the family of God. Despite the consequence of sin, by faith, I believe that Jesus paid the penalty of sin by dying on the cross for me. By believing Jesus took the punishment

I deserve, and through having faith in Him, I know my sin has been removed forever and that I am declared righteous by God. I have received freedom from the silence that engulfed me for so many years.

He wants to make YOU unshakable in Him, just like He made me.

Unshakable Under Attack

By Leecy Barnett

In the Bible, God gives us many promises. One of His most unpopular promises is that things won't always go well for us. We are even taught, *Everyone who wants to live a godly life in Christ Jesus will be persecuted* (2 Timothy 3:12 NIV). Who wants to claim that promise? Thankfully, that isn't the end of the story! God reassures us again and again that with Him, we can be unshakable when we are under attack: *"These things I have spoken to you so that in Me you may have peace. In the world you have tribulation, but take courage; I have overcome the world"* (John 16:33 NASB).

Whether we want them or not, we will eventually be attacked by tribulation and persecution. Why? Because we have an enemy. His name is Satan; he is the deceiver and accuser, the evil one. Peter warns us: *Be alert and of sober mind. Your enemy the devil prowls around like a roaring lion looking for someone to devour. Resist him, standing firm in the faith, because you know that the family of* believers throughout the world is undergoing the same kind of sufferings (1 Peter 5:8-9 NIV). All Christians around the world need to learn to stand firm in Christ so they can be unshakable despite being deceived, tempted, and attacked by the devil.

People commonly spend their time fighting against the wrong enemy. Although people come against us and hurt us, the Bible reminds us that every individual was created in the image of God; since Christ died for all of humanity, we are to love even those people we consider to be our enemies. The Apostle Paul reminds us who we should fight: *Our fight is not against human beings. It is against the rulers, the authorities and the powers of this dark world. It is against the spiritual forces of evil in the heavenly world* (Ephesians 6:12 NIRV). We are to be engaged in "spiritual warfare"—so how do we fight what we cannot see?

Paul explained our tactics when he wrote to the church at Corinth: *We do live in the world, but we do not fight in the same way the world fights. We fight with weapons that are different from those the world uses. Our weapons have power from God that can destroy the enemy's strong places* (2 Corinthians 10:3-4 NCV). And in the book of Ephesians, Paul offered further explanation of those weapons by using an illustration of God's armor. We can be unshakable under attack if we armor up!

GOD'S FULL ARMOR (Ephesians 6:13-17):

- *THE BELT OF TRUTH:* Stand against the enemy's lies with God's truth. *Every word of God proves true. He is a shield to all who come to him for protection* (Proverbs 30:5 NLT)
- *THE BREASTPLATE OF RIGHTEOUSNESS.* Live according to God's standard to protect your heart and mind from evil deception. *Pursue righteous living, faithfulness, love, and peace* (2 Timothy 2:22 NLT).
- *SHOES OF PEACE.* Stand firm, sure-footed with stability, and move forward with peace. *Do not be anxious about anything, but in every situation, by prayer and petition, with thanksgiving, present your requests to God. And the peace of God, which transcends all understanding, will guard your hearts and your minds in Christ Jesus* (Philippians 4:6-7).
- *SHIELD OF FAITH.* Put your trust in God into action. He equips you. Be unafraid, without temptation and worry, as you trust Him. *For everyone who has been born of God overcomes the world. And this is the victory that has overcome the world—our faith* (1 John 5:4 ESV).

- *HELMET OF SALVATION.* Protect your mind and body from the enemy's bombardments day and night by using your battle plan to stop negative thoughts. The almighty God has already won the battle, and your salvation is assured in Him. *Surely God is my salvation; I will trust and not be afraid. The Lord, the Lord himself, is my strength and my defense; he has become my salvation* (Isaiah 12:2 NIV).
- *SWORD OF THE SPIRIT.* Offensive and defensive swords are used in close combat. Christians can use God's Word as a two-edged sword to defend against evil advances. *"Blessed rather are those who hear the word of God and obey it"* (Luke 11:28 NIV).

Additional weapons we can use to be unshakable when we are under attack are:

1. *Resistance.* Call on Jesus, saying, "Jesus help me!" (James 4:7).
2. *Focus.* Protect your mind by focusing on God (Philippians 4:8).
3. *Prayer and fasting.* Ask God for strength, wisdom, and understanding (Ezra 8:23).
4. *Worship.* Praise and worshipping God will make the devil flee (Matthew 4:10).
5. *God's Family.* Surround yourself with other believers as protection and support (1 Thessalonians 5:11).

As believers in Almighty God and Christ Jesus, we are given the power and authority to protect ourselves against evil advances. When you are under attack, use these armor tools to protect and defend yourself—your mind, body, and thoughts—from evil schemes and attacks. When you do, you will gain unshakable victory.

Jesus, I know Satan's plan is to steal, kill, and destroy. But You have given me the tools to fend off any attacks that come my way. You are the victory! Protect my faith in You and Your Word so I will be unshakable when I am under attack. In Jesus' name. Amen.

Maria Montalvo

Born and raised in New Jersey and of Puerto Rican descent, Maria Montalvo retired to Florida with her husband. They enjoy spending time with their family and grandchildren.

Maria earned her Certificate of Business from Roberts Walsh Business School in Union, New Jersey, and her Associate's degree in Business Management from Union County College in Cranford, New Jersey. She has held positions in several corporations and investment firms as a client service associate, rebate analyst, and investment administrative assistant.

She has volunteered at the Gateway Pregnancy Center, First Choice Women's Resource Center, and Life Chapel Women's Ministry Team in New Jersey. She also volunteers with the Women at War Ministry Team.

Maria is passionate about sharing her story in hopes God will use it to inspire and encourage women who have experienced the heartbreak of an abortion. Surrendering her secret and receiving God's gift of forgiveness was a giant step toward her freedom!

Surrendering My Secret

By Maria Montalvo

Years ago, I went to the doctor for a minor medical procedure, and the nurse asked me, "How many pregnancies have you had?"

I joyfully answered, "Two. I have a girl and a boy!"

She stared right into my eyes and sternly said, "Those you carried to full term. I asked you how many pregnancies you have had. Have you had any miscarriages or abortions?"

I hesitated in silence for a moment, then said, "I've had four pregnancies. Two, I carried to full term, and two, I terminated."

For the very first time, I had answered that question with the truth. Wow, I thought to myself, *Where is this going, God?*

I had peace in my heart because I had confessed my sins to God; I was saved! I was forgiven! I knew my babies were in heaven. I asked myself, *Is this the enemy reminding me of my past sins and failures?*

Then, I started having dreams of babies. My bedroom would light up. One night, I saw a finger! It wasn't a finger of condemnation pointing at me, but it was more like I was being chosen. I asked God, "You don't want me to share my story, do You? This is our secret!"

I struggled with what people would say if I were to reveal my past. *Would I be judged? What would my family think? My husband? My children were young adults at the time. What would they say? How could I put my family through this?!*

I continued wrestling with God. *No, God, this is our secret. Remember? You forgave me; as far as the east is from the west, You have removed my transgressions from me. Remember, God?*

I would soon learn that we can defeat the enemy by sharing our testimony.

> *And they overcame him by the blood of the Lamb and by the word of their testimony, and they did not love their lives to the death* (Revelation 12:11 NKJV).

Here is my story.

During my teenage years, I was seeing a guy I really liked. I liked him a lot. One day, I said to him, "I think I'm pregnant."

He said something I will never forget—the exact words I wanted to hear.

I was only 16 or 17 years old, and there was no way I was going to have a baby. I was in high school, and I thought my parents would kill me. Besides, I planned on being a somebody; I had to finish school. My parents had come to this country to give me a better life. They sacrificed so much for me, and I couldn't disappoint them. They didn't deserve this. The pressure was on; I was in panic mode and thought I had no choice.

So, my boyfriend and I went to a clinic in Irvington, New Jersey, for a consultation. I spoke with a beautiful woman sitting behind her desk. She asked me a lot of questions. I explained to her I couldn't have this baby. I was in total panic and despair!

Yes, she understood me and agreed with me. As a 16 or 17-year-old, I was convinced I was making the right choice. It wasn't really a baby yet; it was only tissue. But the truth was that I had no idea how far along I was in my pregnancy.

The day came for the procedure. I left home as though I was going to school, but my boyfriend picked me up, and off we went to the clinic. After arriving, I signed some documents. I have no idea what I signed—I just wanted to get it over. My boyfriend had dropped me off, and I was left standing in a long line with girls of all ages and nationalities. I saw a family friend. *Oh my goodness, she knows what I'm about to do,* I thought. She recognized me, but I just looked away with shame. I knew deep down inside what I was about to do was really wrong, but I went ahead and had an abortion anyway.

I remember the sound of a vacuum during the procedure. Afterward, I was in pain. I felt terrible. My boyfriend was there when I came out from the procedure and took me home. After getting home, I lay in bed in a fetal position, all curled up, just feeling this emptiness, coldness, and pain inside of me. But I kept thinking, I'll be fine now! I can start over! Believe it or not, I felt relieved.

But then, I got pregnant AGAIN the following year. I was SO upset at myself! *How could I have let this happen again?*

Just like that, I had another abortion.

I was determined to finish school, get a good job, make my parents proud, get married with a wedding celebration, buy a house, and then have babies. There were no ifs or buts about it.

And I did exactly that, precisely in that order.

I finished school, and a couple of years later, I got married. I thought I had it all together. Oh yeah, I was in control of my life! I thought I was starting over. I felt such a sense of relief.

But after a short time, the feelings of relief wore off, and I was reminded of my actual experience—over and over again. My short-lived post-abortion relief was replaced by guilt, shame, secrecy, sadness, and regret. It was a very strong, sinking experience.

Years went by. The thoughts of those abortions haunted and crippled me. I became full of panic, fear, despair, and anxiety. I was a nervous wreck. I kept thinking, *Somehow, someone is going to discover the truth.* I avoided the topic at all costs, maintaining the stance that "Women have the right to their bodies."

I couldn't be around babies. I felt extremely uncomfortable around them and couldn't even look at them. And it was heart-wrenching to speak with any woman who was having difficulty conceiving a baby or had experienced the heartbreak of a miscarriage.

The woman who led me to Christ had been married for 20 years and had been trying to have babies but had not been able to. The subject was very painful for both of us. I knew what I had done was wrong. I had grown up going to a church. *How could I have done this?* I asked myself many times. I had regrets, yes, but there was no way I could have...should have...

Before the two children I carried to term were born, I often thought, *Well, I'd better prepare myself because I will never be able to have any babies now.* I thought God was surely going to punish me! My mind was invaded by lies. I battled with this secret for many years. Lies, after lies, after lies...

For years, I was in denial. I wouldn't acknowledge that I had murdered my babies. I just "terminated a couple of pregnancies." I justified my sin by thinking, If it is legal, it's ok.

The devil is a liar! When he lies, it is consistent with his character. He is the father of lies (John 8:44). Regardless of how much I justified my actions, it was still a sin against God, and I could never be free of its damage without repentance.

The emotions I felt after the abortions were real. I was mourning my babies! I was in deep pain and felt an acute sense of loss. The guilt led me into a deep depression. But I couldn't share this with anyone because it had been my choice. I was embarrassed. *Who would understand? I would certainly be rejected.*

I always wondered if my babies were boys. Or girls. I wondered what my life would be like if I had carried them to term. *What would they look like? What would they be like?* But I had made my decision, and now it was time for me to pay. Those were the lies I believed. I couldn't forgive myself. My guilt was overwhelming; my burden was too heavy to bear.

In John 10:10, the Bible tells us the thief (Satan, our enemy) comes only to steal and kill and destroy. The enemy is a deceiver; he deceives us into believing lies instead of truth. He tempts us to fall into sin and then accuses us. I had sinned, and now I believed the lie that I could never be forgiven. The accusations were coming like fiery darts towards me. I felt guilty, ashamed, worthless, and depressed. I felt like a murderer, a failure, and a hypocrite. I would sit in the church pew with a mask on, brokenhearted and silently regarding my past abortions. I was lost in my sin, lost in my pain, and lost in my past.

There was growing angst inside me as rage and bitterness took root. My unresolved anger was an invitation to the enemy. I was wounding myself, my loved ones, and all those around me. I was mean, downright cruel, unloving, and unforgiving. These were all the emotions I was dealing with, but I realized these reactions were a result of my poor decisions. I was in deep turmoil! I was in pain! I was also experiencing a spiritual battle in my mind! I couldn't handle keeping this secret any longer.

I finally surrendered my secret to God. Although it was difficult, I confessed my sins and asked Him to forgive me. Before that, I had hoped that if I could ignore my wrongdoings long enough, they would just go away on their own. But sin doesn't fade, and I couldn't remove its power over me without God's help. It was uncomfortable, but when I submitted to His cleansing power, I was made clean and blameless by His grace.

> *If we confess our sins, he is faithful and just to forgive us our sins and to cleanse us from all unrighteousness* (1 John 1:9 NKJV).

> *I acknowledged my sin to You, And my iniquity I have not hidden. I said, "I will confess my transgressions to the Lord," And You forgave the iniquity of my sin* (Psalm 32:5 NKJV).

I was 33 when I accepted Jesus as my Lord and Savior. By then, I had married the young man I really liked, and we had two children. God got ahold of my heart and performed an open-heart surgery. I surrendered to Jesus. God restored my life; I no longer felt shame or unworthiness. God replaced all the lies with the truth through His Holy Spirit and His Living Word.

The truth is Jesus loves us. When we give our lives to Him, He frees us from all our sins by His Blood. We are washed clean as white as snow and covered by the blood of the Lamb!

> *To console those who mourn in Zion, To give them beauty for ashes, The oil of joy for mourning, The garment of praise for the spirit of heaviness* (Isaiah 61:3 NKJV).

> *"I, even I, am He who blots out your transgressions for My own sake; And I will not remember your sins"* (Isaiah 43:25 NKJV).

One day, while sitting in church, I heard about a pregnancy center in the inner city of Irvington, New Jersey, which needed volunteers. I immediately signed up. As I drove to my very first class, I got off the exit of the New Jersey Parkway into Irvington, which took me right to Ball Street. I began thinking that the street name sounded familiar. I came to a stop at a red light, and when I looked over to my right, I remembered. Everything came back to me. This was the place. The parking lot. This is where I had my abortions. The clinic had been here at this very same location!

I couldn't believe it. I cried. I was here, on the very same street in Irvington, New Jersey, approximately 30 years later!

I attended the class and started my healing process.

As I sat in class one day, we saw a video and a picture of the actual size of a fully formed fetus. It was very small, but it was perfect. I could see and recognize the tiny toes and tiny fingers. I caught my breath. *Oh my. And I believed it was just tissue! But it was not tissue. Or a "blob."* I realized then how human my unborn babies were when I aborted them.

> *For You formed my inward parts; You covered me in my mother's womb* (Psalm 139:13 NKJV).

> *"Before I formed you in the womb I knew you, Before you were born, I sanctified you; I ordained you as a prophet to the nations"* (Jeremiah 1:5 NKJV).

Since that moment, God has opened doors for me to share my story in small groups, Bible studies, one-on-one, and even at Women at War events. And I've learned that when I share my story, not only do I experience healing, but I am also a catalyst for others who may feel as if their stories are unforgivable.

There was nothing, absolutely nothing, I could have done to make things right before God. But when I brought it to Him in repentance, He offered me true forgiveness. God's gift of forgiveness is what changed everything.

> *For by grace you have been saved through faith, and that not of yourselves; it is the gift of God, not of works, lest anyone should boast* (Ephesians 2:8-9 (NKJV).

We all suffer consequences from our actions, but we get a fresh start every day with God because His mercies are New every morning!

> *Through the Lord's mercies we are not consumed, Because His compassions fail not. They are new every morning; Great is Your faithfulness* (Lamentations 3:22-23 NKJV).

Perhaps you are hiding something you don't want others to know about, something you are ashamed of. The enemy knows as long as he can keep you bound by your silence and secrets, as long as he keeps you isolated and separated from others, he can keep you from the freedom God offers.

I broke the power of silence and secrecy that held me captive for so long. I took the mask off and accepted God's forgiveness. When we repent, He forgives us and remembers our sins no more. Receiving God's forgiveness was a giant step toward my freedom. Sharing my story was a second step.

And that freedom is what makes my faith in Him unshakable.

> *Therefore if the Son makes you free, you shall be free indeed* (John 8:36 NKJV).

No matter what you may be hiding, know that our heavenly Father is a loving and forgiving Father who adores and treasures you. You can go to Him. He already knows everything—every secret.

> *The Lord executes righteousness And justice for all who are oppressed. He made known His ways to Moses, His acts to the children of Israel. The Lord is merciful and gracious, Slow to anger, and abounding in mercy. He will not always strive with us, Nor will He keep His anger forever. He has not dealt with us according to our sins, Nor punished us according to our iniquities. For as the heavens are high above the earth, So great is His mercy toward those who fear Him; As far as the east is from the west, So far has He removed our transgressions from us* (Psalm 103:6-12 NKJV).

> *"Come now, and let us reason together," Says the Lord, "Though your sins are like scarlet, They shall be as white as snow; Though they are red like crimson, They shall be as wool"* (Isaiah 1:18 NKJV).

I have learned that God uses unthinkable pain, redeems desperate stories, and turns hopeless circumstances around to bless us and others.

Don't take my word for it. GOD teaches these things in His Word:

- You are accepted in Christ. He calls you to be His child (John 1:12).
- Through Jesus' blood, you are redeemed and forgiven (Colossians 1:14).
- You are complete in Christ (Colossians 2:10).
- By going to Jesus, you are declared free from condemnation (Romans 8:1-2).

- You can trust that God will work all things according to His purpose as you follow Him (Romans 8:28).
- Nothing can separate you from the love of God (Romans 8:35-39).
- God has work for you to do. He calls you to be the salt and light of the world (Matthew 5:13-14).
- Despite your sins, by giving your life to Christ, he raises you up and seats you with Him in the heavenly realm (Ephesians 2:6).
- You can approach God with freedom and confidence (Ephesians 3:12).

I surrendered my secret and replaced all the lies the devil told me with God's truth. And so can you.

- Replace anger with the love of Christ!
- Replace fear with courage!
- Replace shame and guilt with confidence in Christ Jesus!
- Replace depression with the joy of the Lord!

> *"Come to Me, all you who labor and are heavy laden, and I will give you rest. Take My yoke upon you and learn from Me, for I am gentle and lowly in heart, and you will find rest for your souls. For My yoke is easy and My burden is light"* (Matthew 11:28-30 NKJV).

Today, my confidence, courage, worth, and identity are based on the finished work of the cross, thanks to Jesus Christ. I stand on a firm foundation of solid rock. I have found hope, peace, forgiveness, and freedom in Christ!

Today, the joy of the Lord is my strength! I have been blessed with a wonderful husband, two incredible young adult children, a beautiful daughter-in-law, and two precious grandsons.

Accepting God's forgiveness, made possible by love and Jesus' sacrifice on the cross, has allowed me to live a courageous and unshakable life.

No matter what your story is, He is waiting to redeem you, too.

Unshakable When You Are Worried and Fearful

By Donna Whartenby

"Keep me safe, Lord!"

How many times have you spoken those words? Perhaps in the middle of the night or during a hair-raising situation, you have said, *"Lord, help me!"*

David, the Old Testament psalmist, cried out: *Keep me safe, my God, for in you I take refuge* (Psalm 16:1 NIV). King Saul was jealous of David, so the king ordered his soldiers to hunt and kill him. David ran away from the nation he was anointed to be ruler and king of, hiding in the desert and caves for refuge and safety. The Living Bible records David's plea: *Save me, O God, because I have come to you for refuge* (Psalm 16:8 TLB). David feared for his life; his only refuge was with the Lord. *I keep my eyes always on the Lord.* (Psalm 16:8 NIV). David kept his eyes on God out of fear of being captured and worry of being killed. He knew God was the only one who could rescue him from peril.

What worries you? Where do you turn when you are fearful? Scripture insightfully teaches us to keep our eyes on God during times of worry and fear. 1 Peter 5:7 says: *Cast all your anxiety on him because he cares for you* (NIV). God not only cares for you, but He also loves you as His child. Isn't it wonderful that you have a God who cares so much about you that He wants you to give your worries and fears to Him? Isn't it comforting to know He will guide you, give you peace in your circumstances, and take your fears and worries away? All you need to do is ask Him to protect and *keep you safe.* Then, wait for Him to move in your life.

When we are worried or fearful, it's good to find a place of refuge, as David did. While we are there, we can talk to the Lord. Turn over our cares to Him and trust He will provide—trust in an unshakable way in His goodness and wisdom. Remember that God is in complete control; continually put Him and His commands first in your life.

No matter what you go through or where you are, God is always present at your side. The psalmist speaks to God, saying: *Yet I am always with you; you hold me by my right hand. You guide me with your counsel, and afterward, you take me into glory* (Psalm 73:23-24 NIV). The Hebrew word for right hand is yamin (yaw meen). One meaning is a place of honor or status. God is at your right hand, at your side. Meanwhile, scripture tells us Christ is seated at God's right hand. Another meaning of right hand refers to giving sustaining help (Psalm 18:35 NIV). God is at your right hand, and His strength and power will carry you through your worry and fear. WOW! Don't you feel safer and protected knowing God, who has all power and authority, is at your side? God has a special Hebrew name, *Jehovah Jireh,* meaning the God who provides—yesterday, today, and tomorrow.

Psalm 16:8 (NIV) goes on to explain that because you keep your eyes on God, and you know He is at your right hand, *[you] will not be shaken.* You will not stumble or lose your balance. You will not be moved or stagger or totter. You can stand firm, stand unshakable. God will sustain you without fear or worry.

When you turn to God in your worry and fear, He may calm and comfort you, even though your circumstances remain unchanged, or He may take the situation away altogether. But you can be assured that God will always stay at your side and lead you to safety, helping you learn and grow from every experience.

Focus on the Lord, watching as He accomplishes His will in your daily living. Remember, He is always there with you, even in your worry and fear. He is at your right hand, leading you through each day and circumstance.

With Him, we will not be shaken. The Living Bible translates the psalmist's words: *I am always thinking of the Lord; and because he is so near, I never need to stumble or fall* (Psalm 16:8 TLB). God will guide you, giving you unshakable confidence that you are safe in His protection. He will take your worries and fears away—if you let Him. With God at your side, you can be unshakable.

Thank You, God, that You are at my right hand, and I am under Your protection. When I am tempted not to trust You, allowing fear and worry to become my obsession, remind me to pray and focus on You. Grant me unshakable faith in You—my almighty God. Amen.

Connie A. VanHorn

Connie A. VanHorn has a heart for encouraging others to find their God-given purpose. She serves on the Women World Leaders' Leadership Team as an ambassador and administrative assistant, is a best-selling author, and writes for *Voice of Truth* magazine. Hoping her story will help someone else, Connie passionately shares how her amazing and loving God spared her, an ordinary woman, and gave her new life.

Connie resides in Winston-Salem, North Carolina, where she has participated in several discipleship classes and taught Sunday school to international students. She has also attended Bible classes at Vintage Bible College.

Being a mother is by far Connie's greatest accomplishment and her first, best ministry. She dreams of changing the world by sharing Jesus and raising world-changers who have a kingdom perspective.

She enjoys being active with her children, making bracelets, journaling, and spending most of her time with her family. Connie wants her readers to know that it's ok to be broken—it's in our broken place that we find God. See past messy, see past broken, and you might just see a miracle.

Daydreaming with My Eyes Open

By Connie A. VanHorn

When I was a little girl, I had this dream...

Life was hard. My siblings and I endured incredibly tough circumstances that made me feel as though I would not survive. I questioned the fairness of it all, and as the years passed, life only seemed to get more challenging. I would find myself constantly comparing myself to my peers; it appeared as though their lives were effortless, and I longed for that ease. I was raised in a broken environment. My parents had four children by the time they were 22 years old, even as they were still dealing with their own childhood wounds. Meanwhile, they were unaware of the trauma their children were experiencing.

Due to the anguish I experienced in my childhood, I built very tall walls. Layers and layers of these walls were buried deep inside my own heart for years to come. I resorted to one thing I knew how to do well—daydreaming of a life where everything was easy and peaceful. I created an effortless world far from my own reality. I daydreamed with my eyes open.

I felt safe in my daydreams. My siblings did not have this same way of coping. I wish that I had invited them into my world. My sisters turned to destructive coping mechanisms to ease their inner pain and the turmoil going on around them, while I would often run off alone, finding peace within my imagination. Although this habit caused me harm because I learned to avoid dealing with reality, it also helped me develop a sense of resilience. In my unsettling childhood environment, I discovered a way to become immune to the disturbing things thrown at me as a young girl. I found a way to become UNSHAKABLE!

What does it mean to be unshakable? For me, it means having a firm foundation in God that cannot be easily destroyed by the storms of life. As a child, I faced a traumatic and chaotic upbringing, but I found hope in my daydreams. I would envision a world of beauty and peace, far removed from the war around me. Despite not fully understanding who God was, I would still call out to Him in my bedtime prayers, unknowingly planting seeds of faith in my own heart. These prayers taught me very early on and became a constant without which I couldn't fall asleep. Each night, I would recite the same words, "Now I lay me down to sleep; I pray to the Lord my soul to keep..."

Even though I did not realize it at the time, my heart was set on God from a young age. It just took thirty-plus years for me to see that God had been there all along. The journey to becoming unshakable is not always easy. The world has a way of pulling us under, making us feel like we are drowning in rough seas without a life jacket. However, when God builds something within us early on, what I like to call built-in-courage, He prepares us for a lifetime of being unshakable. This courage becomes the foundation on which we can stand strong when the storm strikes.

> *"Have I not commanded you? Be strong and courageous. Do not be afraid; do not be discouraged, for the Lord your God will be with you wherever you go"* (Joshua 1:9 NIV).

The day I heard gunshots go off in my house, I was just past my toddler years. I can barely remember the actual event. I remember mostly hearing the gunshots and hiding. Then, being taken away to live with a stranger. She was not very kind. The room was dark, and I slept in a crib next to my baby sister. We spent a lot of time in that room, and we cried for hours on end. When we finally returned home, I learned that prayer.

"Now I lay me down to sleep."

After that, I never went to bed without reciting it to myself and my siblings. It was a prayer but also a dream I held onto. If something were to happen, I would be safe. I felt safe in that prayer. That is where my daydreaming began.

In those early years, I had regular feelings of fear and anxiety—always on edge and worried about what might happen. I was constantly on alert, checking corners and feeling a sense of unease. Living in a constant state of fight-or-flight, I was unsure what awaited around the next corner or what the future held. My life felt unstable and shaky. I realized at a young age that something wasn't quite right. I discovered that I had the power to change it, but only in my mind. Life seemed to go by rather quickly. We moved around a lot, and nothing ever felt stable or settled.

Facing the teenage years can be challenging for anyone. For me, every ounce of self-worth, stability, and normalcy seemed to have been sucked out of me before I had reached those fragile years. I built walls higher than the Eiffel Tower and created a mask thicker than clay to hide my true self and the emotions and secrets bubbling inside. The mask became a shield, allowing me to put on a fake air of happiness and strength every day, even when I felt broken and lost inside. Though seemingly unshakable, the mask was built on shaky ground, leading to an unhealthy and even harder road ahead.

During those difficult years, going to school became an almost unbearable experience. A fear of facing people and a desire to fit in led me to isolate myself. I regularly avoided social situations and often resorted to hiding in a bathroom stall far away from people on the other side of the school campus. Inside that stall, I let my imagination run wild—I escaped the harsh reality of my surroundings. Even the thought of walking into the cafeteria during lunch seemed daunting. I would have rather been tossed into a lion's den. Despite being good at school, my fear of being noticed and the pressure of keeping up with my peers made each day a struggle. Middle school was hard, but it did not compare to what I would soon face.

High school brought more problems and a sense of forced interaction. I felt like I was drowning in a sea of people, and hiding seemed even more necessary. I was lucky to find a single locked stall where I could retreat and be alone with my daydreams. Daydreaming became my sanctuary, where I could find peace in the chaos of my reality.

I struggled with feelings of loneliness and unworthiness during my time in school, which made me dread going to class. More than anything else, I yearned to be accepted. The one class I did enjoy was Latin. I excelled in learning the written language quickly and was chosen to attend a Latin conference where I won several ribbons—the first I'd won in my life. However, my fear of being called upon by the teacher led me to withdraw and avoid participation. I even approached my teacher one day and asked him politely not to call me out in class. I believed he was intentionally trying to make me uncomfortable. In hindsight, his intentions may have been different.

I could not wait to get off the school bus in the afternoons. I was excited to ride my bike to my favorite park. Sitting against the eight-foot cement wall by the water became my routine. It allowed me to escape into my own effortless world. I was always alone at the park; that was how I liked it. I created my surroundings and the people in it. My favorite daydream was that I was a successful and popular college student with many friends, nice clothes, and a smile I was not constantly trying to hide.

However, as the academic challenges grew in my real life, I fell further behind, eventually facing the reality of repeating ninth grade. The weight of this realization hit me hard. I cried out for help, begging for someone to rescue me from a pit that was getting deeper. I felt alone, embarrassed, and ashamed.

Struggling with unstable emotions from my buried trauma made it difficult to focus on the present and prioritize what was important—my education. The issues I faced extended far beyond the confines of school; they were deeply rooted within me, affecting every aspect of my life. I realized I would never find a clear path in my current environment. I wanted out of that storm and the sea of people.

So, I just left...

I remember the exact day I left the campus and vowed never to return. I can honestly tell you it is the one thing in my life that I wish I could do over. I was good at school. I wanted to be a cheerleader and go to college, but I was on a boat that wasn't prepared for sea.

As I was approaching adulthood, only one bright light could guide me out of the darkness—God. However, my journey to find Him was not a straightforward path. I had more storms in the sea to survive. It took many years of wrong decisions and searching for something beyond myself before I truly saw and heard God calling out to me. After cutting short my school journey, I could not wait until the day I would turn eighteen. I came up with a new dream: becoming a movie star or singer and moving to Los Angeles, California. I envisioned leaving behind the pain and people of my past, seeking visibility and recognition in a place far from my small town in Florida.

So I went to California, but California had a different plan for me than I had envisioned. The glitz and glamor of Hollywood only served to highlight the trauma-filled places in me, leading to further disappointment. Despite encountering celebrities and having many really cool experiences, I realized that my dream of stardom was merely a daydream, not a true calling. Returning to Florida, I was forced to confront my reality and try to understand what was holding me back from a life of freedom and hope—the life I had envisioned by the water's edge as a child. Only now, I was going to be responsible for another human being. I had returned to Florida pregnant! I was unwed, uneducated, and expecting a child. I could barely navigate adulthood. How was I going to be a mom?

They say the first five years of a child's life are crucial in laying the foundation for their future emotional, cognitive, and social development. The first five years of a child's life hold the power to shape a lifetime of stability or instability. The foundational experiences and environment during this period can impact the trajectory of a person's life. So, even as I was now raising a child through those formative years, I knew I must find a way to rebuild my own foundation. God was there for me. In August of 2014, I gave my whole heart to Jesus. (BEST DECISION EVER!) That day was the first day of my new life and view of myself. My worth and identity became solely defined by God and His love for me.

Through the pain, insecurity, and challenges I endured, I began to realize that God had been forging an unshakable spirit within me for a greater purpose—a life of kingdom work. I knew that if I were to be anything in this world, it would be for God.

God does not seek the most educated, successful, or popular individuals to be His leaders; He looks for hearts willing and ready to answer His call and serve His kingdom. He looks for people who will lean on Him and keep going no matter what life throws at them. He wants us to cry out to Him at night but be ready for battle at dawn. That is exactly what I had been doing for so many years. After giving my life to Christ, the difference was that God said, "I will carry you." He promises to go through the storm with us; He did not make us to walk this life alone. All of my struggles and pain had been leading me straight to Him. I no longer had to hide behind a fake smile and an invisible wall.

"The Lord himself goes before you and will be with you; he will never leave you nor forsake you. Do not be afraid; do not be discouraged" (Deuteronomy 31:8 NIV).

While, by the world's definition, I lacked success or achievement, God saw beyond my shortcomings and declared that I was exactly who He was looking for. With a willing heart and an unshaken spirit, I was called to continue the mission that had begun long ago. God wants us to come as we are. True leadership, in the eyes of God, requires bold faith, resilience, and a steadfast commitment to His purpose. Though we may stumble and fall along the way, the spirit that God has put within us enables us to rise again and again in pursuit of His will.

As I look back on the early part of my life, I realize that the hard things empowered me to be unshakable. It does not matter what you have or where you come from; God can and will use you if you let Him. I had nothing when I reached for His hand. Absolutely nothing. Yet He chose me. And He chooses you, too. It is not our worldly accomplishments, degrees, or accolades that define our worth in the eyes of God, but rather our willingness to hear His call, to rise above the hard things, and to continue our journey with faith and courage. In the end, it is this unshakable spirit, rooted in the love and grace of God, that propels us forward on the path of His purpose.

I keep my eyes always on the Lord. With him at my right hand, I will not be shaken (Psalm 16:8 NIV).

When we keep our focus on God, we can withstand any storm that comes our way. Our faith in Him becomes our anchor, holding us steady even through the chaos of life.

My life is not perfect. I still have days when I feel discouraged and defeated and want to run into a locked bathroom stall. However, I am constantly reminded that my faith in God sustains me. The foundation under me is UNSHAKABLE! It takes a lot to shake me because I have now built my life on the unchanging truth of God's love and faithfulness. I continue to keep going, knowing that God is with me every step of the way. We will all encounter seasons of deep waters—when we find ourselves surrounded by darkness, feeling like we are drowning, choking, and suffocating under the weight of our struggles. In those moments when the storms rage and the waters seem so deep, God promises to be right there with us. The things we encounter are not meant to break us but to build within us a foundation of unshakable faith. Built-in-courage!

You can trust God is molding you into a vessel of strength—making you an unshakable warrior.

> *For the Lord God is a sun and a shield; the Lord bestows favor and honor; no good thing does he withhold from those whose walk is blameless* (Psalm 84:11, NIV).

This is the first time I am openly sharing my school journey. For many years, I felt ashamed, like I was a quitter. I made several attempts to complete my degree but struggled with the math portion of the exam. While I understand basic math, I struggle with more complex concepts. It took someone very special to tell me that my struggle with the math portion may be a part of God's plan for me as He uses my life as a testimony.

I believe education is crucial, and I stress its importance to my own children, but I no longer see it as a definitive factor in my life. I trust that God is constantly providing me with the necessary tools to fulfill my purpose.

After having a daydream about becoming a writer, a relative began sending me grammar books—not even knowing about my visions. I used those books (and others) to educate myself on proper writing techniques. I found a Bible College that allowed me to take Bible courses. And I continue to learn constantly through podcasts, online teachings, and the good-ole Bible.

God doesn't just call the qualified; He equips all those He calls. Instead of focusing on my shortcomings, I now choose to use what I have and trust in God's plan. I aim to be an example of UNSHAKABLE FAITH!

Being unshakable is a choice we make each day to trust in God's promises and hold fast to His Word. Being unshakable is a testament to our faith in the face of war. As we walk through the hard things in this life, we can use that built-in-courage to stand firm, unshaken by anything that may come our way.

The world may not understand what is just between you and God. No matter how messy the vision (or you) looks to the world, no matter how hopeless your condition, how much you lack, or how much you want to give up, you can trust that God is in control. Listen for His voice and do whatever it takes to follow His plan. He will never leave you alone!

See past the messy. See past the broken. See through the eyes of God and see a miracle. Allow God to move, and He will make an UNSHAKABLE WARRIOR out of you.

Now I have a new dream...

Stay tuned!

Unshakable When Turning Obstacles Into Victories!

By Donna Whartenby

When facing an obstacle, it can be easy to react by turning and going the other way. I often find myself in this place. Years ago, I would run from, ignore, be afraid of, or lack action when I encountered obstacles. I was not confident in overcoming obstacles and became discouraged when they got in the way. But God offers us another way. He offers us a way to face our obstacles head-on and use our hardship experiences to help others.

We are not guaranteed an easy life. We all encounter the storms of life that may seem insurmountable. So, how do we face what seems to be overwhelming obstacles? Some people are afraid and run, some are discouraged, and some give up in hopelessness. As believers in God, we have the power to turn these obstacles into victories by placing our trust in Him.

When we face these obstacles, it is easy to become discouraged and lose our faith. By shifting our perspective and seeing these as challenges for growth and transformation, we can overcome them with the help of God. *When troubles...come your way, consider it an opportunity for great joy. For... when your faith is tested, your endurance has a chance to grow... for when your endurance is fully developed, you will be perfect and complete* (James 1:2-4 NLT).

In all things God works for the good of those who love him (Romans 8:28 NIV). One of the best ways to be unshakable in trusting in God's purpose and plan is to believe He is always working for our good. Even in the face of adversity, we can find strength and courage in knowing that God is with us every step of the way. Philippians 4:13 advises, *I can do all this through him who gives me strength.* (NIV).

By shifting our focus away from the obstacles and ourselves, we see God's true power and purpose. We shift our focus to the God who is greater than any storm. We can turn what once seemed impossible into a victorious testimony of God's faithfulness and provision and help so many others. Proverbs 3:6 (NLT) explains, *Seek his will in all you do, and he will show you which path to take.* That path is to VICTORY! This is UNSHAKABLE FAITH!

We can turn our pain from trials and obstacles into a greater purpose.

So, please hold tight to God's promises and His message that we are unshakable when we choose to trust Him to turn our obstacles into victories. We can find comfort and strength in knowing that God is always by our side, leading us toward a brighter and more victorious future.

> *"Have I not commanded you? Be strong and courageous. Do not be afraid; do not be discouraged, for the Lord your God will be with you wherever you go"* (Joshua 1:9 NIV).

This powerful verse in the book of Joshua is the Lord's reminder that we, as believers, can be strong and courageous in the face of obstacles because we have the assurance that He is with us wherever we go. When we trust in God and His promises, we can turn our obstacles into victories, knowing He is always by our side.

Just as Joshua was commanded to be strong and courageous as he led the Israelites into the promised land, we, too, can take on challenges with confidence and faith, knowing that God is with us every step of the way. This verse encourages us not to be afraid or discouraged but to trust in the Lord and His strength to overcome any obstacle that comes our way.

This verse is a reminder that God can carry you through the greatest of storms; cling to it daily!

You can be unshakable in God, allowing Him to turn your obstacles into victories as you rely, in faith, on His presence and love for you!

Father, show me which path to take to overcome the obstacles I am currently facing. I will look at these obstacles as an opportunity to choose joy in my life. I will be strong and courageous because I know You are with me in every situation. Thank You for giving me the strength to overcome any obstacle that comes my way.

Mary Kay Inglis

Mary Katherine "Kay" Inglis was born in West Covina, California, adopted by a pastor and his wife, and grew up in Oxnard, California. Her deep love for Jesus was the cornerstone of her life. Her passion was sharing Jesus' love, a message she lived and breathed. Mary Kay has six exceptional children, whom she taught to lean on God for all their needs and trust Him for everything.

Mary Kay's journey took a significant turn when she began working in a ministry in Mexico. Daily, she visited a local dump to provide food and care for the homeless and share the Gospel and Jesus's love with families living in dire conditions. Her hands-on approach and unwavering commitment significantly impacted the lives of those she served.

Mary Kay's passion for sharing the Word of God continued to grow, even when she was diagnosed with cancer. Her faith was tested, but it only strengthened her resolve to spread the message of Jesus's love. Her journey with cancer became a testament to her unwavering faith and her belief in the power of God's love. On September 13, 2023, Mary Kay passed away.

Becoming a Proverbs 31 Woman

By Kimberly Ewell

As you will read, Mary Kay Inglis should have been the author of this chapter. If she had written her story, she would have given full glory to our amazing God, who transformed her into a Proverbs 31 Woman. But my best friend, Mary Kay, has a new address now. She is spending eternity with our Lord and Savior. So, I wrote this on her behalf, using some of her own words but sharing much of her life through my lens. May her story bless you!

~Kimberly Ewell

KIMBERLY

How does one become a Proverbs 31 Woman? If you were to have asked me this question twelve years ago, I would've told you that I hadn't a clue! I was far from being that woman (an entrepreneur, generous, honorable and wise, a praiseworthy worshipper of God—all as described in the last chapter of the book of Proverbs), and never in a million years would I have thought

I could become one—until I met Mary Kay Inglis. Mary Kay's life journey, a testament to God's transformative power, was a personal witness for me. Her story is one of inspiration and hope, a beacon of light in the darkest of times. It's a journey that underscores the transformative power of faith and the paramount importance of a strong relationship with God in personal growth.

In 2023, Mary Kay, or as we affectionately called her, MK, and I embarked on a joint writing project. This project was about sharing our personal journeys of faith and transformation, as we intended to inspire others and deepen our own understanding of our walk with God. Through this project, we looked forward to reflecting on our pasts, understanding our present, and envisioning our future. I will let her share our first meeting in her own words, which marked the beginning of our very unique friendship.

. . . .

MK

OOOOh boy! My friendship with Kimberly has been a friendship like no other. The first day I met Kimberly, I thought, "Here comes the Ventura (California) princess!" I saw the beautiful blonde-haired woman wearing all her cute little silver jewelry, minimal makeup, and a perfectly put-together outfit to look cute but still comfortable. She was my lifetime nemesis. I, on the other hand, was homeless at the time, feeling self-conscious and awkward. Little did I realize she would become my warrior princess, sister in Christ, and prayer buddy! Before I get into all that, let me explain more about our beginnings.

That first day we met was at a church to feed the homeless. We struck up a friendship as we grabbed the supplies and walked to the various hotels, feeding and ministering to people. She was just an ordinary woman! Not the princess I thought she was. She had kids and a past, and we had many of the same interests. As a short time passed, our friendship grew and grew. I eventually became her neighbor. She lived just a few doors over from me, so we would have coffee together and sit and talk about our issues. I was married to a very abusive drug addict, and she was working things out after the death of her son. We had some problems to talk about!

KIMBERLY

When I met Mary Kay, I didn't know she was homeless. However, she was serving the homeless every weekend with our church. I wasn't aware of her dark secrets of being married to an abuser. She kept reticent about her personal life. I, too, recall the day we met. When I saw MK, I thought to myself, *This woman is going to kill me.* She was throwing daggers at me with her eyes, which penetrated my soul. She was a bleach-blonde beautiful woman raised in California and had lived a rough life. MK was hard-core and wouldn't take any garbage from anyone. I prayed, "Lord, DO NOT make me pair up with this woman!" I was so afraid of her. Well, the Lord purposefully paired us together.

As we ventured out to the run-down hotels, I witnessed the true heart of Mary Kay. She had compassion for those who were less fortunate. I watched her pray from her heart over people in need. Not once did she nag, complain, or ask for any help for herself, though she was also homeless and struggled to feed her family and herself. Little did I know she would become my dearest friend, my example of a godly woman, and I'd witness God's handiwork as He transformed her from her brokenness to the most selfless and whole woman I've ever met. Her transformation was genuinely inspiring and filled me with hope. She had a complicated past, but through her unwavering faith, she overcame her struggles and became a shining example of how the power of faith in God can overcome life's challenges.

A pastor and his wife adopted Mary Kay at a young age; they taught her everything she knew about God—including the value of her relationship with the Lord and His love for her—and about the enemy, preparing her to fight spiritual warfare.

MK

My daddy used to call me "the poor little rich girl." We weren't rich by any means, but my parents served a HUGE God, and He ALWAYS provided. After Sunday night church, sometimes we would drive to Farrell's for ice cream, or on a whim, my dad would say, "Let's get dinner and drive up north to Jocko's for some steaks." He'd take me for walks—telling me the names of all the flowers we would pass and teaching me the Spanish word for everything we would see. We'd go to museums for fun, and he would read EVERY plaque/sign in the place so I would learn!

KIMBERLY

Mary Kay's mother was a true Proverbs 31 Woman, a role model who instilled the values of faith, character, strength, and honor in her daughter. Her mother's example set the standard for Mary Kay's spiritual journey, demonstrating the profound influence of parental guidance when God is at the center of personal development.

As the years passed, our spiritual journey continued to evolve. The Lord was teaching me about honesty, and Mary Kay was learning about the power of her words. We both had our struggles, but we also had each other to learn from. Our relationship transcended mere friendship; spiritually, we were so connected that God often spoke to her about me and vice versa. Our profound spiritual connection and the lessons we learned from each other were instrumental in our personal growth and transformation.

When I moved to Florida in 2015, our conversations became less frequent. But when we did talk, it was for hours, and it always seemed to be at the exact moment the Holy Spirit prompted us to call each other. There was always a message for one of us from the Lord. She even dreamed about the house I would move into in 2022.

From afar, I saw the change in my friend; I noticed the gossip decrease, and I saw her heart grow for serving others who were homeless. At one point, she moved to Mexico to help the people who lived in the dump. The people built their homes on the landfill and ate from the leftover trash dumped daily. She described the stench as highly overwhelming. She shared how the ministry she was a part of would bring fresh food and clothes and build new places for them to sleep. She shared how families with children of all ages grew up on this dump, which was "home" to them. For MK, this became her "home." It was where she served the Lord, shared His goodness with the homeless, and allowed His light to flow through her.

I could see what God was doing with my friend. I witnessed her transform into a Proverbs 31 Woman, but to fully appreciate it, I wanted to understand her motivation, fuel, and secret weapon.

> *Charm is deceitful, and beauty is passing, But a woman who fears the Lord, she shall be praised* (Proverbs 31:30 NKJV).

Above all, Mary Kay feared the Lord. Everything she did was by His power and energy. Her compassion, kindness, and loving heart were all a reflection of Him. Her impact on the world was astonishing, but her accomplishments were not a result of her own striving; they stemmed directly from her relationship with the Lord. Mary Kay was fully committed to God's creative plans and submitted willingly to His instructions for her life. Her strength and courage were derived from her faith, which was a source of empowerment and encouragement for us all.

What does it mean to fear the Lord? Fearing the Lord is about reverence and standing in awe of Him as He is all-powerful, all-knowing, and holy. He is majestic. He is the creator of the cosmos—heaven and earth—and He created us. God was constantly on MK's mind. We talked about the Lord in all our conversations. God received all the glory in everything she did. The Lord gave her the power and ability to do the things she couldn't do alone. In all this, she was still confronting her past. She was still becoming the woman she was meant to be.

It was 2019 when MK had her dream about me moving into a house. As she described it, the front of the house was white. Past the front door and through the entryway, double glass doors led to my office, where she saw me sitting at a desk with a man standing next to me. She said it looked as if this man was supporting a ministry of mine. He was overweight and not in the best health because of it. She felt that this was my husband. I didn't have a husband when she had the dream, nor did I want one, but I listened. She shared that the man was in this condition due to the rich food he loved to cook. At that moment, I heard the name of this man, "Aubrey!" I knew who this man was!

Then, in February 2022, I texted MK the images of the house she had seen in her dream four years prior. The double glass doors were my office for the ministry the Lord had given me. There was one thing missing, however: the man she had described, who possibly was to be my husband, wasn't there.

One week after I moved into my new home, I received devastating news from Mary Kay that she had been diagnosed with colon cancer. I broke down and cried out to God, "NO, God, NO! She can't die! God, please help; there's so much more for us to do, so much more!"

In a still, small voice, I heard the Lord say, "She will not die."

I knew she wasn't going anywhere, and her work would be completed.

> *Strength and honor are her clothing; She shall rejoice in time to come* (Proverbs 31:25 NKJV).

MK knew what was coming. She knew the battle she would face with cancer, the chemo, a low immune system, and her physical strength. Yet, she rejoiced for the time that was to come. Her words were, "Not today, Satan!" She held on to God's promise that she was healed and that He was her strength. Not once did she fall into the trap of Satan's deceptive lies. She leaned on the Lord and knew she had already been healed.

MK did not need to fear or worry about her future because she was courageous enough to trust the Lord. Her unwavering trust in Him, knowing that He was the one who would order her steps, brought a sense of peace and reassurance in her life.

She knew God's plans were for her good, so she trusted Him with her tomorrow and received the peace to move forward in her journey. Did this mean MK wasn't nervous or afraid of the unknown? Of course not. However, strength and honor were her clothing, and she depended on the promises of God from whom she drew her strength. By His nature and promise, God is our provider. Mary Kay's faith reassured her that He would take care of every need she and her children would have, including clothing, finances, food, and shelter. She knew her God would never leave or forsake her or the kids.

> *She perceives that her merchandise is good, And her lamp does not go out by night* (Proverbs 31:18 NKJV).

In Matthew 25, Jesus tells the parable of the ten virgins, by which He teaches us to be ready for the coming of the Lord—don't let your light go out. MK was always ready to heed the Lord's instructions. She served Him with her ministry, constantly sharing what it was to be a woman of God. She testified about her life failures, wanting others to learn from the lessons she gained through her heartaches and mistakes. Most of all, she glorified God, passionately sharing her transformation from a shaken, messed-up life to completely surrendering to her unshakable God. She was ready for the return of Her Lord. MK's lamp was always lit, fueled by her relationship with the Lord as she sought Him for comfort, love, and guidance in everything. She didn't care what the world thought of her. Instead, she stayed steadfast in the Lord, knowing that He was her foundation and the source of her hope—even as she fought cancer.

On a gorgeous June day in 2023, as I was chilling out on my couch, pondering what God wanted me to write for this book, I heard the Lord say to me clearly, "Bring Mary Kay to Florida!"

I asked Him, "What, Lord?"

And again, He said, "Bring Mary Kay to Florida!"

There was no mistake. I would be flying her from California to Florida.

I paused a moment, then called MK. I said, "Girl! This may sound crazy, but God told me to bring you to Florida."

When I heard her giggle and say, "OMG!" I knew God was up to something! With so much life and excitement, she said, "The Lord just told me to LIVE LIFE! Let's do it!"

I didn't tell her the Lord told me she was to fly the BEST. I booked a first-class flight for my dear friend. I didn't have the means to pay for a first-class flight; however, because of obedience, He provided. When we trust God's plans, He will not only provide but also bring us a sense of comfort as He reassures us He will do a mighty thing!

When MK arrived in Florida, we had no idea why she was there, but we believed and knew God had a purpose. I felt a tug in my heart that MK was to write her story. I handed MK a Voice of Truth magazine, published through Women World Leaders. She giggled, saying, "OMG! Before coming to Florida, I kept seeing yellow butterflies. Look! The magazine has butterflies on the cover." There was no doubt God was confirming what I suspected.

Just days later, MK was sharing her heart and story with Kimberly Hobbs, the founder of Women World Leaders. They arranged for Kimberly to interview MK for the *Women World Leaders' Podcast* and for MK to write her story for *Unshakable.* Watching God orchestrate His purpose through the two of them was an honor.

A couple of months before bringing MK to Florida, I had seen a vision of Mary Kay and heard the name Alfred in my spirit. Alfred was her now ex-husband, who had severely abused her for years. The Holy Spirit stirred in my gut that I should tell MK she had to forgive him. I knew MK had, so I didn't understand. I called her and told her what the Lord had said and that I believed she still had to forgive Alfred. She listened, and she, too, thought she had already done so.

Not long after MK arrived, we learned her purpose for being in Florida. We were driving in an unfamiliar area and found ourselves going around and around, ending up in the same place repeatedly. That was when we looked up and saw a street sign that read, "Alfred." We both knew for certain at that moment that MK had to forgive Alfred. The next day, she surrendered to the Lord, and I witnessed the Lord move in her heart and release all of her pain, bitterness, and anger, bringing her freedom.

MK was hospitalized with pneumonia only a couple of weeks after returning home. She kept me updated on her condition, and on September 12, 2024, I was on a flight to California. We texted during the flight; her text read, "Hurry, please."

I encouraged her to hold on, that I was almost there. I prayed, "Lord, You said she wouldn't die!"

In a small voice, I heard, "She already made her choice." I knew she was leaving and was ready to go. Her faith and belief in being healed never wavered, and even though God may have had a different plan, she was tired of fighting.

When I arrived at the hospital, I saw my best friend struggling with her breathing. She looked at me and said, "I waited for you; I love you!" God opened my eyes as she said these words. Not only did I see MK, I saw Jesus. I saw the selfless love the Father has for every one of us and realized that, whatever stage of spiritual growth we are in throughout our lives, God sees us as fully transformed by His glory and power. By giving our lives to God, by His grace we become full-fledged Proverbs 31 Women even as, by the world's standards, we are still growing.

Mary Kay passed away on September 14, 2023. She had given me the greatest gifts: selflessness, agape love, and a front-row seat to witness her surrender to the Lord as she allowed Him to transform her into a godly woman. God brought her back into alignment with Him despite her imperfect life. Being a Proverbs 31 Woman isn't about being perfect or performing perfect acts; it is about putting God first in your life. It's about doing our best to live as a reflection of His character, with honor, dignity, love, and selflessness.

Just months after MK's passing, I married the man in her dream, Aubrey. And by God's grace and my submission, I am also becoming a Proverbs 31 Woman.

Beloved, do not conform to the world's ways, but be transformed by renewing your mind. Refrain from carrying the weight of having to work to be perfect. Surrender, let go, and let God transform you effortlessly to become the Proverbs 31 Woman He has made you to be.

Unshakable in God's Word

By Leecy Barnett

Years ago, I was visiting Switzerland during their national holiday. My friends and I decided to join a group of Swiss teens who were going to Schynige Platte to celebrate the holiday. In the late afternoon, we took the train as far as we could and then hiked up a trail on the side of the mountain until we reached our destination. When it was time to leave, it was pitch dark and starting to rain. Fortunately, someone handed me a torch so I could see where I was going. The light the torch provided was the only thing that kept me from straying from the path and falling off the cliff to my death.

Everyday life is like that treacherous walk down the mountain—it is hard to see what is ahead, and it is easy to stray off the path and fall into trouble. Fortunately, we have been given a torch to show us the way. *Your word is a lamp for my feet and a light on my path* (Psalm 119:105 CSB).

Using God's Word to become unshakable in life takes more than simply flipping a switch to turn on a light, but it isn't complicated. Thankfully—and perhaps ironically—in His Word, God instructs us how to integrate His Word into our lives.

LISTEN

In our world full of distractions, paying attention to God's Word takes discipline. But God insists that everyone listens to what He has to say. Come here and listen, O nations of the earth. *Let the world and everything in it hear my words* (Isaiah 34:1 NLT).

We have so many different options for hearing God's Word today. We can listen to Scripture when the message is preached in church, we hear it on podcasts and other recordings, and when we read the Bible ourselves, we understand what we are reading as the Holy Spirit, whose job is to show us the truth, brings it alive for us.

If you have absolutely no desire to listen to God's Word, I invite you to pray and ask God to give you a thirst for His Word, and then begin by simply opening your Bible and reading a small section of Scripture each day.

STUDY AND MEDITATE

For some people, the word "study" may bring back bad memories from their school days. But in the Bible, the word translated study means "to be eager, to make an effort, do your best" at understanding God's Word. We are encouraged to *Study this Book of Instruction continually. Meditate on it day and night so you will be sure to obey everything written in it. Only then will you prosper and succeed in all you do* (Joshua 1:8 NLT). If you don't know where to start with Bible study, seek someone to help you in this area or join a group committed to understanding the Word of God. You have already taken your first step by reading the teachings in this book filled with Scripture!

Meditation often has the connotation of the Eastern religious practice of emptying your mind. But Christian meditation is exactly the opposite—biblical meditation fills our minds with God's Word. Those who meditate on God and His Word, *love the Lord's teachings, and they think about those teachings day and night* (Psalm 1:2 NCV).

REPEAT AND TEACH

We take a step further in absorbing the Word of God when we pass it along to others.

First, we are told to instruct our children in God's Word. *These words that*

I am giving you today are to be in your heart. Repeat them to your children. Talk about them when you sit in your house and when you walk along the road, when you lie down and when you get up (Deuteronomy 6:6-7 CSB).

Second, we are told to encourage our fellow believers with the Word. *Let the word of Christ dwell richly among you, in all wisdom teaching and admonishing one another* (Colossians 3:16 CSB).

OBEY

It is not enough just to know the Word. To be transformed, we must obey God's Word. *But don't just listen to God's word. You must do what it says. Otherwise, you are only fooling yourselves* (James 1:22 NLT). Pastor Rick Warren puts it plainly, "The only parts of the Bible you truly believe are the parts you put into practice."[1] Ask God to show you one way today you can follow His Word.

Jesus tells us we will be unshakable, standing on solid ground, if we obey His Word: *"Anyone who hears and obeys these teachings of mine is like a wise person who built a house on solid rock. Rain poured down, rivers flooded, and winds beat against that house. But it was built on solid rock, and so it did not fall"* (Matthew 7:24-25 CEV).

God's Word is a gift that has the power to make you unshakable. Listen to it. Study and meditate on it. Repeat and teach it. And obey it.

Lord Jesus, I thank You for the precious gift of Your eternal Word. I want to know Your Word by listening, studying, meditating, repeating, teaching, and, most importantly, obeying it. Help me become a person who is unshakably standing on Your Word.

[1]Warren, R. (2020, July 3). *God's Word: What you believe, you do.* https://pastorrick.com/gods-word-what-you-believe-you-do/

Gina Rogean

Gina Rogean is a Florida native; she resides there with her husband, Travis, and their daughter, Gabby. With a desire to write for a magazine, she originally went to college to study journalism. After helping run a family business for a few years, Gina found herself going back to school to pursue a career in healthcare. After completing her Master's Degree in Nursing in 2022, she now works as a Nurse Practitioner in Functional Medicine.

When she is not working, Gina enjoys the beach, loves cooking, and is an exercise enthusiast. Gina is passionate about Jesus, her family, and helping people thrive.

Relying on God in the Fire

By Gina Rogean

In this life, trials of fire will come, the rain will pour, and we will be challenged. Probably like you, I have experienced all of these. In the Bible, Jesus tells us what to expect here on earth: *"I have told you these things, so that in Me you may have [perfect] peace. In the world you have tribulation and distress and suffering, but be courageous [be confident, be undaunted, be filled with joy]; I have overcome the world. [My conquest is accomplished, My victory abiding.]"* (John 16:33 AMP). In my trying times, I relied on the truth of God's Word, knowing that I was not alone. And He was always there in the fire with me.

You may have heard the saying, "God doesn't give us more than we can handle." I believe this is far from the truth. The truth is that God does give us more than we can handle, teaching us to rely on His strength. In faith, He enables us to do the hard things. Of the many trials I have faced in my life, I want to share a path that God took me on, showing me just how important it is to have a relationship with Jesus, which makes us unshakable.

My husband Travis and I got married when I was 23 years old and he was 25. We were both raised in "religion," but neither one of us had a "relationship" with God. A few years into our marriage, we felt something was missing. We tried to fill that void with friends, things, and parties, but nothing ever satisfied. Then we decided to go to church and quickly realized that a relationship with our creator was the missing piece. We both chose to start a relationship with Jesus. We began reading the Bible, jumped into small group Bible studies, and attended church regularly. Our lives began to look very different. We became filled with peace, joy, and contentment that could only come from God. Things that were dragging us down, like unhealthy friendships and a lifestyle of partying, were slowly replaced. This was a huge turning point in our lives, which laid a foundation for the years ahead. □□□

About eight years into our marriage, we started trying for a baby. The weeks turned into months, the months turned into years, and still nothing. Doctors told us that we had 0.001% chance of conceiving. We did not let that steal our faith. We prayed. We waited. And it finally happened. We were pregnant! The joy was overwhelming. This long-awaited answered prayer was finally here.

Then, it came time for my ten-week pregnancy checkup. As the doctor looked on the screen at the ultrasound picture, she asked if my conception timeline was correct. Her face said it all, and my heart sank. I was measuring six weeks, and there was no heartbeat. Our indescribable joy turned into sadness. Happy tears turned to tears of grief. This wasn't the first trial I had experienced since becoming a Christian, but it was certainly the hardest.

Immediately after the loss, I began to blame myself. *Was it something that I did? Was it something that I didn't do?* My husband and I continued to pray and dug even deeper into God's Word, meditating on the many promises He has given us. We would pray together daily, thanking God for His peace. We trusted that He had a plan in everything. It took some time, but as we kept our eyes on God, the storm dissipated. Because we truly believed His many promises, we had supernatural peace.

Trouble often comes when we take our eyes off Jesus and focus only on our circumstances. A great biblical example is when Jesus told Peter to walk out on the water to meet Him. As Peter walked out, he took his eyes off Jesus and looked at the arising circumstances. *But when he saw the wind, he was afraid and, beginning to sink, cried out, "Lord, save me!"* (Matthew 14:30 NIV).

When we keep our focus on God, He will enable us to handle all the storms in our lives. Sometimes, however, we get caught up in *the why* when Jesus wants to show us *The Way*—that we can trust Him unconditionally. When I lost my baby, I remember asking God, Why? This is such a tough question, but sometimes we just want an explanation for the things we don't understand, the pain we endure, and the prayers God doesn't answer as we would like. During that trial, God brought me to a place of knowing that I won't always know or understand the why, but I can always trust God, whose ways are higher than mine.

My husband and I knew that God had promised us a child, and we also had faith that nothing is too difficult for Him. We wrote Bible verses on note cards and spoke them out loud. One of the verses we stood firm on was Psalm 126:5: *Those who sow in tears Shall reap in joy* (NKJV).

We tried to conceive again two months later, and God kept His promise. Today, we have an amazing eight-year-old daughter, Gabby, and an awesome story of God's faithfulness. The Bible is full of promises God has for us, and we can take Him at His Word. We can hold on to His promises by memorizing, reading, and repeating scripture—essentially hiding His Word in our hearts. Doing this will strengthen and steady us through any storm, helping us experience an unshakable life. It's like making deposits in the bank for that rainy day. When the rain comes, you are able to make a withdrawal without going bankrupt.

I also learned through this process that few women talk about miscarriage, despite the estimate that about one of every five women experience this type of loss in their lives. I found that when I began sharing my story, it allowed others to be vulnerable enough to share theirs. Talking about our hurts allows healing to take place. Processing the pain through the lens of Christ repairs wounds. We all have wounds, but we do not need to live wounded. Meditating on His Word and allowing His truth to blossom in our hearts is the beginning of transformation. The verses we wrote on the note cards were all around the house and helped me stay focused on faith. Here are a few of the verses that gave me comfort in His Word and peace in the storm:

Your word is a lamp to my feet And a light to my path...
You are my hiding place and my shield; I hope in Your word...
I rise before the dawning of the morning, And cry for help; I hope in Your word...
Great peace have those who love Your law, And nothing causes them to stumble.
(Psalm 119:105, 114, 147, 165 NKJV)

> *And we know that all things work together for good to those who love God, to those who are the called according to His purpose* (Romans 8:28 NKJV).

This last verse reminds us that ALL things, not just those we like or enjoy, work together for the good of those who love God. And I can attest that God has always, without fail, used every single trial I have experienced for good.

I am a big fan of journaling. If you don't journal, I highly recommend it. Even if you just write one sentence per day, getting your thoughts, prayers, and experiences down on paper can be an important part of healing. After the trial has passed, you will be able to look back and see how God redeemed your loss, made a way through the darkness, and created something even better than you imagined. Reading your own words allows you to reflect on your trials and fully acknowledge that God always keeps His promises and never wastes anything. Trust the process and trust that your heavenly Father wants the best for you.

After a few years of being parents, things got rocky in our marriage. My husband and I started to disagree about almost everything. We were acting more like roommates than a married couple. I remember just wanting to be alone. My husband wasn't happy, I wasn't happy, and life was very challenging. We had been together for 11 years before we became parents, and suddenly becoming mom and dad was a tough adjustment, resulting in us neglecting each other.

We rarely had date nights, grew cold toward each other, and stopped praying together. What scared me the most was the possibility that our daughter would grow up in a broken home. The thought of my daughter being around another woman made me sick to my stomach, yet I just wanted to be alone. Neither my husband nor I grew up with good examples of a healthy marriage, and we were headed in the same direction as our parents—toward divorce.

I prayed for years that my husband would step up to be the spiritual leader of our family, but it wasn't looking good. I thought to myself, *What is taking so long? Are my prayers just bouncing off of the walls?* How many years do I have to endure living like this? I had so many ideas about how a good husband should act, speak, and treat me, yet I was failing miserably at being his wife. I was not a good listener, dismissing him when he shared difficult situations. I talked over him when he spoke to our daughter, not respecting his authority, which caused our daughter to listen to me over him. She started disrespecting him, which I knew was my fault, but I didn't care. Although he would tell me what I was doing wrong, I could not see outside myself. And although I told him what he was doing wrong, he couldn't see outside himself. We were both blinded by each other's issues and couldn't see the need to fix what was wrong in ourselves.

Knowing we needed guidance to survive as a family, we sought outside help. We started Christian counseling and attended studies on marriage together, but it wasn't until I was at my end that I did something that would begin to change the course of our relationship. I decided to look into myself and stop looking into him. I went to an inner healing ministry session.

During my two-day experience, the gracious facilitators showed me who I was supposed to be as my husband's wife. They helped me take an inventory of my life and my thoughts about what marriage should be. They showed me the reality of how I was living—in a state of blaming my husband for my unhappiness. They also helped me adjust the lens through which I was viewing my husband and the role God had created me to fulfill in our marriage. Let me explain. You see, in the book of Genesis, when God was creating woman, He called her the helper. *The Lord God said, "It is not good for the man to be alone. I will make a helper suitable for him."* (Genesis 2:18 NIV). When I heard this, I burst into tears. I had been denying my husband his helper! I was not loving him through his wounds or allowing him a safe place to bring the hurts of his past or his present. I was expecting him to be the husband that I dreamed of while I was not being the wife that he needed. The wife was created to be the helper of the husband. This was a true revelation for me and the pivotal lesson I needed to learn to move forward in our relationship with hope.

With my new mindset of being the helper, things began to change. My husband noticed the difference in me. As I started to become a better listener, respect him more, and let him lead us, I began to see a change in him as well. We started praying together again, making date nights a priority, and communicating in healthy ways that fostered deep, healing conversations.

A few months later, we signed up for a weekend marriage retreat. It was a two-night, three-day camping event through a Christian ministry called JH Outback, designed to bring couples closer to each other and Jesus. We went into the weekend in a very good place in our marriage, the best it had been until that point. We spent time worshipping, praying, and learning. I can't explain what happened, but a divine healing took place in my husband. He fully surrendered to all that God wanted to do in him. In a moment, my prayers for him were fully answered—he transformed into the spiritual leader of our home.

We now have confidence in knowing that our marriage is unshakable. We have been brought to a place of reconciliation and restoration like no other. Prayerfully investing in our marriage—in ways such as fully participating in marriage retreats and doing the work of inner healing in my own life—allowed God to produce the fruit we desired in our marriage. God wants to bring good, not chaos or confusion, out of what He has brought together.

Keeping God's Word in front of us helps us become more aware of when something within us needs attention. Living fully submitted to God requires studying His Word and allowing it to transform our thoughts and renew our minds, changing how we think and view the world. Knowing God's Word, having it hidden in our hearts, helps us to discern His will. The Bible assures us that God Himself established marriage and that He desires all marriages to be healthy and thrive. *A person standing alone can be attacked and defeated, but two can stand back-to-back and conquer. Three are even better, for a triple-braided cord is not easily broken* (Ecclesiastes 4:12, NLT). By adding Jesus, your marriage becomes a triple-braided cord that is not easily broken.

When we were told we had miscarried our first child, it felt like we were passing through waters and coming close to drowning. I often recalled the Lord's words from Isaiah, which still bring me strength and comfort on rainy days.

> *"When you pass through the waters, I will be with you; And through the rivers, they shall not overflow you. When you walk through the fire, you shall not be burned, Nor shall the flame scorch you"* (Isaiah 43:2 NKJV).

When I was contemplating a divorce and felt like I was in a fiery furnace and coming close to burning up, I remembered Daniel and his friends who were thrown into the fiery furnace. The Bible tells us that Jesus was in the fire with them. *"Look!...I see four men loose, walking in the midst of the fire; and they are not hurt, and the form of the fourth is like the Son of God"* (Daniel 3:25 NKJV). Daniel and his friends survived that fire without a trace of smoke on them. When we go through trials, we, too, can trust that God is in the fire with us.

Going through these trials was difficult for me and my husband, but they refined me; they refined us.

Being unshakable is about being so centered in Christ that no matter what life throws at you, you are grounded in the knowledge of who you are in Him. Being unshakable is about knowing you have victory and nothing can separate you from God's love. Being unshakable is about living out who you are called to be—the daughter of the King!

Being, knowing, and living an unshakable life starts with having His Word planted in your heart. Soak Him in as much and as often as you can. I encourage you to write out verses on cards and study them until you know them in your heart and mind. I also encourage you to journal—start with a few sentences about how God is moving in your life, strengthening your faith, or just loving you. Through your own words, you will begin to see the story God is weaving in your life.

I will leave you with my two life verses for you to memorize and meditate on. An unshakable life is in your grasp.

> *Trust in the Lord with all your heart, And lean not on your own understanding; In all your ways acknowledge Him, And He shall direct your paths* (Proverbs 3:5-6 NKJV).

> *Delight yourself also in the Lord, And He shall give you the desires of your heart. Commit your way to the Lord, Trust also in Him, And He shall bring it to pass* (Psalm 37:4-5 NKJV).

Unshakable When You Are Lonely

By Leecy Barnett

In 2023, the United States Surgeon General declared a loneliness epidemic. That same year, a global study found that loneliness can shorten a person's life span. But loneliness is nothing new; being alone originated in the Garden of Eden. God created everything good, but even in that perfect world, there was something not good: The Lord God said, "It is not good for the man to be alone. I will make a helper suitable for him" (Genesis 2:18 NIV). So, He created Eve. Man and woman walked in the Garden with God and did not suffer loneliness again until sin entered the picture and banished them from the Garden. Ever since, human beings have struggled with feeling alone at times—even when surrounded by people.

David, who wrote many of the psalms—the prayers of the Bible—cried out to God, *Turn to me and be gracious to me, for I am lonely and afflicted* (Psalm 25:16 NASB). Another psalm writer described his isolation: *I am like an owl in the desert, like a little owl in a far-off wilderness. I lie awake, lonely as a solitary bird on the roof* (Psalm 102:6-7 NLT).

God sustains us in our loneliness in two ways.

First, God assures us of His constant presence in our lives. He said, *"I will never leave you or abandon you" (Hebrews 13:5 CSB).* And we are reminded through His Word, *Even if my father and mother abandon me, the Lord will hold me close* (Psalm 27:10 NLT).

When we are lonely, we tend to think no one cares about us or remembers us, that we are out of sight, out of mind. But we are never out of God's mind. David tells us: *How precious are your thoughts about me, O God. They cannot be numbered! I can't even count them; they outnumber the grains of sand! And when I wake up, you are still with me* (Psalm 139:17-18 NLT). And Hagar, when she was alone in the desert, said, *"You are the God who sees me"* (Genesis 16:13 NIV).

Jesus knew His disciples would be lonely when He left earth to be with His Father in heaven, so He promised, *"I will ask the Father and he will give you another Comforter, and he will never leave you. He [the Comforter] is the Holy Spirit, the Spirit who leads into all truth"* (John 14: 15-17 TLB). The Holy Spirit lives in believers; He teaches, guides, and comforts us. Because we have the Holy Spirit, we are never truly alone.

Second, God sustains His children in their loneliness by providing a spiritual family: *God places the lonely in families* (Psalm 68:6a NLT). No matter who you are or what your status is—single, married, widowed, divorced—God has a family for you. His! When you become a follower of Christ, you also are adopted as a child of God. *You received God's Spirit when he adopted you as his own children. Now we call him, "Abba, Father." For his Spirit joins with our spirit to affirm that we are God's children (Romans 8:15-16 NLT).* The Apostle Paul explains, *You are citizens along with all of God's holy people. You are members of God's family* (Ephesians 2:19 NLT).

God's family consists of people who trust Christ as their Savior. God's original cure for being alone was to create another human for Adam, the first man. His cure today is to connect us with other believers in His family. Loving the brothers and sisters God brings our way demonstrates that we love God: *No one has ever seen God; but if we love one another, God lives in us and his love is made complete in us* (1 John 4:12 NIV).

Being part of God's family includes taking on certain responsibilities. For instance, we need to show up for one another: *Let us consider how to inspire each other to greater love and to righteous deeds, not forgetting to gather as a community...but encouraging each other* (Hebrews 10:24-25 VOICE). We are to accept each other: *Accept one another, then, just as Christ accepted you, in order to bring praise to God* (Romans 15:7 NIV). We are also to provide support for each other: *Carry each other's burdens, and in this way, you will fulfill the law of Christ* (Galatians 6:2 NIV).

In the world today, love, concern, help, encouragement, acceptance, and support are desperately needed by those suffering from loneliness. As Christians, God has made a way for us to be unshakable even in our loneliness by recognizing His presence in our lives and reaching out to His family—our family—the community of Christian believers.

Father, I am so glad You are always with me, so I am never alone. When I feel lonely and sad, I will call Your name to feel Your presence. Surround me with Your love. Thank You for sending the Holy Spirit to be with me and in me. When I am feeling alone, help me stop focusing on myself and step out and connect with a local church where I can get to know my brothers and sisters in Christ. Thank You for allowing us together as Your family to be unshakable as we trust in You.

Alicia Renee' Roberts

Alicia Renee' Roberts is a resilient woman who has triumphed over heartbreak and life's challenges. Balancing the roles of a single mom of a child on the autism spectrum, corporate finance professional, and entrepreneur, she remains committed to empowering women and helping them get unstuck. She blends faith and practicality to guide others through emotional healing and confidence-building so they begin to prioritize themselves, their dreams, and aspirations.

Alicia Renee' is not just a best-selling author, but also a YouVersion author, speaker, host of the *She Exudes Now* podcast, and a certified inner-healing and confidence coach. In 2020, she founded The Confident Lily, a global personal development company dedicated to unleashing women's personal power and transforming lives.

You can find out more about Alicia and download free resources at www.confidentlily.com.

Unshakable Confidence, Even in Brokenness

By Alicia Renee' Roberts

Broken crayons still color.

I've heard the phrase many times and always thought, *Of course they do, but I prefer the nice, non-broken ones!* Let's be honest. Sure, broken crayons still work, but whole crayons, in all their glory, look better. Right? It wasn't until I really digested the message and had my own experience with brokenness that I understood the phrase on a much deeper level.

See, there have been a few times when my spirit felt broken, and I didn't look *so great.* There have been times when my self-esteem was low and my confidence wavered so much that I didn't recognize myself. My actions and thoughts were not of the happy and optimistic person I was once. There have been times when my inner will to do couldn't do! I was overall different. Eventually, with God's grace, I began to pick up the broken pieces in my life, and my confidence was restored. Even though I had been rocked a bit and my appearance looked a little odd, I was able to color a beautiful, new picture that meant more to me than any I'd ever created before.

In the past, I'd created a picture of how I thought a happy life would look:

God's favor, a promising career, a happy marriage with one or two children complete with the house and the car, and all the other good stuff! My picture didn't include any hardships or strife. I mean, who would create a picture like that? I believe the same is true for why God doesn't show us the "big picture" of our lives all at once. If He were to show us the many hills we'd have to climb or the bumps along the way, would we want to go on the journey? If He were to show us the tears we'd cry and the pain we would endure, would we allow ourselves to go through it?

God didn't initially reveal to me that my "happy life" would look different than what I'd hoped for all those years ago. Instead, He gave me glimpses in small doses. Today, I have one child, a great career, a house, a car, and the favor of God, but I'm not married. I've had to endure many hardships, like divorce, single-parenting a child with special needs, navigating through toxic relationships, losing a significant other in an accident, and more—*BUT* here I am! The picture looks different. Many of my crayons are broken, but as I cultivate more confidence every day, I am happy, and my faith in God keeps me moving forward each day.

So, you are probably wondering how my confidence became "unshakable," remaining intact during my ups and downs. Let me preface this story by telling you that it did not constantly stay intact and that, at times I've been more shaken up than one of those old Etch-a-Sketch drawing gadgets. But just like the gadget, I could erase the pictures I was not happy with and start over with a fresh canvas and renewed confidence that only God could provide.

THE SHAKING

It was happening again. I found myself at my wit's end and ready to leave again. I was in a toxic relationship but had trouble letting it go. This wasn't my first rodeo. I'd experienced verbal and emotional trauma before in a previous relationship, but this one was different. It was supposed to work out. This one seemed so hopeful; to others, we appeared to be a "picture-perfect" couple.

What started off as a happily-ever-after fairy tale began to transform into a series of plot twists and bad dreams. One moment, my ex and I were on a high love cloud, and the next moment, we were arguing over the most trivial things—our whole day ruined.

The marriage had potential, but we did not demonstrate agape love or unconditional love, as mentioned in the Bible. 1 Corinthians 13:4-7 says, *Love is patient, love is kind. It does not envy, it does not boast, it is not proud. It does not dishonor others, it is not self-seeking, it is not easily angered, it keeps no record of wrongs. Love does not delight in evil but rejoices with the truth. It always protects, always trusts, always hopes, always perseveres* (NIV). There were many moments of unkindness, pride, and dishonoring. We kept a list of wrongdoings and allowed anger and resentment to set in. We were two broken people who had not totally addressed our wounds individually before coming together.

Many false accusations and let-downs made me doubt my intentions, worth, and value. The shaking began to occur. God was trying to show me something and I began to be honest with my feelings.

I was unhappy, confused, and sad as I considered leaving the person who was supposed to be my "knight in shining armor," my friend, and, at one point, the love of my life. To leave was such a tough decision as there was so much unknown ahead, and the unknown was a scary place for me.

But I became determined to listen to God's voice. I thought about God's best for me and my son. I knew I wasn't perfect, but I took comfort in the words that kept going through my mind: *I am a child of God, too. God wants His best for me and my son.*

I felt that all options had been exhausted, and regardless of how much we loved each other, we were doing too much damage to each other. It was time for us to go our separate ways. I chose peace for me and my son.

Sometimes, our perception and judgment are off when our world is shifting and things are shaking up. The picture of our lives gets messy, and we become uncertain whether we are making the right decisions. I didn't know how I would make it financially after having made the decision to leave. I wasn't sure what the future held and whether or not I would recover from the heartbreak. I wasn't sure if I would ever find love again or if I was even loveable. I believed that God would forgive me for walking away from my marriage, but I wasn't sure what that forgiveness looked like.

Several times, I wanted to recant my decision because of fear and not wanting to be alone. However, whenever I had second thoughts, God would give me a sign that retreating was not an option. When I considered settling, I looked at my son, thought about his happiness, and cast the thought away. The Lord provided everything I needed when I thought I would struggle to make it. Settling would've been a convenient and comfortable decision, but I knew deep down inside that it was not God's best for me. I felt a still, small voice telling me to be patient and not to look back. I was determined that there had to be *more* ahead, and I wanted to find it.

Years before the separation occurred, I had thoughts of moving out of state, writing, and starting a support group for women to help them overcome difficult situations with tenacity. Those thoughts became dreams, and the tug on my heart to help women became greater. I had no idea how I would do it as I had no formal training in writing or counseling. I simply believed that those dreams might become a reality for me one day.

> *You are the God who performs miracles; you display your power among the peoples. With your mighty arm you redeemed your people, the descendants of Jacob and Joseph* (Psalm 77:14-15 NIV).

Nothing is more miraculous than seeing the faithfulness of God manifest when we are least expecting it. While separated, I was contacted by someone I did not know who was recruiting for a job in the state I'd been dreaming of moving to. I decided to go through the motions of pursuing the job, but I didn't really care whether I received an offer. Remember, my life was in a bit of shambles, and I had no idea what was next for me in life.

I got the job, and the favor with it was a sure answer to my worries.

THE BREAKDOWN & REPAIR

To say that I was afraid and a little concerned about the move out of state would be an understatement. I was overwhelmed with all sorts of anxious thoughts. Once my family returned home from helping me move in, all I could do was cry. At that moment, I knew there was no turning back; I had to face this new challenge alone. It was just the two of us, my son and me, and I had to be his rock to comfort him during this transition. I was in a new state, with a new job and surroundings, a smaller home, and a new routine. Yikes! It was a lot to adjust to. Not to mention, I was still grieving.

There were many times when I would put my son to sleep at night and stay up crying and praying to the Lord for help and guidance. I was truly afraid—afraid that I'd made a mistake, afraid of the new environment and having no resources around, and afraid that I'd fail again. As I wiped my tears, I clung to the scripture that says, *weeping may endure for the night, but joy comes in the morning* (Psalm 30:5 NIV). I needed some serious joy. I wished the pain and mess in my life would subside. Little did I know, there was still a bit more to endure.

The month following my move, it was over. My divorce was final. The flurry of feelings that filled my heart and mind was overwhelming. On the one hand, I was relieved and surprised at how smoothly and quickly the process went. On the other hand, I was distraught. I truly felt like I experienced three deaths: the death of my marriage, the loss of someone that I once truly cared about, and the death of life as I once knew it. My heart was broken, and I mourned the loss of all three. I yearned for the shaking of my world to stop, but the rumble continued.

Less than a month after my divorce was final, the United States confirmed that the global health emergency, COVID-19, had spread throughout the country and had already affected thousands of people. The crisis escalated into a pandemic, and travel bans were enforced. States across the country began to shut down, and fear wreaked havoc all over. This virus added an even greater level of fear of the unknown for me. I began to question the decisions I'd made just a few short months before to step out on faith into new territory. How could I possibly survive a national lockdown, avoid catching the virus, remain employed in my new role, comfort and take care of a child, and grieve without any family or friends to support me? I had to rethink some things!

I decided to spend some time in quarantine with my parents. My son and I packed our things, including our electronic devices, and returned to my home state. We were able to work and go to school remotely; it felt so good to be surrounded by loved ones during that chaotic time. As I watched the news and heard all of the reports of those falling fatally ill to the virus, I was so grateful for the health and safety of me and my family. My heart may have been broken, but I was thankful it was still beating. Gratitude changed my perspective during this dark time, and after a month of staying with my parents, I felt that it was time to return to my "new home" and figure things out.

I returned, a little skeptical yet determined to give the new home and city a chance. There was still a pandemic, and things were getting worse in the world each day, but I mustered up enough courage to try to understand what God was doing in my life. I wanted so badly to know the purpose of all the disappointment and upset I had been experiencing. I believed He was with me and that His grace and mercy still covered me.

I'd heard a phrase that said, "Do it afraid!" I added my own twist to it and said, "Do it afraid until I am no longer afraid!"

I began to repeat the scripture in 2 Timothy 1:7 that says, *For God hath not given us the spirit of fear; but of power, and of love, and of a sound mind* (KJV). That verse became an affirmation and mantra for me. I reminded myself of it every time I felt afraid and powerless. I needed that scripture whenever I felt weak and as if I would lose my mind. When I wondered if I would ever find love again, Jesus reminded me that He was love and that I was capable of showing love and being loved the right way!

There was one good thing about the quarantine—I had plenty of time to reflect! For the first time in a long time, I started journaling again. I took my journaling a step further and began studying God's promises from the Bible. I even joined an online Bible study group. I was thirsty for knowledge, community, and healing.

As I started compiling a list of scriptures that spoke life to me, I realized I was beginning to feel relieved. The weight of grief on my shoulders was lifting. Life didn't seem so dark, and my self-confidence was increasing. As I wrote more and encouraged myself through the Word, my faith strengthened, and I had an awakening. The beginnings of a self-help book emerged from months of reflection, studying, praying, and devotion. I knew then that I would turn all that into a devotional to help other broken women. She Exudes: *A Confidence Awakening Devotional and Journal* was born! My dream of writing and becoming an author was coming to life!

BECOMING UNSHAKABLE

It is said that seven is God's complete number. Seven months after my divorce was final, I officially started writing a devotional, started a business called *The Confident Lily*—which later became a ministry, and created an inspirational coloring book called *Oh, So Confident!* One of the things that had been missing in my life for a long time was confidence. I understood that even when I didn't feel confident in myself or my abilities, I could be confident in God, who never fails. Hebrews 13:6 states, *So we say with confidence, "The Lord is my helper; I will not be afraid. What can mere mortals do to me?"* (NIV). I knew and believed I could do all things with the Lord, but left up to my own strength, I could do nothing. I had been a wreck earlier that year, but just seven months later, I had hope and a sense of purpose!

As God restored my confidence and spirit, it became clear that my purpose was to motivate and assist other women in finding theirs. I wanted to encourage them to be resilient, never give up on themselves, and trust God without ceasing. I had to share the message of pushing even when it hurt. I wanted to let others know they weren't broken beyond repair.

As I was thinking about names for the business, the lily flower came to mind. I discovered that this beautiful flower could grow in adverse conditions. It is also highly revered in the Bible, and each color represents an attractive quality women should have. For example, orange represents confidence, and pink represents abundance. Additionally, as I thought about inspirations in my life, I thought about my mother, Lillie, one of the most resilient women I know. She is also responsible for the deep roots of my faith, which is one of the best gifts she could have given me.

Healing from the brokenness of divorce was no easy journey, and it didn't stop when I decided to write a book. It took much work and prayer. In fact, I still work to maintain my healing today. My life was shaken to a point where I didn't know if or how I'd ever be able to get it back on track. I fell many times, but God always helped me get back up. I learned that when shaking occurs in your life, you may need to shake loose some attachments, mentalities, and other things that are not conducive to the life God wants you to have. When we listen and follow God's wisdom, He will bless us.

Being shaken up is often unavoidable and sometimes even necessary. Still, we can rest assured that we will be secure if we hold on to God. He will never let go of us. We must cultivate unshakable confidence in the Lord's ability to provide, deliver, heal, and make all things right.

> *And we know that in all things God works for the good of those who love him, who have been called to his purpose* (Romans 8:28 NIV).

I encourage you to love God unconditionally, seek His will for your life, and walk in your purpose even when things get tough. We know that in the end, it will all work out for the good if we remain unshakable in our belief. After all, God is a beautiful artist, even when He is working with broken crayons!

Unshakable When You Are Empowered

By Donna Whartenby

God empowers us when we need strength, courage, and wisdom to do His will. In Joshua 1:9 the Lord instructs, *"Be strong and courageous. Do not be afraid; do not be discouraged, for the Lord your God will be with you wherever you go"* (NIV). As a believer in God, He is always with you.

God empowered Joshua to lead the Israelites to march around the city walls of Jericho for six days. You may have heard or sung the song as a child telling this biblical story about Jericho. After their march on the seventh day, when the horns blew, the Israelites shouted, and the walls came tumbling down (Joshua 6:1-20). The Israelites overthrew the city. Joshua trusted God's instructions and, without using physical weapons, took the city in victory.

God empowered David to bring victory to Israel with warring nations. David was *a man after his [God's] own heart and appointed him ruler of his people (1 Samuel 13:14 NIV).* Scripture is clear, *In everything he [David] did he had great success, because the Lord was with him* (1 Samuel 18:14 NIV). God empowered David with unshakable wisdom, devotion, obedience, and love. Because of David's trust and faith in Him, God made David the king of Israel.

God causes everything to work together for the good of those who love God and are called according to his purpose for them (Romans 8:28 NLT). When God empowers us, all things work for good when we are in His will.

God also empowers us as we go through obstacles and trials, as He did for Joseph in the Old Testament. Joseph was sold into slavery by his envious brothers, imprisoned and forgotten, until God empowered Joseph to interpret a dream of Pharoah's, and in turn, placed Joseph as the second in command of Egypt. God used Joseph during a time of famine to save his family and God's covenant people, the Israelites, from starvation. Joseph's testimony in Genesis 50:20 (NLT) demonstrates, *You intended to harm me, but God intended it all for good. He brought me to this position so I could save the lives of many people.* Despite obstacles and trials, God's power and authority placed and empowered Joseph, turning his circumstances for good. God used regional famine to allow Joseph's actions to save lives. As in this story, even when deception and evil come at us, God can turn the circumstances for His good by empowering and using us.

Peter, who denied knowing Jesus three times in one night, was later empowered to care for Jesus' followers by teaching them God's Word, spreading the gospel news to those who did not know about Jesus, and leading the believers in the ways Jesus taught. *God has given us everything we need for living a godly life. We have received all of this by coming to know him* (2 Peter 1:3 NLT). God empowers us to accomplish all we need to do His will. Some of that power is found in knowing God's Word and living the life God desires for us.

God uses believers in Christ to share the gospel news of who Jesus is. We do not share the gospel using our own abilities, but we use the power of God working in us through the Holy Spirit. This Spirit of God empowers and encourages us to reach out to others to tell them the gospel message. The power of God can help people understand the gospel of Jesus' death, burial, and resurrection, turning them away from sinful ways. We have faith and trust in God as He empowers us to unshakably lead others to know Christ.

I can do all this through him who gives me strength (Philippians 4:13 NIV). This verse tells us we have unlimited potential to do God's will when we have faith in Him. This should encourage us to step out in trust, move away from our comfort zones in faith, and allow God to empower us to accomplish His will in our and others' lives. When we are empowered, we glorify God in His grace, power, and authority as our Sovereign Lord.

We walk in faith and will, allowing Him to empower us to accomplish the tasks He gives us for His purpose.

Lord, thank You for empowering me to do Your will. Because I know You are with me, I can be unshakable in accomplishing the tasks You give me with unshakable trust and strength. In Jesus' name. AMEN.

Kaye Hollings

After completing Journalism studies and a Diploma of Theology, Kaye Hollings became a freelance writer/editor, tracing journeys of ruin to renewal. She became a Mental Health Chaplain and then a Funeral Director/Celebrant, caring deeply about hurting people.

Kaye currently facilitates grief workshops and volunteers with disabled adults. She is a published author of four books, *Dawn of Hope, Kept by Love, Shaped, and Shafts of Light* (www.kayehollings.com), about real people with real problems and how God makes life make sense.

Kaye is married with two daughters and two grandchildren and lives on the Gold Coast in Australia. She loves writing, reading, and spending time in nature with God.

Kaye Hollings
PO Box 3662
Robina Town Centre Drive
Robina, QLD 4230 Australia
Mobile: (61) 0422 111 809
Email: enquiries@kayehollings.com
Website: www.kayehollings.com

My Ocean Walk

By Kaye Hollings

Sitting on a rock at the base of the headland with the sun warming my shoulders and gentle waves splashing between my toes, I praised God for the wonderful world He has made. I have always lived near the ocean and love being in it, on it, and under it—nature therapy at its best! I've observed its many moods and rhythms, breathed in its salty, invigorating scent, and pondered its power. I'm happiest when I'm wet!

Thanking God for His creation led me to recall when I became a new creation in Christ. I met Him when I was a fearful teenager living with my grandmother and father, who both struggled with mental illness. It was through these growing-up experiences that God called me to be a caregiver and hospital chaplain for the mentally ill.

As I reminisced by the water, a very touching story came to mind of a young boy throwing stranded starfish back into the sea and, when challenged as to the hopelessness of his actions because there were simply too many starfish for his small efforts to make a difference, he said, "I made a difference to that one!" My goal has always been to make a difference wherever God calls me, whether that calling is big or small.

God nudged me to start walking down the beach. Looking up, seagulls were flying above, noisily chatting with me. Looking down, I stepped over shells, some whole and beautiful, others damaged and rejected. I saw the first starfish of the day, which took my mind back to Barry, one of my new contacts—a permanent resident in a psychiatric facility. The ocean still looked calm, but in my mind, I saw a sign that said STRONG RIPS, and I thought about Barry's confusion beneath the surface and a life of trying to stay afloat and not be swept away by forces he couldn't control.

Working with Barry was challenging. What do you say to a 60-year-old non-verbal man who knows no other home than his hospital room with its walled exercise yard? How do you relate to a man whose sole earthly possessions consist of a few plastic combs and a collection of scratched toy cars in a scruffy overnight bag that never leaves his side? When I began working with Barry, I was told never to touch his bag. He was so closed off that despite many visits, I couldn't even encourage him to look up at me.

One day, many weeks after we first met, I was greatly moved to see Barry smiling warmly at me. Then, to my amazement, he opened the precious black bag and, one by one, handed me his toy cars, sharing his limited world with me. I placed each car carefully on the ground while Barry quickly re-positioned them in the right order—his order—before packing them away again. This interaction was repeated every time I saw him. His smile made my day.

I had become Barry's friend, although no words were ever spoken. Just being there with him had made a difference, and I was so thankful.

As the months progressed, so did my God-given love for those trapped in a confused turmoil of ideas that refused to make any sense. Locked in with my new friends as a mental health chaplain, I sensed what a frightening existence they led, and my own fears fled. One invaluable life lesson I learned was not to judge by appearances. By looking deeper below the surface, I often discovered a very valid reason for a person's seemingly bizarre behaviour.

Then there was Perry. Perry was a little man with greying hair, a very uneven gait, and often spittle combined with the remains of breakfast around his mouth. My first reaction to Perry was filled with caution, distance, and uncertainty. As he approached me, I smiled hesitantly and said hello. He grunted, waved his arms around wildly, and kept going. What was I to say to a developmentally disabled person who had lived in a mental institution all his life and whose speech I couldn't understand?

I would see Perry sitting under a tree with a crumpled comic he couldn't read and an unlit cigarette he couldn't smoke. He was copying others, showing how much he longed to belong. Often, he would emerge from the kitchen with a banana and a few slices of cold meat hanging out of his pocket.

One day when I was in a meeting, Perry burst through the door looking for the usual "cuppa" and being his noisy self. He abruptly stopped when he saw we were praying and stood in the middle of the room with his eyes closed and hands pressed together until we had finished. Then he quietly left, the cup of tea forgotten. I saw God's unsurpassed love in action. Somehow, somewhere in Perry's confused mind, he had met God and been touched by Him. We understand so little about how divine influence touches troubled hearts and minds. I learnt never to assume. No one is beyond God's reach. We all hold a unique place in our world. Perry was clearly stating, "I'm one with you and with our God."

My contact with Barry and Perry began with wondering what to say and ended with the realization that words weren't necessary. I communicated through body language and an attitude of love, and God did the rest. Did I do enough or say enough? I didn't think so, and I often felt hopeless, but God worked while I watched. It was a ministry of presence, and for 12 years, He gave me many assurances from His Word as I worked in psychiatric wards. Like this very special one:

> *I will give you the treasures of darkness, riches stored in secret places, so that you may know that I am the Lord* (Isaiah 45:3 NIV).

What an unshakable promise. Mental illness is a very dark place!

I continued on my walk, knowing a storm was approaching as menacing dark clouds blocked the sun and frantic waves began to lash the beach. Picking up my second starfish, I remembered that heart-breaking day after I had become a funeral director and funeral celebrant when I met with the distressed family of Ben, a cheeky four-year-old, and took his service. There was nowhere to hide, no safe direction, as they tried to chart a course through smashing breakers and ongoing turbulence.

Surrounded by colourful balloons, teddies, and toys, I began, so grateful for a group of friends who were praying for me. The overhead photo presentation and accompanying music, all favorite songs the little boy loved to sing, were heart-wrenching as we relived his all-too-few Christmas and birthday celebrations, saw his infectious smile beaming down on us again and again, and heard his innocent giggles. Usually, the laughter of a child is pure delight. That day, it was agony. The poem I had practised many times caught in my throat, and my tears broke through. The celebrant is the one usually looked to for strength, but I knew my audience would understand another mother's heart.

It had been a long apprenticeship to forgive the hurts from my own childhood, but now I was emotionally mature, having learnt to deal with my feelings in a healthier manner and to trust Him to empower me in all situations and turn fear into faith. This is so important when reaching out to a world in pain.

Upon arriving home after the funeral, I sobbed the remainder of my tears for this broken family and then fell into an exhausted sleep. On waking, I knew that out of devastation grows strength. Only God. Only God.

During my ten years in the funeral industry, I conducted over 100 services. This was a wonderful opportunity to be a channel of God's love to hurting families who may not have ever thought about the One who holds life and death in His hands and is the Comforter in all of life's tragedies. Did anyone find faith in Jesus after these funeral services? Not to my knowledge, but I prayed that the spirits of these shattered families would be touched by God's hand and that something heard or seen would draw them to pursue Him. When I struggled, *He made a way through the sea, a path through the mighty waters* (Isaiah 43:16 NIV). God saw my inadequacies and met them with His power.

As I pushed ahead, the wind over the moderately choppy water began to lessen. I saw my third starfish and a lifeboat drawing near, both of which reminded me of *Princess for A Day,* a beautiful program that pampers disadvantaged women trying to rise above mental health issues, domestic violence, and poverty. Our volunteers are like the workers on that lifeboat—standing ready to rescue anyone in danger of sinking. Our lifesaving tools may look a bit different, taking the form of free haircuts, massages, facials, manicures, makeup, and delicious food. There are free Bibles on offer and many opportunities to pray with the women. These gifts of time and talents help improve self-esteem, make smiles appear on sad, tired faces, and straighten hunched shoulders as women are valued and included. No questions asked—just a focus on allowing the sun to shine for a short time.

As we help it's like watering wilting roses, seeing women spring back to life. Although no one is waiting at home to compliment them on their outward appearance, inside and out, each one leaves feeling like a princess. A little love and care can achieve so much when we allow the divine Caregiver to work through us. I longed for them to learn the truth of Isaiah 43:2: *When you go through deep waters, I will be with you. When you go through rivers of difficulty, you will not drown* (NLT).

I stop for a rest. I've been on this walk for 50 years, but I am humbled and want to continue.

Smiling, I walk on and pick up the fourth starfish, seeing my special friends at Crossroads—a program for disabled (differently abled) adults. My heart warms as I anticipate meeting with them again next Friday. The boy who walks around with a guitar he can't play exudes his love of music and teaches me to absorb every note I hear. The young woman with a doll always in her arms reveals her longing for the child she will never have and reminds me to cherish my children. The smiling woman wearing the iridescent pink hat is shouting, "I'm here. Please don't ignore me," and it's a joy to share in her effervescence. The man who loves to conduct the singing with an empty music stand lights up with enthusiasm. My heart breaks as he tries to find purpose in life.

As I befriend and observe, it is profoundly clear that no one has a disabled soul, and I know God is beaming as we dance and laugh together. Music certainly is the universal language. The joy we see on these happy faces as they sing karaoke, uninhibited and doing life together, ensures that the helpers are truly blessed and uplifted as well. Does God care if some of the words are incorrect? Does it matter if the melody becomes lost in the excited cacophony? We always receive more than we give.

It's a privilege to share in both their happiness and their pain. They hurt when one of their friends dies or when someone is sick, and each week they ask us to pray for their special needs. God is very important to many of them, and they have embraced our weekly prayer times and made them personal. Such simple faith is so touching and beautiful. The following is one such conversation:

"Kaye, will you please pray for my sore finger?"

"Sure, Robert. What happened to it?"

"I was bitten by a pelican."

"How did that happen?"

"He was so cute that I tried to pick him up and carry him home with me."

I know God was smiling as I tried to keep a straight face while praying and choking on my laughter as I visualized this hilarious interaction, but I'm sure that even a pelican bite is not beyond His compassion.

I walked on, noticing that although the sea was quite calm again and the sun had broken through the clouds, there was still the danger of being strangled by strands of suffocating seaweed or being tossed by rogue waves that rise unexpectedly and can flatten with their force, leaving pain and exhaustion. But God's promise renews me, the carers, and participants as we share struggles: *He reached down from on high and took hold of me; he drew me out of deep waters* (Psalm 18:16 NIV).

A large group, my fifth starfish, catches my attention. They are all stuck in the sand, unable to move towards the incoming tide. I sit among them. Flashing through my mind are so many faces who have participated in the *Grief and Loss Course* that I've facilitated for the last six years. I see them striving to find new meaning and courage to reinvest in living while struggling not to be shipwrecked on the rocks of pain.

The course has no magic formula that will bring instant healing to the mum whose 19-year-old son committed suicide, leaving devastating heartache and a young baby behind, or to the distraught woman unable to say goodbye to her husband after his fatal plane crash left an empty chair at the table, an empty space in the bed, and damaged hearts that may never fully heal.

There is no quick fix for the beautiful young girl who was planning her wedding, now sitting shattered and broken in the room after her fiancé died in a motorcycle accident on the way to work. Her dreams are smashed, and her future is stripped bare.

But I remembered Psalm 93:4: *But mightier than the violent raging of the seas, mightier than the breakers on the shore—the Lord above is mightier than these!* (NLT).

Only God can renew and restore hope in this depth of despair. My constant prayer is that they'll discover the immense power of God and find Him to be bigger than their pain. Grief is an ocean only He fully understands.

For the past eight years, my husband has been living with prostate cancer, and he has become my sixth starfish. We were shattered by this diagnosis as, at the time, we were trying to sell his accountancy practice so we could retire and move interstate and had arrangements in place that couldn't be changed. We had to pack up a large suite of rooms that accommodated seven staff, organise shredding of hundreds of files, sell all office furniture, pack up our home, search online in our spare time to find a new house, and face a 2-day drive to get there while exhausted. "Why now Lord? How will we cope? Couldn't You have chosen a better time?" I sobbed into my pillow.

Is there ever a right time for cancer or grief??? This was an unexpected emotional tsunami that knocked us off our feet for a while, but God held our heads above the water and brought us through safely. We were so grateful for His strength and guidance which enabled us to survive.

Then in 2022, I was diagnosed with aggressive breast cancer. Both of us? Me, now having to accept care rather than give it? Requiring invasive and unwanted confidence-stripping treatments? I saw wild waves mirroring my wild thoughts. I was in shock, slowed down, my pause button firmly pressed!

So now I have become the seventh starfish. I really appreciated those who were picking me up and carefully placing me back in the cool water to help me keep swimming rather than letting me burn up on the beach. I'm learning to accept all offers of help graciously rather than insisting on doing everything myself.

When I woke up after surgery, God promised to be my shield and protection. While I was having chemotherapy, friends prayed me through many months of bad days, provided a loving chauffeur service to treatments, and filled my home with flowers and delicious meals. Yet, while having radiation in 2023, I was fearful and stressed—then I looked up and saw that a divinely inspired painter had coloured the ceiling sky blue with fluffy white clouds. In my mind I saw Jesus leaning down, arms outstretched, holding me on the metal machine.

Why did I doubt? I've realized yet again that because He is unshakable, I can be, too. He will keep me living above the waves and will always take me to where I'm meant to be.

None of us know our future, but as we walk, God gives us new ways to reach out—what we are called to do for His glory is as important to others as the boy was to the individual starfish he threw back into the sea. I know God's power will enable me to continue to care for my husband as his health declines and to patiently accept all the ongoing medical appointments for both of us and some limitations we now experience. However, I am still the mentor He called me to be all those years ago as I'm being led to others, newly diagnosed, who need a driver to their oncologist or encouragement and reassurance while having treatment. God is good.

> *Truly he is my rock and my salvation; he is my fortress, I will never be shaken* (Psalm 62:2 NIV).

Keep walking along your beach, helping a few starfish survive life's times and tides. You will find yourself changed as you yield to and put your confidence in our unshakable God. And you will certainly make a difference to those you encounter and be truly blessed.

---

[1]This story was inspired by Eiseley, L. C. (1979). *The Star Thrower,* Harcourt Brace & Company

Unshakable Relationships

By Donna Whartenby

Do you realize that Almighty God, the creator of the cosmos, also created humankind, both male and female?

God made Adam. Then He said Adam should not be alone and created Eve so that they could relate to God as well as to each other (Genesis 2:18). Do you know why? God wants to have an unshakable relationship with us! Our God is majestic and all-powerful, yet He loves, cares personally for, and longs to be actively involved in the lives of each of His children—all those who have come willingly under His care.

Hebrews 1:3 (NLT) tells us God *sustains everything by the mighty power of his command.* Yet 1 John 4:8 tells us the fundamental truth that *God is love.* God's love is the basis of His desire to have a relationship with all creation. That all-powerful, mighty God loves and longs for a relationship with you, me, your spouse and children, His heavenly angels—ALL of creation!

John 3:16 (NLT) proclaims that *God so loved the world.* There was never a time when God was not filled with love that He shared joyfully and freely. Love is the foundation of all God does. And because He created us in His image, like Him in mind and spirit, we were also created to have unshakable relationships with others and God Himself. You were created for the purpose of having a relationship with the living God who created the universe!

One of God's many attributes is that He is omnipresent, which means He lives among His people everywhere. Understanding this helps us grasp how important relationships are to Him. 2 Timothy 1:7 (KJV) teaches us that God has given us the *spirit...of power, and of love, and of a sound mind.*

We can more fully experience God's love and express our love for Him by intentionally developing our relationships with Him and others. One way we can do both is through prayer. Prayer is simply a conversation with God—which helps us get to know Him and His will for our lives.

Reading the Bible and following God's instructions in the Bible also helps us grow in love. 1 John 3:11 (NIV) instructs us to *love one another.* Likewise, Jesus commands us to *"Love each other as I have loved you"* (John 15:12 NIV). Further, He tells us that loving one another will demonstrate that we are God's children (John 13:34-35). Jesus also teaches that one of the greatest commandments is to *Love your neighbor as yourself* (Mark 12:31 NIV). Your relationships are important to God!

A frequently quoted scripture from Jesus' teaching is, *"Do to others as you would like them to do to you"* (Luke 6:31 NLT). Like all scripture, it is essential for us not to gloss over this teaching but to ask God to help us understand what it *really* means. This scripture comes under the main teaching that we are to love our enemies. Sometimes, we must push aside our feelings and opinions to be compassionate to others. We are called to love those with humble needs—those who are hungry and thirsty or need warmth, clothing, or transportation. We are to love others with compassion and grace, showing them God's light in their darkness. We are even to love those who hate us. Our relational God directs us to do as He does: offer unshakable love. He knows that by our love, others will be drawn into relationships.

If you have children, you have a golden opportunity to teach them the importance of relationships. You can begin by your example of showing kindness, compassion, and love for others. Teach the young ones God has entrusted to you to be aware of others who need a helping hand and how easy it is to brighten someone's day by opening a door or carrying their groceries. It's important for children to learn that unshakable relationships are built one moment at a time.

There is a warning in Romans 12:9—our love must be sincere, not fake, artificial, or contrived. We must hate what is evil or sinful, and cling to what is good. 1 Corinthians 13:4-7 (NLV) teaches us, *Love is kind. Love is not jealous. Love does not put itself up as being important. Love has no pride. Love does not do the wrong thing. Love never thinks of itself. Love does not get angry. Love does not remember the suffering that comes from being hurt by someone. Love is not happy with sin, but is happy with the truth. Love takes everything that comes without giving up. Love believes all things. Love hopes for all things.*

Understanding and reflecting God's love is the beginning of building unshakable relationships.

Thank You, Lord, for wanting to have a relationship with me. I accept Your invitation to come into my life and teach me Your ways. Teach me to love better each day—generously, not with timidity, and with strength and compassion for others in need. Help me to encourage my children, grandchildren, and others in a loving, kind, and compassionate way that builds strong relationships. In Your precious, Holy Name. Amen.

Dr. Violet E. Taylor

Dr. Violet E. Taylor is a leadership subject matter expert (SME), the outcome of a God-directed journey to defy statistics for her children while raising them as a single parent. She is the founder and CEO of EmpowerUp Solutions, a leadership development consulting company. Taylor is also a John Maxwell certified coach, teacher, trainer, and speaker, and she is passionate about valuing and empowering others.

Taylor empowered leaders locally for numerous years on topics such as single parenting, self-talk, healing and transformation, and leadership. God expanded her reach to Global platforms where Taylor's accomplishments include co-presentations and motivational speaking on topics such as Leading Authentically, Ethical Decision-Making, Diversity, Equity and Inclusion, Ethics and Diversity, and Self-Leadership.

She previously contributed chapters to published works, and her manuscript, *Owning My Scars: A Transformational Journey to Effective Leadership,* affirms her prowess in self-leadership and is now pending publication.

Taylor enjoys spending time with God, her two wonderful children, and her family. Her life is a testament to God's unshakable faithfulness, goodness, and love.

Our Unshakable God

By Dr. Violet E. Taylor

In the Bible, God reminds us that we will have trouble in this world (John 16:33). Many of us cope well with the usual struggles, such as problems in traffic and time management. However, there are instances when life throws us a curve ball and knocks us off our feet. When this happens, many of us keep up a facade of faith, claiming we're blessed and not stressed, but that behavior is not taught in the Bible.

Jesus, Son of God, admitted He was enduring a hard place (Matthew 26:38). Facades impede growth and often lead to our hurting each other because pain needs an escape. When the weight bears heavy on us, it is better to admit we're in a hard place and run to God—our rock, fortress, and deliverer (Psalm 18:2). It is here, at our end, where God begins.

Indeed, problems are conduits for a closer walk with God, for they build our faith and open our eyes to see His ever-present help in our times of need (Psalm 46:1).

The hardest times and the darkest nights teach us to rely on our unshakable God.

MY STORY

After recommitting my life to Christ, I had a newfound joy I wanted to spread. In the excitement of my new faith and learning about a relationship with God, I began serving in four ministries within Christian organizations that served other local organizations. I also welcomed others into my home, becoming a drop-in babysitter, Motel 6, and the train rest stop. You name it, and I was it. I was finally raising my children in Christ and doing what the Word of God instructs.

Despite financial hardships, other life struggles, and being a single parent, I was overjoyed. I was a babe in Christ with a joy-filled heart and expected everything to go well—peaches, cream, and kumbayas.

However, I learned that just as I come broken, others also come broken. And we show our brokenness in different ways. My wounds led to a broken voice: I was unable to speak up for myself, while some people's brokenness was displayed in bullying and poor treatment of others. In this clash of brokenness, I simply accepted and tolerated the poor behavior aimed at me. I never objected to the mistreatment and accepted that we are all imperfect.

I had suffered complex childhood trauma and other adversities that extended into adulthood. My trauma began at nine years old when I was assaulted by a neighbor and trusted family friend. To deal with my experience, I unknowingly began to overeat, resulting in excessive weight gain. In my culture at the time, the older generation viewed being fat as being loved and cared for. However, children viewed it differently, so I was mocked daily on my long walks to and from school.

Accordingly, I became aware of and accustomed to childhood bullying; however, I never considered adult bullying. Was that even a thing, and in a Christian establishment? I would have never expected it.

To this end, I suffered bullying and emotional abuse in community volunteer assignments from 2001 to 2020. It began in my second week of volunteering when one of my leaders openly belittled me. Due to my background that fostered a broken voice and fear when faced with certain approaches, along with my babe-in-Christ understanding of God's Word, I watched the subsequent laughter in silence. I then forgave my tormentor.

I thought forgiveness meant I had to continue fellowshipping with this individual. So, I proceeded, and the behavior continued and grew worse, taking the form of announcements in larger groups. For the first couple of years, I was labeled as weak, and the delivery was usually accompanied by uncontrollable laughter. Individuals in my circle also criticized and bullied my children to no avail.

There were times I smiled when I wanted to cry and showed up when I wanted to hide. Yet, my experience in these volunteer opportunities also included great moments. A few individuals encouraged me, and I felt such a sense of belonging that I did not focus on the poor treatment. I kept serving, forgiving, and fellowshipping.

For many years, I thought I was being a great Christian, "bearing with others," as the Bible taught me (Colossians 3:13). And let's not forget living unoffended! However, I was tolerating poor behavior and embracing emotional abuse—operating in my comfort zone.

As time passed, some people grew beyond this behavior, and we moved on. However, the enemy continued to use one individual, and the behavior worsened. This person began calling me weak, insecure, pitiful, and toxic. Around the 17-year mark of continuous emotional attacks and humiliation, I finally stepped away because being around that individual was just too expensive. It cost me my peace and my sanity, and it was pushing me away from God. However, stepping away from this individual produced more attacks, and I eventually asked the individual, in front of a witness, to stop attacking me. I explained that their behavior was a trigger to my past abuse and impacted me negatively.

Following the meeting, this bully continued to do what I asked them not to do. Their harassment extended into public settings in other organizations. Ultimately, I was accosted in front of a group of individuals I had recently met. I was so mortified. I'd previously embarked on my healing process, and through counseling, I developed a phrase to demand respect for my boundaries, but my voice did not matter. The onslaught continued with attempts to convince me that I had totally misread the situation. In the days to follow, I received partial apologies filled with half-truths—admitting to things I viewed as trivial while lying about the things that mattered. Of everything that happened, I was most devastated by the lies.

I spent the next couple of months questioning God: *Why? How? Lord, I was in the process of serving Your people. How could You allow this? Why didn't You stop it?* Then I offered suggestions to God: *You could have created a decoy.* For the first time in my life, I regretted the connections I made, regretted serving, and regretted attending that event. I was angry, which had not happened in numerous years.

I was so humiliated that I took a short break from serving and later realized I was no longer welcome to serve in a particular area. Then I began wondering, *What did I do that was so wrong? Was it because I asked for my boundaries to be respected? Is that wrong?* I was triggered by their attacks—I cried, I wept, and I continued to search. *What sin did I commit? I think that was the part that hurt most. If I committed such a horrible sin that disqualified me, shouldn't someone care about my soul enough to meet with me, explain it, correct me, teach me, guide me?*

But they didn't.

Again, despite the bullying, I experienced spiritual growth and gained some healthy relationships with people who encouraged me. But I felt lost and confused. I didn't feel like myself. I felt like a castaway. Almost 20 years of belonging abruptly ended, and I didn't understand it. Even non-religious environments have exit conversations, but here in this God-space, there was none. My soul lamented.

I reached out but received no response, and others who volunteered in this area no longer interacted with me. I was completely excluded and isolated, and I felt myself slipping into depression. However, God, in His infinite wisdom, had me on a growth path to defy statistics for my children as I raised them as a single parent. At this juncture, I had completed two years of my doctoral studies and was faced with examinations that would determine whether I proceeded. He used this growth path to capture much of my attention and intentions. Still, I hurt. Oh, but in this crushing, God reminded me that He is my unshakable God.

> *The Lord is my rock, my fortress, and my deliverer; my God is my rock in whom I take refuge* (Psalm 18:2 NIV).

I fasted and cried out to God as always, for His Word says when I cry out to Him, He will answer (Jeremiah 33:3). Today, I testify He is faithful to His Word. God led me back into counseling. I saw God, my Shepherd (Psalm 23:1), guiding me through my Gethsemane moment, where, like Jesus, my soul was filled with grief, and He restored my soul (Psalm 23:3).

Below, I share three of the stages of my journey through grief.

GRIEVE THE LOSS

Like many individuals, when I heard the word grief, I attributed it to the loss of a loved one. However, with God's help, I have learned that grief is attached to any loss, and it is a part of the healing process. I read excerpts of Kübler-Ross's "Stages of Grief" and learned that being angry, for example, reflects grieving.

While it is imperative I did not remain in that state, I needed to allow myself to feel and address the feelings. So, I entered a season of grieving in the arms of my loving Father, my rock—my unshakable God! He is strong enough to take my anger, questions, mixed-up moods, and attitudes.

God then guided me to forgive and reminded me through His Word and His messengers that I can forgive and still establish boundaries that I hold firm. Conversely, I also need to respect the boundaries others establish.

If you have experienced a loss, any loss, do not bypass grieving. Grieving is not a sign of weakness, and it does not mean you are less holy or less blessed. God did not call us to live in pretense, but some of us proceed in this manner, likely feigning perfection or misinterpreting scriptures. However, this behavior is not exemplified in the Bible. My favorite example is when Jesus took Peter, James, and John to the Garden of Gethsemane and told them, *"My soul is overwhelmed with sorrow to the point of death"* (Matthew 26:38 NIV). Friends, whether you are the offender or the victim, grieving is foundational to your healing process, and admitting where you are is the beginning of healing.

If you cover your hurts in facades, you put them in a pressure cooker. Then what happens? The pressure builds, and while you fake it with some people, others, likely those closest to you or those perceived as weak, will receive the steam from that pressure cooker—the impact of the hurt you are attempting to hide. I invite you, as a believer in Jesus Christ, to cry out to God right now and allow Him to do what only He can do from the "inside out." As I cried out to God, as His Word promises, He answered (Psalm 120:1), then lovingly comforted me (Ps. 23:4), showing me where I had lost focus, guiding me back on track, and to healing.

God's might and restoration power are unshakable!

In prayer, place your grief and need for healing in the mighty hands of our unshakable God.

SPEND QUALITY TIME WITH GOD

As God guided me back to emotional and spiritual health, He moved me to spend quality time with Him. Through my intentional time in devotion, God reminded me of Mary and Martha and told me this was my season to be Mary and sit at His feet and learn from Him (Luke 10:38-42). This knowledge led me to accept where I was. He also pointed out that I was grieving the loss of serving in certain ministries with a specific organization; however, He reminded me He needs workers in other parts of the fields, in other regions. So, when He releases me, I know where I will be going.

When we think of devotion, the first thing that often comes to mind is our lack of time. Additionally, often we are put off by an unwritten rule that states that devotion must be tended to in the mornings. However, some of us are not alert in the mornings, so even when we try, it becomes a ritual where we do not experience the connection to Almighty God. Many Christian leaders may suggest this time of day due to scriptures that instruct us to honor God with the first of our resources. I firmly believe that we should pray first thing in the morning, and as life would have it, most days, I pray throughout the day. However, our quality time of reading and reflecting on God's Word can be any time of the day—even on our lunch break, in the evening, or at night.

I have heard pastors liken our not spending time with God to a marriage. If spouses do not spend time together, their relationships suffer. But the quality of that time is important. A couple can sit at the dinner table and be in two separate worlds. They spent time together, but it was not quality time and produced no depth to their relationship. It's the same for us with God. If you're reading a devotion in the mornings but your mind is on the laundry, making breakfast, or the honey-do list, you have performed an act, but that's all it was. You did not experience a connection with God.

Going through the motions in the mornings only to follow a suggested rule or to get it off your checklist is not honoring God. It's not the time of day but the quality of your time that honors God. God wants a relationship with each of us. Whatever time of day is your best time, He is waiting to meet with you. He neither sleeps nor slumbers (Psalm 121:3-4).

God's patience is unshakable!

Spending quality time with God allows you to recognize His unshakable presence, developing your unshakable character.

PRACTICE GRATITUDE EVEN IN THE WILDERNESS

Amid my loss in 2020, God gave me the word *gratitude* for my word of the year 2021. I thought, *Really, God?* I am smiling as I write this, understanding that His ways and thoughts are so much higher than mine (Isaiah 55:9).

I wrote the word *gratitude* where I could see it throughout the day, but in case I forgot to look, God often reminded me. What a good God He is! His love is unshakable.

Without even trying, my attention was drawn to His many blessings, experiencing new beneficial triggers, praise God. Each blessing triggered my memory of His Word. For example, one day, I sat at my dining table, listening to the birds and watching them frolicking in my yard. I began to thank God for the ability to hear them singing and see their beauty. Just then, God reminded me that although He is faithful to the birds, He values me much more.

> *Look at the birds of the air; they do not sow or reap or store away in barns, and yet your heavenly Father feeds them. Are you not much more valuable than they?* (Matthew 6:26 NIV).

I daily recalled His benefits of forgiving, healing, redeeming, satisfying and crowning me with love and compassion (Psalm 103:2-5 NIV).

I recommitted to my life verse: *I will bless the Lord at all times: his praise shall continually be in my mouth* (Psalm 34:1 KJV).

Friends, gratitude is an expression of joy and celebration in thankfulness for all God's blessings. It takes your focus off the problem and puts it onto The Problem Solver. Gratitude reminds us that He is our helper.

I encourage you to observe the small things you often overlook, like the painting of the sky, the different shades of green among the trees, and the blessing of beholding them. Reflect on what He has done; look how far He has brought you. He is the same God; He is unchanging. Be grateful for His faithfulness.

You may be going through a storm as you read this chapter. I am not saying you don't acknowledge what's *not* going well. Please acknowledge it and bring it to Him in prayer, but also be intentional in seeing God in every situation. Take note of how He is keeping and providing for you in the midst of it all. See Him carrying you in the storm, walking with you through your Gethsemane moment of hardship or grief, and offer Him thanksgiving. Friends, let's *Give thanks to the Lord; for He is good* (Psalm 136:1 NIV) in and out of season.

God's faithfulness is unshakable.

Gratitude removes our focus from the problem and places it on the faithfulness of our unshakable God.

FINAL WORD

Many of us have heard the saying, "If God allowed it, there's a purpose."

This statement is very accurate, but it does not negate that life's trials bring pain that sometimes knocks us off our feet. However, our God is faithful, and if we run to Him—our rock, fortress, and deliverer—painful experiences can be foundational for restoration and growth for both offenders and victims. Indeed, when we rely on our unshakable God, we recognize Him as our ever-present help in our times of need (Psalm 46:1).

Today, I am grateful for the experience in the story I shared. I am grateful that I was kicked out and excluded; I am grateful for the season of isolation. God used this time to nurture me, and I experienced Him in a greater way. He is my best friend.

Additionally, He used this time to help me focus on my health and complete the growth path He orchestrated for me.

Today, I am Dr. Violet Taylor.

God's goodness is unshakable.

Whether you are the offender, victim, or both, know that God loves you. His love is unshakable.

My prayer is that you seek our unshakable God so you may experience His restoration power.

Unshakable When Life Is Unfair

By Leecy Barnett

Perhaps you had been working hard for your company for five years when the promotion you deserved went to the boss's nephew, who had just joined the company six weeks prior.

Maybe you and your husband had been praying for a child for a decade when, suddenly, your neighbor, who really didn't want children, got pregnant.

Or it may be that your sibling who smokes like a chimney is in perfect health, while you, who have never smoked a day in your life, got diagnosed with cancer.

Do any of these scenarios sound familiar? These are just a few situations that might make us scream, "Life is unfair!" And you would be correct: life is *not* fair. When we encounter unfairness, it can be tempting to let envy and bitterness consume us and shake our faith in God. We may even mistakenly believe that because we have faithfully served God, He owes us. Asaph, a Hebrew religious leader and psalm writer, fell into this trap:

But as for me, my feet almost slipped;
my steps nearly went astray.
For I envied the arrogant;
I saw the prosperity of the wicked.
They have an easy time until they die,
and their bodies are well fed.
They are not in trouble like others;

they are not afflicted like most people
(Psalm 73:2-5 CSB).

Comparison almost led Asaph astray. When he saw the ungodly living lives of ease, he resented them. He took his eyes off God and envied those who live only for themselves and their own pleasure. This made him doubt whether a life of serving God was worth it:

Did I purify my heart
and wash my hands in innocence for nothing?
For I am afflicted all day long
and punished every morning
(Psalm 73:13-14 CSB).

Maybe Asaph had been seduced by an Old Testament version of the "health and wealth" gospel some people teach today. Perhaps he expected that since he was a religious leader in God's service, God was obligated to smooth his path through life. But instead, he faced adversity. Asaph's experience did not line up with His understanding of God:

When I tried to understand all this,
it seemed hopeless
until I entered God's sanctuary.
Then I understood their destiny....
Those far from you will certainly perish;
you destroy all who are unfaithful to you.
But as for me, God's presence is my good.
I have made the Lord God my refuge,
so I can tell about all you do
(Psalm 73:16-17, 27-28 CSB).

Entering the Temple reminded Asaph that he was meant to serve God. No matter how unfair life seemed at the moment, God's presence was all he needed. Finding refuge in God made Asaph *unshakable.*

The world likes to tell us, "You deserve it." If we don't get what we feel our actions merit, our natural response is, "That's not fair." However, when we take our eyes off the unfairness of this world and turn our eyes on Jesus, we can be thankful that God does not treat us fairly: *He does not treat us as our sins deserve or repay us according to our iniquities* (Psalm 103:10 NIV). None of us deserve God's forgiveness, love, and grace. Comprehending this truth will help us to be unshakable when life is unfair.

Father, forgive me for evaluating my life by comparing it with others. Help me to fix my eyes on Your amazing love and grace. Don't let the unfairness of the world shake my faith in You.

Karen Sierra

Karen Sierra was born in Colombia, raised in Canada, and has lived in the United States of America for over twenty-six years. The Lord blessed Karen with many talents that started at a young age. He made her into a beautiful butterfly, creating a special design in her. Karen has become a pure, godly woman. She has surrendered her life to our Savior and loves hearing the Word of God. Karen was saved by the holy blood of Jesus Christ and is on her way back to heaven. Her story will inspire you to believe in the strength that can only come from the love of God.

Karen shows us in her testimony how our heavenly Father has sustained her through a life of trauma in His loving arms. The Lord is healing her inner self. God is an awesome God; we worship and praise Jesus Christ and await His return to bring us back to heaven with all our loved ones whom we truly miss.

Only God Sustained Me

By Karen Sierra

Have you ever realized how awesome our God is and that He can sustain us through everything? Scripture tells us to *Cast your cares on the Lord and he will sustain you; he will never let the righteous be shaken* (Psalm 55:22 NIV). God has sustained me. Upon reading my story, I pray you hear God's voice and place your faith completely in Him.

Satan tried to do everything to rob me of my innocence at a young age—even destroying my family and killing my son. But God has been faithful to me throughout my whole life and has sustained me through all my storms in an unshakable way. The definition of unshakable from the dictionary is "(of a belief, feeling, or opinion) strongly felt and unable to be changed."

I hope to be just like the Apostle John, who said he was *the one who testifies to everything he saw—that is, the word of God and the testimony of Jesus* Christ (Revelation 1:2 NIV). This is my story.

Bad circumstances have surrounded my life as far back as I can remember. My family immigrated to Canada from Colombia when my twin brother and I were a couple of months old. My mother didn't speak English very well at that time, and we lived in poverty. My mother did her best to make ends meet, and God blessed her.

As a little girl, I was robbed of my innocence by my biological father, who started sexually abusing me when I was a very young age. A child has no voice and understanding of what is happening to them when they are abused. A child should learn what is right and wrong from their parents.

Confusing messages were taught to me and my brothers while we were growing up. We went to church every Sunday, read the Bible, and memorized Bible verses. But my father had a demon inside and was really abusive towards us, even though we prayed every day and went to church. How does an abused child grasp the message of God's love when it is not being shown in the home?

Growing up in an abusive home where one of the parents was abusive and the other parent didn't have a voice really traumatized me. My father abused me sexually, physically, emotionally, mentally, and verbally. He would say evil things to us, such as we were Satan's kids and that the devil would appear to us. We did not understand what the devil and demons were.

When I revealed to my mother what my father had been doing to me from age 9, my parents sent me to Cali, Colombia, because my dad said I was possessed and making things up. There, I went to church with my grandma and was introduced to exorcism. My grandma had a pastor pray for me, and I acted like I was touched, although I really didn't understand what was going on.

During our childhood, despite being abusive, my father was studying to become a pastor. He graduated from seminary, and we relocated to Sedalia, Missouri, USA, from St. Catharines, Ontario, Canada. My father started a church called Amigos de Cristo, Friends of Christ. He continued being a monster behind closed doors, and then he would preach the Word of God at church.

As awful as my childhood was, I do remember a few good things. God blessed my beautiful mother for allowing us to be children and to enjoy life. My mother took me to ballet, piano, and swimming lessons when I was young. I became musically adept because of my mother.

After reaching my 15th birthday, I was raped by a stranger. I had no idea what to say or who to tell, so I kept it a secret. When I mentioned to my mother that I wanted to kill myself or run away, she took me to see a counselor. After opening up about all my abuse, I was removed from my family home and placed into foster care.

I became very depressed and hated myself. I felt used, worthless, abandoned, and rejected. I felt hopeless and neglected. I was lonely. I grew to hate my mother because the foster care family said that my mother didn't protect me from my father's abuse. My caseworker would not allow me to speak to my mother for this same reason.

My mental illness developed at the age of 16 when I made my first suicide attempt. I had refilled my anti-depressant and nightmare medications and tried to overdose by taking 120 pills. I heard God's voice say to me, "Karen, get up." I knew it was God because the voice I heard was a man's, and the foster home I was living in only had girls and a woman. Because I knew God cared about me so much, I survived, but I was still kept in mental hospitals for a while.

I was very angry at life. I was confused about how my parents and caretakers had treated me, and I rebelled against my parents. My father had fled the country when our case was being investigated, and my mother had moved to Florida. Life did not seem fair to me, and it was really difficult to love myself after being broken and bruised. Later I learned from the Bible that *Though my father and mother forsake me, the Lord will receive me* (Psalm 27:10 NIV). God was sustaining me. Unfortunately, I didn't understand this at the time.

Because my adolescence was so hard, I became angry at God. I didn't understand why I felt so unloved. I was introduced to smoking cigarettes and marijuana at the age of 13 and started making friends with drug addicts and rebellious teens. While in foster care, I was bounced around to ten different living arrangements, and I felt very confused about love.

After getting out of foster care at 17 and a half, I became promiscuous and got pregnant. Even though many people advised me to abort the baby, saying I wasn't ready to be a mother, I chose to keep my baby boy. I was a senior in high school, and it was uncomfortable being the only teenager pregnant. People gossipped about me and gave me nasty looks. I didn't care, though. For the first time in my life, I felt that I had a reason to live. I got a chance to feel my first-born child's unconditional love.

I gave birth to my beautiful baby boy, Jovanni, shortly before I graduated from high school. After graduation, Jovanni and I relocated from Missouri to Florida. My mother was living in Florida with her 2nd husband. I didn't know who Jovanni's father was, so I took a DNA test. The father turned out to be an ex-boyfriend I had in Florida who was still into women, drugs, and alcohol. So, I became a single teen mom at 18. Not receiving all the support I needed, I went into postpartum depression. Once I started taking medications again, I was able to take care of my baby boy. I realize now that God was once again sustaining me by showing me His love in giving me my precious son.

My Jovanni was a happy baby. He was very lovable. He was beautiful. He was very smart. I started working two jobs and going back to school so I could provide my son with a good life. Even though I had been traumatized as a child, I did my very best to be a good mother. My desire was to be the best mother I could be for my son.

When Jovanni was about three years old, I met a man I fell in love with at first sight. We moved in together. I was madly in love with him, and I got pregnant. Because we were attending church, we wanted to honor God and have our daughter born in a blessed home, so we got married a few weeks before the baby was due. My pregnancy with my daughter was very beautiful. I was excited to have a baby girl because I had grown up surrounded by boys. We were blessed with our beautiful baby girl, whom we welcomed into the world in November 2009. I felt complete and happy.

Married to my husband with my son and daughter, I felt blessed to be a part of a family. We attended church and a Bible study group regularly. Life was good.

During that time, I felt God's sustaining presence in my life. But those feelings wouldn't last. I didn't know that *life is lived by faith. We do not live by what we see in front of us* (2 Corinthians 5:7 NLV).

Our happy home didn't last long as I began to see a different side to my husband. He didn't think highly of me and became abusive and unfaithful. My husband and I separated. I was so upset I was drinking and driving with my daughter in the car. Therefore, I lost custody of both my kids. I lost my mind and went through a really hard time as my husband and I got divorced.

Because the Department of Children and Families gave me the proper help that I needed, I was able to get my children back two years later. My ex-husband asked me to try again, and we remarried. I thought I could forgive him and show him more love so he would stay with me, but he never wanted me; he wanted another woman. I pray he seeks God and that he is saved and forgiven. I can say that I tried my best to keep my family together.

Although heart-wrenching, the loss from my divorce was nowhere near as big as the next loss I am about to tell you.

My beloved son Jovanni was murdered.

On his 13th birthday, a group of family, friends, and acquaintances gathered for a dinner to celebrate my son. Afterward, Jovanni went to spend the night at one of his friends' homes. That night, he was killed by an older boy who was also staying at that home.

My son's killer had been sitting at Jovanni's birthday dinner while, unknown to us, plotting his move. He had been manipulated by a religious fanatic who told him he had to kill three nonbelievers of the Quaran in order to have a place in heaven with the 76 virgins. And he tried. The terrorist who murdered my son also attempted to murder two others. The mother of my son's friend was the second victim. She was stabbed, but she survived. My son's friend was the third victim. He was also stabbed numerous times and had damage to his kidney, liver, and arm. After surgeries and intensive care, he also survived.

But my son did not survive after this older boy stabbed him numerous times and slit his throat. It was the worst nightmare in history. As far as I knew, my son had been having an innocent sleepover with a friend. When I heard the news of his death, I was completely shocked. My only comfort was knowing that as much as I loved my son, God loved him just as much or more.

It took almost four years for my son's killer to be sentenced to life in prison in January 2022.

I had been traumatized most of my life, but losing my son was the worst trauma I have ever experienced. It was the worst pain I have known in my life. I am sure that my son is with our heavenly Father above, but I still do miss him a lot.

After losing my son, my ex-husband removed our daughter from being around me. She was relocated to Miami to be with her aunt and paternal grandmother. This made my grief so much worse. I was searching for answers. I was angry at God. I lost my mind again. I walked through hell, and Jesus rescued me back.

While I was waiting for the trial, God sustained me in many ways. I was grieving; I was confused and torn apart. I lost my mind. I didn't see how God was always faithful to me, even after losing both of my children. My ex-husband went on with his life. He was living with our neighbor while I became homeless.

Becoming homeless caused me to start believing and have faith that God was in control of everything. God already knew that the killer was going to get sentenced to life in prison. That was something I didn't fear. But the nightmare played in my mind as many questions arose. Sitting through the trial and hearing all the details of that night was so difficult. It was excruciating to be in the same room with the killer who had taken my baby boy's life. I had to learn how to surrender and to forgive. I had to learn to let go and let God help me mend. No matter how many times the devil attacked me, God's army was always fighting for me by praying for me and guiding me in a better direction. By not losing my faith, I was able to survive what I believed was a nightmare.

God will always be our protector. God was sustaining me through all of my darkest times.

After my son's killer was sentenced and I was divorced, my eyes were opened to everything the Lord revealed to me. In my own flesh, I am not perfect. I got another DUI, and I went to jail as a result of it. Yes, I am an alcoholic, and I did turn to the bad stuff amidst my pain. I have been listening more and more to God's guidance, and I am not ashamed to say that I had to pay the price for my missteps.

Jail is a terrible place. Being there was traumatizing. It was like a horror film happening right in front of me. But I requested and received a Bible. And I got on my knees to pray and worship God. I was not afraid to say that I loved Jesus and that He made the ultimate sacrifice for my salvation. I kept praying and having faith that I would get out of jail soon. I kept praying for forgiveness, too. Finally, I gained my freedom from jail. It was so beautiful. I fully opened my eyes and saw that God knows us completely. Matthew 10:30 tells us that He knows us so well that He even keeps track of all the hairs on our heads. God makes no mistakes (Psalm 18:30). And He loves us beyond what we can imagine.

> *For God so loved the world that he gave his one and only son, that whosoever believes in him shall not perish but have eternal life* (John 3:16 NIV).

I have seen God's miraculous hand on my life, and I am getting better each and every day. Jesus promised us, *"If you have faith as small as a mustard seed, you can say to this mulberry tree, 'Be uprooted and planted in the sea,' and it will obey you"* (Luke 17: 6 NIV). Through my pain and turmoil, I held onto my faith as much as I could. Thankfully, that's all we need to do to allow God to move mountains on our behalf. I am proof of this. Without my faith, I would not still be alive to tell this.

I now walk the best way I know how toward my ultimate goal: being reunited with my son and all the loved ones who have gone before with the Lord in heaven. I know my name is written in the Book of Life, so I am ready for the second coming of Jesus.

I pray for you to believe that everything is possible through Christ, our Lord. As a woman who has suffered a lot of sexual trauma throughout my whole life, there was a time when I couldn't see my worth or love myself. I couldn't respect myself. I didn't know I had a voice. Today, I can say that I am proud of how far I have come with the strength God has given me.

I learned to receive God's forgiveness and forgive everyone who has hurt me. I have done a lot of healing, and I no longer dwell on my past. Instead, I praise God every day for still allowing me to be alive, and I am grateful for all my blessings. Only Christ our Lord can help us get through the trials and tribulations of life. I am sober today, and I love having a clear mind. I love being able to spend quality time with the ones I love. I thank God for everything because life is a learning lesson, and with God and through God, we are able to grow and do better.

So, I end as I began—by saying God is an awesome God and He can sustain us through everything. I've learned that God's love never lets us down.

> *"Though the mountains be shaken, and the hills be removed, yet my unfailing love for you will not be shaken nor my covenant of peace be removed," says the LORD, who has compassion on you* (Isaiah 54:10 NIV).

I have prayed over this story, and I bless you in Jesus' name, that you will seek God for everything and that you will come to understand as I have just how much God loves you.

I pray that you may seek the Lord our God with all your heart and keep the faith. Whatever hardship has been placed on you, know that the Lord will see you through. The mercy and love of our heavenly Father is what enables us all to live an unshakable, purposeful life.

Unshakable in God's Hands

By Leecy Barnett

I have a niece and nephew who were adopted. Just like natural-born children, these two disappointed, frustrated, and even grieved their parents from time to time. But never once did my sister and her husband consider sending them back, nor did they ever contemplate disinheriting them.

The Bible teaches us that we have been adopted into God's family:

> *But when the right time came, God sent his Son...so that he could adopt us as his very own children. And because we are his children, God has sent the Spirit of his Son into our hearts, prompting us to call out, "Abba, Father." Now you are no longer a slave but God's own child. And since you are his child, God has made you his heir* (Galatians 4:4-7 NLT).

After God adopted us as His children, no matter what we do, He will never consider sending us back, nor will He ever contemplate disinheriting us. God will never leave us, even when we turn our backs on Him, disappoint Him, or grieve Him. He promises us: *"Can a mother forget the baby at her breast and have no compassion for the child she has borne? Though she may forget, I will not forget you! See, I have engraved you on the palms of my hands"* (Isaiah 49:15-16a NIV).

God holds us unshakably in His mighty hands. He pledges, *"I will take you by the hand and guard you"* (Isaiah 42:6b NLT). Jesus said of His followers: "I give them eternal life, and they shall never perish; no one will snatch them out of my hand. My Father, who has given them to me, is greater than all; no one can snatch them out of my Father's hand" (John 10:28-29 NIV). Think about it! No one, not even you, can pry open God's hands to pluck you away from Him.

You may be thinking that the women whose stories you have been reading are unshakable in a way you could never be. But we are all human. I know that I stumble and fall on a regular basis. If you stumble, too, take heart. God is always faithful; He never abandons us. He reminds us, *"I have hidden you safely in my hand"* (Isaiah 51:16 NLT).

God will never let you go!

Furthermore, we are unshakable in God's hands because, metaphorically, His power emanates from His hands: *His coming is as brilliant as the sunrise. Rays of light flash from his hands, where his awesome power is hidden* (Habakkuk 3:4 NLT). We don't have to be shaken no matter what happens to us because, as a good friend of mine always says, "God's got this." Fear is unnecessary because God always holds our hand: *"Don't be afraid, for I am with you. Don't be discouraged, for I am your God. I will strengthen you and help you. I will hold you up with my victorious right hand...For I hold you by your right hand—I, the Lord your God. And I say to you, 'Don't be afraid. I am here to help you'"* (Isaiah 41:10, 13 NLT).

I cannot think of a better place to be than in the almighty, secure hands of my heavenly Father!

Father, thank You for holding me in Your hands. I can be unshakable because You are holding on to me. Even when I stumble and fall, You are right there to pick me up. I don't need to be afraid because You've got me.

Afterword

As you read the final pages of *Unshakable: God Will Sustain You,* we pray that you have drawn inspiration from our stories and experiences and feel empowered to continue steadfastly on the unshakable path God has designed specifically for you.

In an effort to motivate you to trust God and stand unshakable in your faith, these remarkable authors have courageously shared how God sustained them during their challenging journeys. It can take years of trials and tribulations to forge a foundation strong enough to withstand any storm, but by sharing our stories, we can lend our strength to each other and stand strong together in faith.

Life sometimes leads us through valleys of darkness and shadows of doubt, but through it all, God uses adversities to help us grow and learn to trust His love. Like a sculptor who uses sharp tools to chisel rough stone into a beautiful work of art, God uses difficult circumstances to shape us, mold us, and make us who He created us to be.

In the center of adversity, we can find our strength and learn to stand unshakable in our faith. Through storms and struggles, we can build resilience anchored in God's grace. Every single trial and triumph can become a lesson that helps us harness our deepening faith and trust in God.

If you turn to Him, God will provide you with His strength, which is beyond comparison. Through your struggles and the shadows of strife, God is able to build an unshakable foundation on which He promises to sustain you.

This book is a reminder that you are never alone; God is always with you. The women who have written within the pages of this book chose to step out in faith to give this hope to you. Through sharing our stories, God has reminded us of His steadfast goodness. Now, our prayer is that He didn't just transform us through our adversity and writing but that the result, this book, has also ignited a flame of strength and power in your life.

May that flame empower you to embark boldly on the unshakable faith journey God is calling you to.

We trust that as you turned the pages of this book, your heart was deeply touched in a way that will linger within you. We pray you will be empowered to bravely face the hard things and that as you emerge with unshakable faith, heightened spiritual growth, and boundless trust in God, you will boldly and courageously step forward and share your story to empower others.

God is longing to become part of your life. He wants to walk with you and lay the foundation for an unshakable faith and a testimony you can share with others.

To you, dear reader, we express our heartfelt gratitude. Thank you for embracing these stories, becoming part of our unshakable community of believers, and joining us on this journey of hope. May you carry these stories with you as you travel on your own journey, allowing them to grow and encourage your own faith. Thank you for your courage, vulnerability, and willingness to show up and read this powerful book.

Together, we stand firm in our faith and unshakable in God's love, knowing He will always sustain us.

Dear Heavenly Father, thank You for opening my eyes to the journeys others face in times of uncertainty, impossible circumstances, and pain. Thank You for putting this book into my hands to discover who You are. I long for Your love. I ask You to come into my life because I want to know You more. Strengthen my faith so I may become unshakable in You. Sustain me during times of uncertainty, difficult circumstances, and pain so that I may have unshakable joy and peace. Give me the courage to share this discovery with others so that we might journey this life of faith together. In Your Holy name. Amen.

More WPP Anthologies!

The authors of *Unseen: You Are Not Alone* share their struggles of feeling isolated and unnoticed and detail how our awesome God helped them overcome every obstacle to find what truly matters: Him. These stories and devotional teachings shed light on the truth of your significance and value. You are never alone!

Despite all the adversities we face throughout our lives, God is the source of our hope. As you read the pages of this book, you will see firsthand how God brings *Hope Alive* to every person who is yearning for a reason to go on. Like a broken tree in a dark place is primed for new growth, God can use the rich soil of your dark place to prepare a new life to sprout in you.

The authors of *Miracle Mindset: Finding Hope in the Chaos*, have experienced the wonders of God's provision, protection, and guidance. These stories and teachings will ignite a spark within you, propelling you to encounter the marvel of God's miracles, even in the chaos.

Life is full of storms and rough waters. The stories in *Navigating Your Storm: By United Men of Honor* will give you the ability to see the light of God and navigate your storm victoriously.

With *Joy Unspeakable: Regardless of Your Circumstances,* you will learn how joy and sorrow can dance together during adversity. The words in this book will encourage, inspire, motivate, and give you hope, joy, and peace.

Surrendered: Yielded With Purpose will help you recognize with awe that surrendering to God is far more effective than striving alone. When we let go of our own attempts to earn God's favor and rely on Jesus Christ, we receive a deeper intimacy with Him and a greater power to serve Him.

United Men of Honor: Overcoming Adversity Through Faith will help you armor up, become fit to fight, and move forward with what it takes to be an honorable leader. Over twenty authors in this book share their accounts of God's provision, care, and power as they proclaim His Word.

Embrace the Journey: Your Path to Spiritual Growth will strengthen and empower you to step boldly in faith. These stories, along with expertly placed expositional teachings will remind you that no matter what we encounter, we can always look to God, trusting HIS provision, strength, and direction.

Victories: Claiming Freedom in Christ presents expository teaching coupled with individual stories that testify to battles conquered victoriously through the power of Jesus Christ. The words in this book will motivate and inspire you and give you hope as God awakens you to your victory!

WPP's Mission

World Publishing and Productions was birthed in obedience to God's call. Our mission is to empower writers to walk in their God-given purpose as they share their God story with the world. We offer one-on-one coaching and a complete publishing experience. To find out more about how we can help you become a published author or to purchase books written to share God's glory, please visit: **worldpublishingandproductions.com**

At seventeen, Audrey Marie experienced a sudden and relentless excruciating firestorm of pain. *Chronically Unstoppable* tells of her true-life journey as she faced pain, developed strength, and battled forward with hope.

The world has become a place where we don't have a millisecond to think for ourselves, often leaving us feeling lost or overwhelmed. That is why Max Gold wrote *Planestorming!*—a straightforward guide to help you evaluate and change your life for the better. It's time to get to work and make the rest of your life the BEST of your life.

THE BULLIED STUDENT
WHO CHANGED ALL THE RULES

A NOVEL BY
ROBERT M. FISHBEIN

Riley Rossey is not your everyday bullied student, but one who discovers how to utilize his talents to assist other shy and picked-on individuals. Journey with Riley as he meets bullying head-on and becomes a God-given blessing to so many in *The Bullied Student Who Changed All the Rules* by Robert M. Fishbein.